# WORKING WITH FAMILIES

# WORKING WITH FAMILIES

## A Guide for Health and Human Services Professionals

### Second Edition

*Patricia Spindel*

CANADIAN
SCHOLARS

Toronto | Vancouver

**Working with Families: A Guide for Health and Human Services Professionals,
Second Edition**
Patricia Spindel

First published in 2020 by
**Canadian Scholars, an imprint of CSP Books Inc.**
425 Adelaide Street West, Suite 200
Toronto, Ontario
M5V 3C1

www.canadianscholars.ca

**Library and Archives Canada Cataloguing in Publication**

Title: Working with families : a guide for health and human services professionals / Patricia
    Spindel.
Names: Spindel, Patricia, 1948- author.
Description: Second edition. | Includes bibliographical references and index.
Identifiers: Canadiana (print) 20190226323 | Canadiana (ebook) 20190226366 |
    ISBN 9781773381848 (softcover) | ISBN 9781773381862 (PDF) |
    ISBN 9781773381855 (EPUB)
Subjects: LCSH: Families—Health and hygiene—Case studies. | LCSH:
    Public health—Case studies. | LCSH: Human services—Case studies. |
    LCGFT: Case studies.
Classification: LCC RA418.5.F3 S65 2020 | DDC 306.85—dc23

Page layout: S4Carlisle Publishing Services
Cover design: Em Dash


Printed and bound in Ontario, Canada

Canada

# Contents

# Introduction

Today's definition of the family is no longer straightforward. The notion of family—what it is, its purpose, and how it should function—has become a contentious subject. Where decades ago families usually consisted of a mother, a father, and 2.5 children, the families of today may have only a mother or father and children, parents may be gay or lesbian, and children of different relationships and marriages may be living with new moms, dads, and step siblings. Some individuals are choosing to live together in "families of choice" where no blood ties exist.

Irrespective of what definition or form it takes, today's family remains the bedrock of society. Human Resources Development Canada (2013) refers to the family as "an essential building block in Canadian society [that] serves fundamental social and economic roles (learning, caring, parenting, reproduction, and participating in community)."

Families are highly complex groups of individuals who live together and try to function as one unit. The family unit is fraught with conflict and with joy. Some families are sanctuaries, and some are dangerous places. Either way, they are launching pads for new generations of adults who will either function well in society, or endure difficulty and hardship in their lives because of the early impact of the family in which they grew up.

Because families are such a fundamental part of society, attempting to ensure that they function well and remain healthy is an important task often assigned to health and human services professionals.

This book provides those studying for this field, as well as professionals already working in the health and human services, with a wealth of information about how families are structured, including the challenges and opportunities inherent in gay and lesbian, single-parent, Indigenous, blended, refugee, and immigrant families. The disorienting effects of immigration and trauma for immigrant and refugee families, the challenges inherent in their interactions with social institutions such as schools, and the impact of discrimination by the wider society are explored, as are the lives of military families, and families where one or both parents have a disability. The special challenges facing Indigenous families because of colonialism and oppression, as well as the abuse suffered in residential schools, are also discussed.

The theoretical and practical strategies used to promote positive family functioning include process-oriented approaches, and newer models such as the strengths and ecological approaches. Readers will learn about how building on a family's strengths can positively affect family functioning and increase the well-being of individual family members. The impact of environment and how to enrich environments for families is also examined. Recent research on how to promote family resilience—the ability to bounce back from challenges and adversity—is included, as are positive, practical strategies for how professionals can help families work together in optimal ways.

Stages of family development across the lifespan and the impact of grief and loss on family functioning are also explained.

Case examples cited in this book arise from the author's work. Some are compilations of situations described to her, and others are based upon her observations. All have been altered to eliminate identifiable information in order to respect the privacy of individuals and families. These case studies are intended to demonstrate struggles that individuals often have in their families of origin and relationships, which may come up in clinical practice. Most readers will be able to relate to many of these issues because they are so common.

Chapters 1 through 4 present issues that can act as barriers to families remaining healthy and being able to effectively carry out their roles, including the impact on the psychological and physical development of children of constructive and destructive patterns of interpersonal family relationships, as well as external social forces. Common dynamics found in families, and how these appear in various communication styles that can positively and negatively affect how families function, are also described.

Chapter 5 outlines the roles individuals in families take on, and what impact birth order, gender (including same-sex parenting), and cultural and ethnic background can have on how roles are determined in families. These roles may become disrupted through the process of immigration and acculturation. The special situation of Indigenous families is discussed.

Chapter 6 examines family belief systems, scripts (specifically parenting, grieving, and disrupted scripts), legacies in families, and how family members are defined and treated across generations. Suggestions on how scripts can be rewritten and used to promote positive family functioning and new legacies are included.

Chapter 7 explains how power works in families, which members tend to be scapegoated and why, and what impact various kinds of power dynamics have on a family's ability to solve problems and carry out their purposes. It is now common knowledge that the quality of early attachment by children to their parents has lifelong effects on children's well-being and ability to take their proper place in society. The chapter includes information on how attachment issues can develop and what protective factors may also be present.

Of major importance in family functioning is how well couples interact. The strengths or weaknesses in a marriage, same-sex or opposite-sex union, single-parent, or blended family can have a significant impact on how well children develop, on their ability to adjust to the demands placed upon them, and on their long-term ability to function in society. The impact of prolonged exposure to marital conflict and divorce on children and its implications regarding their emotional, social, physiological, and cognitive development is explored in chapter 8.

The presence of mental health, developmental, and other disabilities can leave families struggling, often without sufficient community or governmental support. This can greatly increase the stress for parents of children with disabilities and in some cases lead to family breakdown. Chapter 9 describes the kinds of challenges that families in these situations face and how professionals can best help them.

Chapter 10 explores the factors that contribute to family violence, and the legal and ethical responsibilities professionals have when working with violent families.

Addiction can destroy a family or, if successfully overcome, can bring families closer together. Chapter 11 presents an overview of the dynamics present in families struggling with addiction, the impact of addiction on individual family members, and the roles they often feel forced to embrace. It also discusses pathways back from addiction.

Chapter 12 includes an overview of various approaches to assessment of families and the theoretical bases for them.

Chapter 13 explores ways of working with families that build on their strengths and help build resilience. Older professional approaches are included and contrasted with more modern methods.

Chapter 14 looks in detail at the challenges and opportunities facing families where a parent has a developmental disability or mental illness. The impact of these parental disabilities on children and a discussion of how professionals can assist to mitigate these effects and strengthen parents' coping capacities are discussed.

Chapter 15 covers the special situation of military families and the impact of relocation, deployment, and return. Each aspect of military life presents challenges, and approaches that may ease the lives of these families are examined.

Chapter 16 looks at the grieving family, and includes the stages of grief, complicated grief, and how social support and professional intervention can be helpful.

Chapter 17 describes the kinds of dilemmas professionals themselves confront when working with families, as the dynamics in some families resonate with their own childhood challenges. Strategies for overcoming these kinds of pitfalls are discussed.

## REFERENCE

Human Resources Development Canada. (2013). Family life—Marriage. *Indicators of well-being in Canada*. Retrieved from http://www4.hrsdc.gc.ca/h.4m.2@-eng.jsp

## CHAPTER 1

# The Changing Structure of Families

*You don't choose your family. They are God's gift to you, as you are to them.*
—Desmond Tutu

## CHAPTER OVERVIEW

Canadian families are more diverse now than they have ever been, and this requires that professionals who work with them demonstrate cultural competence, understanding of different kinds of families, and respect for their traditions, beliefs, and values. In this chapter, readers will learn about how much families have changed based upon statistical information, and the new challenges and opportunities modern families experience.

From the 1950s through the 1970s, TV programs such as *Ozzie and Harriet*, *Leave It to Beaver*, and *The Partridge Family* portrayed a world where the mom stayed home with the kids, the dad went out to work, divorces did not occur, and even mischievous kids were not all that problematic. The families portrayed were Caucasian, and their antics were alternately funny or entertaining.

Those families we saw in the popular culture of 40 to 60 years ago bear little resemblance to the modern family. The social transformation of the last five decades has completely altered earlier social roles and functions. It has created new definitions of family, where gay and lesbian families are generally accepted, where ethnic diversity and interracial marriages are now common, where many families are led by single parents, and where both men and women are employed, get married, and divorce if a marriage is not working.

In Canada and in most of the Western world, the nature of families has changed significantly. Many factors have played a role in this change. According to Statistics Canada (2013), "By the end of the 1960's, events such as the legalization of the birth control pill, the introduction of 'no fault' divorce, as well as the growing participation of women in higher education and in the paid labour force may have contributed to delayed family formation, smaller family size, and an increased diversity of family structures."

## CHANGES IN CANADIAN FAMILIES

According to the 2016 census, family composition has changed appreciably from earlier decades: 28 percent now live in a one-person household, 26 percent are couples without children, 26 percent are couples with children, 9 percent are lone-parent families, 4 percent are non-family households of two or more, 4 percent are other family households, and 3 percent are multigenerational households (Statistics Canada, 2016b).

On average, 21 percent of Canadians are in common-law unions, with the highest percentages being 40 percent in Quebec, 50 percent in Nunavut, 37 percent in the Northwest Territories, and 32 percent in Yukon. Ontario has one of the lowest rates of common-law households, at 14 percent, while most other provinces range from 15 to 21 percent common-law households (PEI: 15 percent; Manitoba and Saskatchewan: 16 percent; Newfoundland, Alberta, and British Columbia: 17 percent; Nova Scotia: 19 percent; and New Brunswick: 21 percent) (Statistics Canada, 2016b).

More adults 65 and older are living as a couple and fewer are living alone. In 2001, 57 percent lived as a couple and 29 percent lived alone. By 2016, 63 percent were living as a couple and 26 percent were living alone (Statistics Canada, 2016b).

One of the biggest changes in families is that 35 percent of young adults aged 20 to 34 are living with their parents. In Oshawa and Toronto, one out of two in that age bracket are living with their parents (Statistics Canada, 2016b).

You need only look at the statistic that in 1961, 91.6 percent of families were headed by married couples to see the dramatic alterations in family life in the past 70 years (Statistics Canada, 2016b).

# RACIALLY, CULTURALLY, AND ETHNICALLY DIVERSE FAMILIES

Statistics Canada (2019a) reports that "on January 1, 2019, Canada's population reached 37,314,442, up 71,871 from October 1, 2018, according to preliminary population estimates." This increase is largely driven by international migration, as 71,131 new immigrants made Canada their home in the last quarter of 2018. "Canada grew by 528,421 in 2018, of which 80.5% was due to international migration. This level of increase has not been seen since the 1950s" (Statistics Canada, 2019a).

Many more children in Canada are being raised in immigrant families. Statistics Canada (2017b) reports that "in 2016, close to 2.2 million children under the age of 15, or 37.5% of the total population of children, had at least one foreign-born parent." Children in immigrant families are likely to represent between 39 percent and 49 percent of the total population of Canadian children by 2036 (Statistics Canada, 2017b). More children of diverse backgrounds now attend daycare and public schools than ever before, and they may often be an important cultural bridge between their parents, grandparents, and the society in which they live. The values, social norms, and languages they learn at school and in the larger society may be different from those of their parents and grandparents, and children of immigrant families are also familiar with the values and cultural practices of their family's country of origin. Many live in families that include three or more generations. This gives these children numerous strengths, and the advantage of speaking more than one language, but it may also create cultural stressors with which they and their families must contend.

The cultural diversity of families can be seen clearly in Toronto's (Canada's largest city) ward profiles. Scarborough-Guildwood's Ward 24 has 35,925 households. Of these, 71 percent are members of visible minority groups and 47 percent speak a language other than one of Canada's two official languages. This area is home to 54,785 immigrants, who make up 54 percent of the ward's population, with 71 percent of them having immigrated between 1991 and 2016. Within this group, 42 percent were economic immigrants, 36 percent were sponsored, and 20 percent were refugees (City of Toronto, 2018b). This is a major demographic, cultural, racial, and ethnic shift in less than 30 years.

If we shift to Ward 1, Etobicoke North has 37,890 households: 76 percent are members of visible minority groups and 52 percent speak a language other than one of Canada's two official languages. The ward has 67,865 immigrants—58 percent of the population—with 67 percent having immigrated between 1991 and 2016. Of these, 31 percent were economic immigrants, 41 percent were sponsored, and 27 percent were refugees (City of Toronto, 2018a).

While it is not possible to exactly compare ward profiles for other major Canadian cities, some comparisons are possible. For example, Vancouver has a population of 2,463,431, where 2,440,140 list English as their mother tongue. Of the city's total population, 416,565 also speak Indo-European languages, 82,025 speak Austronesian languages, 66,830 speak Tagalog, 57,625 speak Balto-Slavic languages, 37,825 speak German languages, 24,200 also speak Austro-Asiatic languages, and 22,950 speak Vietnamese, among many others (Statistics Canada, 2016d). So even though English is listed as a mother tongue, there is also significant cultural, racial, and ethnic diversity in Vancouver.

Montreal has a population of 4,098,927, where 2,231,540 speak English or French. In addition, 493,565 speak Indo-European languages, 286,425 speak Italic languages, 176,965 speak Afro-Asiatic languages, 157,015 speak Semitic languages, 151,955 speak Arabic, 58,295 speak Balto-Slavic languages, 33,385 speak Austro-Asiatic languages, 25,430 speak Vietnamese, 20,215 speak Austronesian languages, 14,865 speak Tagalog, 54,205 speak creole languages, and 13,490 speak Tamil (Statistics Canada, 2016a). Clearly, this is a racially, culturally, and ethnically diverse city.

Calgary, with a population of 1,229,220, increased in size by 13 percent, or 142,000 people, between 2011 and 2016, with more people moving out of Calgary in 2016 than moving in. From 2011 to 2016 population growth was due to net migration, but in 2016 population growth was due to natural increases—births over deaths. By 2017, there was a small increase in net migration (City of Calgary, 2016a). Approximately 75 percent spoke mostly English at home, while 30 percent listed their mother tongue as other than English. Tagalog, Spanish, Punjabi, Cantonese, and Mandarin were the languages most often spoken other than English, ranging from 3 to 5 percent of the population (City of Calgary, 2016b).

St. John's, with a population of 205,955, lists 202,690 as English speakers. In addition, 3,030 residents speak Indo-European languages, 1,325 speak Indo-Iranian languages, 1,040 speak Afro-Asiatic languages, 1,000 speak Semitic languages, 555 speak Austronesian languages, 470 speak Tagalog, 440 speak Balto-Slavic languages, and 410 speak Germanic languages, among many others (Statistics Canada, 2016c).

The demographic shifts across Canadian cities toward a much more culturally diverse population are evident in all of the statistics shown above.

Just as there were challenges facing those who lived in the nuclear families of the 1960s, which were dominated by heterosexual couples where the mother did not work, there are also challenges confronting those who live in the differently structured families of the second decade of this century.

The character of families has changed, with differing roles, cultures, and ways of functioning. The impact of external events has also made it difficult for some families. Being part of a military family, with Canada now playing a combat rather than peacekeeping role; a family whose income is below the poverty line; a family living in a ghettoized urban environment; a family that is step or blended—all have an impact on both adults and children growing up in these relatively new environments.

## THE SPECIAL CHALLENGES OF MILITARY FAMILIES

"As of August 2017, there were 66,472 Regular Force personnel with 99,716 additional family dependants (spouses, children and other dependants). In the Reserve Force, there were 47,135 personnel with 38,398 additional family members and dependants" (Manser, 2018, p. i). The highest number of military personnel (24,196) live in Ontario, with 10,896 living in Quebec, 6,838 living in Alberta, 7,405 in Nova Scotia, 5,209 in British Columbia, 4,779 in New Brunswick, and 2,781 in Manitoba. Much smaller numbers were located in the other provinces and territories (Manser, 2018, p. 22).

Rowan-Legg (2017) sets out the issues often experienced by military families, citing several life stressors, including having to move frequently, dealing with extended separations, feeling isolated from the usual social systems—friends and family—as well as family members being deployed to dangerous situations. Deployments are assignments of military personnel to either combat or non-combat zones, and they typically last from 1 to 15 months. They may be routine or unexpected. Canadian military personnel have, over the last number of years, been deployed to very dangerous areas such as Afghanistan and Iraq, and the stress of these kinds of deployments on families should not be underestimated (Rowan-Legg, 2017).

The developmental pressures on children growing up in military families are striking. These can result in strengths but also create challenges for them, including school problems and higher levels of depression and anxiety. Children undergo a variety of emotions when a parent is deployed, but also in the months after they return home. The impact of heightened communication in real time can help, but may also increase anxiety in children and families of deployed family members (Rowan-Legg, 2017).

A higher than average proportion of "female regular force members posted in Canada are single parents (24% of all single parents), caring for a disabled child (28% of all those who have declared a disabled child), and are caring for elderly parents (24% of all those who declared a dependent parent) compared to the total Regular Force proportional female to male ratio (15% female to 85% male)" (Manser, 2018, p. ii).

About 8 percent of Canada's military deployed to Afghanistan suffer symptoms of post-traumatic stress disorder (PTSD), while another 5.5 percent have symptoms of depression. Many critics suggest that the number of returning military personnel with mental health conditions is actually much higher than these statistics indicate. Between October 2001 and 2008, 30,500 men and women under the age of 40 were deployed in Afghanistan. Of those, 158 were killed in action (Auld, 2013). The impact of a returning family member with PTSD and/ or depression is considerable, as is the loss of a parent in combat. Both PTSD and depression are associated with a higher risk of suicide and substance abuse.

Until recently, effective and appropriate additional supports have not been available to either servicemen and -women or their families. The impacts on these families are finally beginning to be recognized, but Canada still has a long way to go to fully address the needs of these children and families. It is important that Canada make available needed assistance considering the number of families involved.

## SINGLE PARENTHOOD

National statistics demonstrate the pressures experienced by single-parent families and the impact on children of living with the increased risk of poverty if they are being raised in one-parent families. It should also be noted, though, that single parents often have the support of former partners and spouses or extended family members, or they may be in committed relationships. Especially in immigrant and Indigenous families, there is often multigenerational support. This kind of social support is critical in ensuring that these children and families thrive.

Nora Spinks (2019), of the Vanier Institute of the Family, has pointed out that "any portrait or discussion of modern lone mothers requires an open mind. One needs to understand that family life is diverse and complex, and families of all kinds are adaptable, strong and resilient. Myths and stereotypes about particular family types only lead to misunderstandings."

## POVERTY CAN BE A CHALLENGE

In Canada today 21 percent of single mothers and 7 percent of single fathers raise children while living in poverty. "Women parenting on their own enter shelters at twice the rate of two-parent families" (Canada Without Poverty, 2019). According to Statistics Canada (2017a), "nearly two in five children in lone-parent families (or 38.9%) lived in a low-income household in 2015. This rate was three and a half times higher than for children in two-parent families (11.2%). Furthermore, the vast majority of children living in a lone-parent family lived with their mother. The low-income rate for these children was much higher than for children who lived with their father (42.0% compared with 25.5%)."

"Canada has the third highest rate of child poverty among 17 similarly developed countries" (Robinson, 2019). One in seven children in Ontario lives in poverty, with income inequality, unemployment, waitlists for social housing, and the need to resort to food banks all increasing across the province. Indigenous people, immigrants, and racialized people are all disproportionately impacted by poverty, thereby increasing their marginalization. Poverty is associated with increased mortality, more chronic illness, adverse effects on child development, and exposure to toxic stress that may increase mental illness and result in poor educational attainment (Robinson, 2019). Some single parents living in poverty may be forced to work two jobs to make ends meet, and this can contribute to difficulty supervising children and place the children at greater risk. Many children growing up in these circumstances manage to develop an array of strengths and are highly resilient, sometimes as a result of having to navigate these challenges. Consequently, they are able to overcome these impacts. Others find it more difficult.

Browne et al. (2017) found that "single parents have the highest rates of emotional problems" and that their "distress appears to be due in large part to the fewer available social resources." This study also found the following:

> Rates of emotional problems systematically varied as a function of gender, income and immigration category. Compared to males, females were more likely to report emotional problems six months after immigration, and their odds of reporting emotional problems increased at a faster rate. Other research has documented a higher prevalence of internalizing psychopathology (depression and anxiety) in females during the period following immigration [and that] rates of emotional problems increased most rapidly for those in lower socioeconomic strata. The effects of socioeconomic status on mental health are complex and multifaceted, operating through a variety of mechanisms including access to resources, health related behaviours, and psychosocial stress. (Browne et al., 2017)

It is important to analyze what these statistics actually indicate. Parents raising children on their own with little to no social support are likely to have increased mental health challenges, especially if they are struggling financially. The worries associated with being able to provide adequately for children would magnify these anxieties. Add the racism and xenophobia experienced by racialized and immigrant parents and the impact is even greater.

Effectively addressing poverty among single parents and Indigenous, immigrant, and racialized communities; ensuring that social support is available; and reinforcing shared beliefs and open and encouraging communication would go a long way toward improving determinants of physical and mental health, and ensuring family resilience (Pogosyan, 2017).

When parents' mental health suffers, it is likely that children's mental health will also suffer. Having said that, many children grow up in homes where one or both parents suffer from a variety of mental health conditions. In some cases, children growing up in homes where this is the case can develop higher levels of empathy and a desire to help others, whereas others will become withdrawn or suffer mental health challenges of their own. To suggest that any study results apply equally to all children growing up in single-parent families, especially those dealing with poverty, would be misleading.

There is no question that stress, loneliness, feeling overwhelmed, and having to deal with the impact of poverty place parents of either gender at higher risk of not being able to parent in a positive way. This has implications for the kinds of interventions that may be helpful to single parents. Dr. Ellen Lipman of McMaster University conducted a study evaluating a social and educational support group for single mothers. The *Toronto Star* revealed that "at the beginning of the study, most mothers reported high levels of stress related to finances and mental health problems. Over the next four months, mothers who were part of the support group reported significant improvements in mood and self-esteem" (Cairney, 2013). This demonstrates the important role that social support can play for single parents.

But perhaps the highest risk is experienced by single fathers. A relatively new study reveals that there is a "startlingly high" death rate among single fathers in Canada, more than twice the national average (CBC News, 2018; Chiu, Rahman, Vigod, Lau, & Cairney, 2018). According to Maria Chiu, of the Institute for Clinical Evaluative Sciences in Toronto, "It's a startlingly high mortality. They were three times higher than single moms and partnered fathers, and five times higher than partnered moms" (CBC News, 2018). Cancer and cardiovascular disease and visits to emergency rooms were higher. Binge drinking and unhealthy eating seemed to contribute to these problems. It seems that single fathers did not take very good care of themselves, and less social support appeared to add to the problem (CBC News, 2018). What this shows is that of all family groups, single fathers with children in their home may be the most at risk and require special assistance. Given the high mortality rates, this may be a concern that has not yet been flagged by social agencies and medical personnel.

## CULTURALLY DIVERSE FAMILIES

It is important to understand that newcomers to Canada are not a homogenous group. Families are affected by their migration stories, their level and quality of education, their income, where they decide to live, and how much social support they have (Canadian Pediatric Society, 2019).

Economic immigrants will have a different experience of integrating into Canadian society than refugee families, who have likely suffered trauma in their countries of origin, and who will require higher levels of support. How well immigrant families adapt and acculturate can often be a direct result of their immigration experience.

Canada's growing levels of cultural diversity place additional stresses on families attempting to integrate into Canadian society. There can be major shifts in roles as families emigrate and attempt to resettle in their chosen country. If economic hardship due to unemployment or underemployment and racial discrimination by the wider society are added to the mix, it can pose severe hardships for immigrant families. Women may, for the first time, become the major wage earners, thereby shifting the male and female roles in the family. Role reversals can also occur as children may be quicker to adopt a new language, thereby becoming translators for their parents. As language gulfs occur, there may also be challenges in parents attempting to transmit their cultural values and beliefs to their children. This may cause a sense of loss and feelings of depression in the older generation (Tyyska, n.d.).

In some families, one member of the family, possibly the father, will emigrate first in order to establish himself economically before bringing his family to the new country. This can create a degree of estrangement that may cause considerable tension once the family arrives and the father attempts to re-establish his authority. Children, some having been fatherless for years, may also be experiencing difficulties because of his absence.

One of the issues that often arises in immigrant families is the interfamilial culture clash that occurs between parents and children as children seek to fit in with peers and appear to surrender some of their cultural heritage to do so. As children press for greater freedoms, differences in dress and deportment, and in some cases unchaperoned contact with the opposite sex, extreme clashes can occur in families. Parents' expectations of high educational performance can add to the stress level children experience.

Visible minority immigrant youth do appear to have high educational aspirations. "National survey data from the 2000 Youth in Transition Survey (YITS) show that the educational aspirations of 15-year-old visible minority immigrant Canadians are much higher than those of their native-born non-visible minority counterparts, even when we control for a wide range of socio-demographic, social psychological, and school performance factors" (Krahn & Taylor, 2005). This is a very positive determinant of their ability to successfully make their way in their adopted country.

Tensions can increase to extremes as gender roles shift and children challenge traditional cultural beliefs and customs. This can raise the spectre of family violence, especially in families where there are strong expectations of girls to be of good reputation, marry within their caste according to their parents' wishes, and comply with parental expectations not to bring shame to their families. This is particularly challenging for the young girls in these families who go to public schools, where they are exposed, on a daily basis, to youth of other cultures and belief systems (Handa, 1997; Kandasamy, 1995).

Parents raised in a collectivist culture may not understand their children's newfound demands as they grow up in a culture that values individual freedom and expression. Since many of these parents are economic immigrants who are seeking a better life for themselves and their children in Canada, their children's efforts to become more integrated can be seen as disrespectful by parents when it is assumed that they do not understand or appreciate the sacrifices made to come to a new country. In response, some children, attempting to avoid fights with their parents, may become secretive, in essence, leading double lives. This can place them at risk as they attempt to survive at a young age without the scrutiny or supervision of adults.

The challenges facing parents attempting to raise children while integrating into a new culture involve attempting to establish influence without exerting too much control. This can be helped by dialogue, where family history, culture, and their dreams and reasons for emigrating are shared in non-confrontational ways.

There appear to be far fewer intergenerational conflicts in non-traditional versus traditional families. Using Toronto's Iranian community as an example, Tyyksa (2003) found that hierarchical families with high expectations of conformity from both girls and boys—where young people, and in particular young women, have little to no influence in family decision making—were more likely to experience high degrees of conflict. Compare to this non-traditional families—that are less hierarchical and where communication is more open, with input from all family members—which had fewer intergenerational problems. Where parents were more willing to be flexible and adaptable, there was increased family harmony.

## SAME-SEX PARENTS

Perceptions of same-sex families in Canada have changed considerably. Studies have shown that children raised by same-sex parents are as well-adjusted and psychologically healthy as those raised in homes with heterosexual parents (Dufur, McKune, Hoffmann, & Bahr, 2007); however, children raised by same-sex parents do continue to face higher levels of discrimination than their peers (Vanier Institute of the Family, 2013).

In 2007, Patterson and Wainright completed a major study on how children adopted into same-sex households fared. Generally, major studies had found "that parent sexual orientation is not a significant predictor of adoptive family functioning, adopted child's behavior, and parent's perceptions of helpfulness from family support networks" (Erich, Leung, & Kindle, 2004, p. 43). Nevertheless, where discrimination is present, adolescents may have lower self-esteem related to social acceptance and self-worth because of the stigma associated with their same-sex parents (Gershon, Tschann, & Jemerin, 1999). Parenting style and the relationship of parents (whether heterosexual or homosexual) with their adolescent children was much more likely to influence outcomes for children. Where a warm, accepting relationship exists between parents and children, children are much more likely to do well in life. Overall, "family processes are more important predictors of adolescent functioning than are structural variables such as family type" (Allen, Moore, Kuperminc, & Bell, 1998).

There can be no doubt that all of the changes in families in the last 50 years have placed a strain on both parents and children. Some families are adapting well to these changes, but others are not. Some will need the assistance of health and human services professionals as they struggle with the challenges of the modern world and the demands being placed upon them by the Information Age. There is no question that the revolution in information technology has had an impact on family life. As children and parents begin to engage in more solitary activities using their smartphones and computers, the glue that once held families together may no longer be present. Parents using their smartphones while supervising their kids at the playground, family members texting rather than interacting while out for dinner, and mothers, fathers, or kids all sitting at computers or watching TV for long periods of time may preclude important and necessary family conversations and contribute to feelings of emotional neglect or abandonment in all family members.

As families struggle with these and many other issues, their ability to function may decline and there may be tension, struggle, and conflict. It is therefore more important than ever for professionals working with families to understand these tensions and be able to work with them in positive and innovative ways.

## CHAPTER SUMMARY

This chapter has provided a general overview of the degree to which families have changed in the past 50 years, from being typical nuclear families with a mother, father, and two children, to a highly diverse group of families. This diversity includes single-parent, LGBTQ, blended, and families of choice with widely varying countries of origin, cultures, and ways of functioning. The chapter has touched on the special struggles of military families and some of the challenges facing children growing up in single-parent families.

## FURTHER READING

Canadian Association of Social Workers. (2018). Understanding social work and child welfare: Canadian survey and interviews with child welfare experts. https://www.casw-acts.ca/sites/default/files/documents/CASW_Child_Welfare_Report_-_2018.pdf

Citizens for Public Justice. (2018). Poverty trends 2018 report. https://cpj.ca/wp-content/uploads/Poverty-Trends-Report-2018.pdf

Financial Accountability Office of Ontario. (2019, Winter). Income in Ontario: Growth, distribution, and mobility. https://www.fao-on.org/en/Blog/Publications/income-report-2019

Immigrant Services Association of Nova Scotia. (2019). Immigrant families: Stages of adaptation to life in Canada. https://www.isans.ca/get-settled/community-wellness-services/stages-of-adapting-to-life-in-canada/

## CLASSROOM RESOURCES

*A kind of family.* (1992). National Film Board of Canada (NFB). https://www.nfb.ca/film/kind_of_family/

*Birth of a family*. (2007). NFB. https://www.nfb.ca/film/birth_of_a_family_edu/

*Children of soldiers*. (2010). NFB. https://www.nfb.ca/film/children_of_soldiers/

*Choosing children*. (1985). New Day Films. https://www.newday.com/film/choosing-children

*Chris and Bernie*. (1974). New Day Films. https://www.newday.com/film/chris-and-bernie

*Daddy and Papa*. (2002). New Day Films. https://www.newday.com/film/daddy-papa

*Family motel*. (2007). NFB. https://www.nfb.ca/film/family_motel/

*Joint custody: A new kind of family*. (2015). New Day Films. https://www.newday.com/film/joint-custody-new-kind-family

*Mimi and Donna*. (2014). New Day Films. https://www.newday.com/film/mimi-and-dona

*That's a family!* (2000). New Day Films. https://www.newday.com/film/thats-family

## CLASSROOM ACTIVITY

### Questions for Groups

1. How well do you think statistics do or do not reflect the lived experience of each of the family groups outlined in this chapter? Give examples of your reasoning.
2. In your experience, have you seen children from any of the family groupings described (i.e., newcomer families, single parent, same-sex parents, military families) discriminated against or bullied? What, if anything, did you want to do about it? What may have stopped you from acting? What action might you take now?
3. Were you raised in any of the family groups described in this chapter? What was your experience, and what would have made your family's life easier? What do you think is preventing Canadian society and government from addressing these issues?

## QUESTIONS FOR REFLECTION

1. Are you the child of immigrant parents, or do you know any children of immigrant parents? If so, are there tensions between the children and their parents as a result of immigration? What are they?
2. How might you help immigrant parents and children navigate these tensions?
3. Have you noticed any special challenges in the single-parent families you know? If so, what is causing them?
4. What, if any, are the special challenges that blended families might face?

## REFERENCES

Allen, J. P., Moore, C., Kuperminc, G., & Bell, L. (1998). Attachment and adolescent psychosocial functioning. *Child Development, 69*, 1406–1419.

Auld, A. (2013, July 2). 14 per cent of Canadian forces in Afghanistan had mental health problems: Study. *Edmonton Journal*. Retrieved from https://www.ctvnews.ca/health/health-headlines/14-per-cent-of-canadian-forces-in-afghanistan-had-mental-health-problems-study-1.1350421

Browne, D. T., Kumar, A., Puente-Duran, S., Georgiades, K., Leckie, G., & Jenkins, J. (2017, April 4). Emotional problems among recent immigrants and parenting status: Findings from a national longitudinal study of immigrants in Canada. Retrieved from https://journals.plos.org/plosone/article?id=10.1371/journal.pone.0175023

Cairney, J. (2013, July 22). In support of single mothers. *Toronto Star*. Retrieved from http://www.thestar.com/opinion/2007/12/26/in_support_of_single_mothers.html

Canada Without Poverty. (2019). Poverty and demographics: Marginalized communities. Retrieved from http://www.cwp-csp.ca/poverty/just-the-facts/

Canadian Pediatric Society. (2019). Adaptation and acculturation. Retrieved from https://www.kidsnewtocanada.ca/culture/adaptation

CBC News. (2018, February 14). Startlingly high mortality among single dads in Canada. Retrieved from https://www.cbc.ca/news/health/single-fathers-mortality-1.4535816

Chiu, M., Rahman, F., Vigod, S., Lau, C., & Cairney, J. (2018, February 14). Mortality in single fathers compared with single mothers and partnered parents: A population based cohort study. *Lancet, 3*(3). Retrieved from https://www.thelancet.com/journals/lanpub/article/PIIS2468-2667(18)30003-3/fulltext

City of Calgary. (2016a). Calgary profile: Chapter 1. Population, age, sex, dwellings and households. Retrieved from http://www.calgary.ca/CSPS/CNS/Documents/Social-research-policy-and-resources/Calgary-Profile-Chapter-1.pdf

City of Calgary. (2016b). Calgary profile: Chapter 3. Language. Retrieved from http://www.calgary.ca/CSPS/CNS/Documents/Social-research-policy-and-resources/calgary-profile-chapter-3-language.pdf

City of Calgary. (2016c). Ward 1 profile. Retrieved from http://www.calgary.ca/CSPS/CNS/Documents/ward_profiles/2019/Ward-1-Profile.pdf

City of Toronto. (2018a). Ward 1 profile. Retrieved from https://www.toronto.ca/wp-content/uploads/2018/09/8f33-City_Planning_2016_Census_Profile_2018_25Wards_Ward01.pdf

City of Toronto. (2018b). Ward 24 profile. Retrieved from https://www.toronto.ca/wp-content/uploads/2018/09/8f23-City_Planning_2016_Census_Profile_2018_25Wards_Ward24.pdf

Dufur, M., McKune, B. A., Hoffmann, J. P., & Bahr, S. J. (2007). *Adolescent outcomes in single parent, heterosexual couple, and homosexual couple families: Findings from a national survey.* Paper presented at the annual meeting of the American Sociological Association, New York, New York City Online. Retrieved from http://citation. allacademic.com/meta/p_mla_apa_research_citation/1/8/4/0/7/p184075_ index.html

Erich, S., Leung, P., & Kindle, P. (2004). A comparative analysis of adoptive family functioning with gay, lesbian and heterosexual parents and their children. *Journal of GLBT Family Studies, 1,* 43–60.

Gershon, T. D., Tschann, J. M., & Jemerin, J. M. (1999). Stigmatization, self-esteem, and coping among the adolescent children of lesbian mothers. *Journal of Adolescent Health, 24,* 437–445.

Government of Canada. (2014). National Defence and the Canadian Armed Forces: Women in the Canadian Armed Forces. Backgrounder. Retrieved from www.forces. gc.ca/en/news/article.page?doc=women-in-the-canadian-armed-forces/hie8w7rm

Handa, A. (1997). *Caught between omissions: Exploring "culture conflict" among second generation South Asian women in Canada* (Unpublished doctoral dissertation). University of Toronto.

Holt-Lunstad, J., Smith, T. B., Baker, M., Harris, T., & Stephenson, D. (2015). Loneliness and social isolation as risk factors for mortality: A meta-analytic review. *Perspectives on Psychological Science, 10,* 227–237.

Kandasamy, B. (1995). *Findings on the Tamil community.* York, ON: York Community Services.

Krahn, H., & Taylor, A. (2005). Resilient teenagers: Explaining the high educational aspirations of visible minority immigrant youth in Canada. Retrieved from https:// www.researchgate.net/profile/Alison_Taylor8/publication/226246196_Resilient_ Teenagers_Explaining_the_High_Educational_Aspirations_of_Visible-Minority_ Youth_in_Canada/links/5444833a0cf2e6f0c0fba43c.pdf

Manser, L. (2018, June). Profile of military families in Canada. Retrieved from https:// www.cafconnection.ca/getmedia/7b46894d-91aa-421b-912f-6293b0cab4b9/ Profile-of-Military-Families-in-Canada-2017-RegF-Demographics-Report- FINAL-June-2018.pdf.aspx

Patterson, C. J., & Wainright, J. L. (2007, November 7). Adolescents with same-sex parents: Findings from the National Longitudinal Study of Adolescent Health. University of Virginia. Retrieved from http://people.virginia.edu/~cjp/articles/ pwInPress.pdf

Pogosyan, M. (October 11, 2017). What makes families resilient? *Psychology Today.* Retrieved from https://www.psychologytoday.com/ca/blog/ between-cultures/201710/what-makes-families-resilient

Ravanera, Z. (2007). Informal networks social capital of fathers: What does the social engagement survey tell us? *Social Indicators Research*, *83*, 351–373.

Robinson, C. (2019, February 25). The impact of poverty on Canadian children: A call for action. Retrieved from https://cmajblogs.com/the-impact-of-poverty-on-canadian-children-a-call-for-action/

Rowan-Legg, A. (2017, May 3). Caring for children and youth from Canadian military families: Special considerations. Retrieved from https://academic.oup.com/pch/article/22/2/e1/3793203

Snyder, V. (2013). Caring for each other together and apart: Canadian military families. Vanier Institute of the Family. *Transition*, *43*(1). Retrieved from vanierinstitute.ca/wp-content/uploads/2015/11/MFAM_2013-11-07_Transition_43-1_Caring-for-each-other-together-apart.pdf

Spinks, N. (2019). Lone mothers and their families in Canada: Diverse, resilient, and strong. Vanier Institute of the Family. Retrieved from https://vanierinstitute.ca/lone-mothers-families-canada-diverse-resilient-strong/

Statistics Canada. (2013). Fifty years of families in Canada: 1961 to 2011. Retrieved from www12.statcan.gc.ca/census-recensement/2011/as-sa/98-312-x/98-312-x2011003_1-eng.cfm

Statistics Canada. (2015, November 27). Lone-parent families. Retrieved from https://www150.statcan.gc.ca/n1/pub/75-006-x/2015001/article/14202/parent-eng.htm

Statistics Canada. (2016a). Montreal census profile. Retrieved from https://www12.statcan.gc.ca/census-recensement/2016/dp-pd/prof/details/page.cfm?Lang=E&Geo1=CMACA&Code1=462&Geo2=PR&Code2=12&Data=Count&SearchText=Montreal&SearchType=Begins&SearchPR=01&B1=All&wbdisable=true

Statistics Canada. (2016b). Portrait of households and families in Canada. Retrieved from https://www150.statcan.gc.ca/n1/pub/11-627-m/11-627-m2017024-eng.htm

Statistics Canada. (2016c). St. John's Census Profile. Retrieved from https://www12.statcan.gc.ca/census-recensement/2016/dp-pd/prof/details/page.cfm?Lang=E&Geo1=CMACA&Code1=001&Geo2=PR&Code2=10&Data=Count&SearchText=St.%20John

Statistics Canada. (2016d). Vancouver census profile. Retrieved from https://www12.statcan.gc.ca/census-recensement/2016/dp-pd/prof/details/page.cfm?Lang=E&Geo1=CMACA&Code1=933&Geo2=PR&Code2=59&Data=Count&SearchText=Vancouver&SearchType=Begins&SearchPR=01&B1=All&TABID=1

Statistics Canada. (2017a, September 13). Children living in low income households. Retrieved from https://www12.statcan.gc.ca/census-recensement/2016/as-sa/98-200-x/2016012/98-200-x2016012-eng.cfm

Statistics Canada. (2017b, October 25). Children with an immigrant background: Bridging cultures. Retrieved from https://www12.statcan.gc.ca/census-recensement/2016/as-sa/98-200-x/2016015/98-200-x2016015-eng.cfm

Statistics Canada. (2017c, August 2). Portrait of children's family life in Canada in 2016. Retrieved from https://www12.statcan.gc.ca/census-recensement/2016/as-sa/98-200-x/2016006/98-200-x2016006-eng.cfm

Statistics Canada. (2017d, August 2). Same-sex couples in Canada in 2016. Retrieved from https://www12.statcan.gc.ca/census-recensement/2016/as-sa/98-200-x/2016007/98-200-x2016007-eng.cfm

Statistics Canada. (2019a, March 21). Canada's population estimates, fourth quarter, 2018. Retrieved from https://www150.statcan.gc.ca/n1/daily-quotidien/190321/dq190321d-eng.htm?indid=4098-1&indgeo=0

Statistics Canada. (2019b, February 20). Families, households, and marital status highlight tables. Retrieved from https://www12.statcan.gc.ca/census-recensement/2016/dp-pd/hlt-fst/fam/Table.cfm?Lang=E&T=42&Geo=00

Statistics Canada. (2019c). Family matters: Grandparents in Canada. Retrieved from https://www150.statcan.gc.ca/n1/en/pub/11-627-m/11-627-m2019001-eng.pdf?st=OHVe1dPH

Taylor, Z. E., & Conger, R. D. (2017, March). Promoting strengths and resilience in single mother families. *Child Development*, *88*(2), 350–358. Retrieved from https://www.ncbi.nlm.nih.gov/pubmed/28139842

Tyyska, V. (n.d.). Parents and teens in immigrant families. *Cultural Diversity.* Retrieved from http://canada.metropolis.net/pdfs/Pgs_can_diversity_parents_spring08_e.pdf

Tyyksa, V. (2003). Solidarity and conflict: Teen-parent relationships in Iranian immigrant families in Toronto. In M. Lynn (Ed.), *Voices: Essays on Canadian families* (2nd ed.). Toronto, ON: Nelson Canada.

Vanier Institute of the Family. (2013, March). Same-sex families raising children. Retrieved from https://vanierinstitute.ca/wp-content/uploads/2015/11/FFAM_2013-03-00_Same-Sex-families-raising-children.pdf

## CHAPTER 2

# Building on Family Strengths and Promoting Resilience

*The oak fought the wind and was broken, the willow bent when it must and survived.*

—Robert Jordan

## CHAPTER OVERVIEW

Individuals and families demonstrate strengths and resilience every day. Unfortunately, these are not always acknowledged by others or by individuals or families themselves. In this chapter, readers will explore why helping families to recognize and acknowledge their own strengths and ability to bounce back from hardship is important.

## RESILIENCE DEFINED

The American Psychological Association (2013) defines resilience as "the process of adapting well in the face of adversity, trauma, tragedy, threats or significant sources of stress—such as family and relationship problems, serious health problems, or workplace and financial stressors. It means 'bouncing back' from difficult experiences."

A popular misconception about resilience is that those who demonstrate it are not in distress. In fact resilience is a journey through emotional and sometimes physical pain while never losing hope, finding ways to carry on, and believing that things will get better. Like everything else, it involves a system of beliefs that lead to particular thoughts, which in turn lead to behaviours and actions that are adaptive rather than personally destructive. All of these can be learned or acquired through life experience or modelling by others.

Children tend to learn their coping strategies from their parents; therefore, a key method used in helping families is for professionals to assist parents in shoring up and strengthening their own coping mechanisms. To do this, professionals themselves need to know what factors contribute to resilience and be able to talk about, teach, and model these.

## WHAT PROMOTES RESILIENCE?

Just as with individuals, one of the primary ways families can promote resilience is through the creation of supportive relationships, both within the family and with others. The goal is for the family to be an oasis of safety and encouragement. The skill of being supportive does not come naturally. It is grounded in a world view that others, and not just oneself, are important and deserve to be valued and cared for. It is much easier to care for others when we care for ourselves and feel supported and loved. Similarly, it is more likely that we will be unkind or cruel to others if we, ourselves, feel hurt, deprived, and uncared for.

Helping families to establish warm and caring relationships with other families is a primary goal in building resilience. Close relationships with others can provide positive role models for children and banish feelings of isolation and loneliness. Assisting families to decide their own paths by locating their strengths and using these to develop plans that address their goals and dreams, as individuals and as a group, helps to promote resilience.

Anne is a single parent of Eastern European descent. She has two children, Anne Jr. and Ralph. Ralph has Down syndrome. Anne recognized that she and her children needed social support, and joined an organization called Extend-A-Family. Extend-A-Family links families of non-disabled children with families in which one or more member has a disability (Extend-A-Family, 2019). Jill and Hank had no children living at home and they were linked to Anne and her family. For years they went on outings with Anne Jr. and Ralph, and invited the family to their home. They became friends and also visited at Anne, Anne Jr., and Ralph's home. The social support that they provided to each other helped both families endure difficult times and built a friendship that lasted for decades. It led to both children developing more resilience and feeling supported, thereby reducing the isolation they had felt. As part of Extend-A-Family there were also yearly events where they were able to meet other families. Soon one of Jill and Hank's neighbours decided he liked Ralph so much he would take him and other children with disabilities swimming. And so the social support spread to others.

No family can work well without a basic understanding of how to communicate and resolve issues and problems together. Most family breakdowns are the result of poor communication and an inability to solve problems in reasonable ways. Solving problems reasonably often requires another factor in the promotion of resilience: emotional regulation—being able to handle sometimes overwhelming feelings and emotions and translate them in a way that others can hear, and to which they can relate (Southwick, Litz, Charney, & Friedman, 2011).

A young Vietnamese woman, now working as a human services professional, made this comment about managing powerful feelings: "My parents taught me to be calm, and to communicate calmly. Sharp words to others are like hammering a nail into a tree. Even when you finally remove it, there will always be a mark there." Sharp words do create wounds and long-term scars that never go away. To prevent family members from harming each other with words, it is important to help them learn how to regulate their emotions and express themselves while taking the feelings of others into account.

## PRACTICAL STRATEGIES FOR PROMOTING RESILIENCE

Psychologists have come up with some strategies that are very helpful in promoting resilience in individuals and families, including teaching children values that foster a positive world view to help them embrace altruistic motives and actions; surrounding children with social supports and promoting their friendships with others; offering encouragement and helping families to identify their strengths and abilities as well as actions that are adaptive and functional; discouraging "catastrophizing" and replacing it with more positive or optimistic thinking to promote emotional regulation (Grohol, 2014); helping families to learn from mistakes and focus also on accomplishments and positive experiences; encouraging families to play together and enjoy fun activities; and, finally, teaching communication skills that are supportive of others, and avoiding common communication pitfalls that shut down interaction.

Saanvi is married to Arjun. He is away a great deal on business. Ansh is her stepson and Arjun's son from his first marriage. Ansh has been running away from home recently, usually during periods that his father is away. Saanvi has been depressed for some time, and spends her time watching daytime television. Both Saanvi and Ansh are very unhappy and argue constantly. When Arjun comes home there are major family fights where Saanvi and he point fingers at each other about what is wrong with the family. Arjun wants Saanvi to look after the home and his son, but Saanvi finds Ansh disrespectful and disobedient.

Connie is with a local youth serving agency and has started working with this family. At the first family meeting, she asked the family to put their disagreements aside for a moment and discuss each other's strengths and the family's strengths. She asked what hopes and aspirations the family had for themselves and for each other. She asked how often the family did things together, what their common interests were, and what they enjoyed doing alone and together. Saanvi wanted to work at least part-time. She had skills in accounting. Arjun enjoyed watching sports and agreed to take his family out to games when he was at home. Ansh enjoyed music, so his parents agreed to buy him a musical instrument, get guitar lessons, and let him join the school band. Saanvi and Arjun attended Ansh's school concert, and they regularly went to hockey and baseball games together. Saanvi began working three days a week at an accounting firm, and agreed to cook traditional family dinners two days a week. She and Arjun also agreed to up the family budget to allow take-out or restaurant meals on the days that Saanvi worked. After only a month, the arguments had greatly decreased, and all of the family members reported feeling happier and more supported. When family members feel valued and see the importance of working together so that each member gets at least some of the things they want, family functioning can improve considerably. Arjun started taking his son to the park to play baseball when he was home, leaving Saanvi time to read—another favourite pastime of hers. After only two months of support, this family was on its way to healing, and Ansh had stopped running away from home.

## TEACHING VALUES

Whenever individuals in families interact, they are teaching each other who they are as people, what they believe, and what and whom they value. Do they believe it is important to be kind or harsh? Do they believe that others matter or that they alone matter? Do they think it is important to give back to the world or just take from it? Do they think that human beings deserve dignity or to be abused? Is sexuality a private thing or something that should be publicly displayed? Is love and sharing important in relationships, or are others just there for their convenience? All of these and many other things are conveyed through the interactions and modelling that happens in families.

A health professional and a student shared similar backgrounds that helped them acquire their "family values." The health professional described their family values as follows:

> Everyone in my family believed that you had to speak up when you saw injustice. My grandfather taught me that evil flourishes when good people say nothing. He ought to have known. He was a Holocaust survivor and often told me about how Hitler came to power and murdered so many people because good people did not stand up and oppose him early on. That left a lifelong impression on me, and I have always worked for social justice because of that. My mother ran for public office and served on a hospital board. My father brought home food from his retail store to give to people on our street who did not have enough to eat. These were very strong values in my family.

Another young man had this to say about the values in his family:

> My family has always believed in hard work. My father and mother were immigrants. They had to start from scratch and built a life for themselves and us kids with their hands and the sweat of their brows. I always admired them for that. They always took care of their family. I guess I have those values too. I love and care for my family as well.

A young male college student also described his family's values:

> We emigrated from the Caribbean and were shocked by the racism we encountered in this country. But my father and mother taught us not to be bitter, but to handle ourselves with grace and dignity, be friendly to others, and always respect ourselves, never stooping to the same kind of behaviour

as some others display. I guess I internalized that because self-respect is very important to me. I think a lot about who I am and who I want to be as a person, and I try to live by that every day. I want a good education, and I want to do important work, and I want to be good to and take care of my family and contribute to society. I believe that my actions will speak louder than any words I could ever say. My parents taught me that. They have done very well since emigrating. They have a big circle of friends, people of all races. I guess in their own way, they overcame racism by being good people and attracting other good people. I learned from that and plan to do the same in my own life.

Families can also transmit negative values, either consciously or unconsciously. One young woman had this to say:

My mother used to hit us, and now I find myself hitting my own children and feel very bad about it. She also used to yell, and everything was about her. I have to fight those tendencies in myself now. She was not a strong woman. She acted like us kids were there to serve her, and often she couldn't be bothered with us. We grew up feeling like we were nothing. I have to struggle so hard to be different with my kids because of all the awful things my mother taught us. I don't want to be like her and have my kids grow up hating me.

It is important for professionals to help families identify what positive values they hold dear, how they demonstrate these, and how the parents transfer their own values to their children through their words and actions. Helping parents to reflect on whether or not they are transmitting the values they would like their children to have is critical.

A professional working in a family services agency gave this example of how the parents in one family with whom she worked were inadvertently giving their children the wrong message:

The parents in this family meant well. They had both come through hardship growing up and suffered abuse at the hands of their own parents. They did not want their children to ever have to go through what they did. Unfortunately they overcompensated for their own personal pain growing up and were very lax with their children when it came to setting limits and disciplining them. Their kids were growing up to be very selfish and self-absorbed, not respecting others' limits or boundaries. The problem was their parents gave them everything, did everything for them, stood up for them when they got in trouble at school, and did not correct them when they were rude or inconsiderate. They were shocked when their kids became insolent adolescents and increasingly got into more and more trouble because they had no respect for authority. It is hard for a family to reintroduce limits when children are adolescents. It is even harder to try to instill good values in children at that age, but nevertheless [it's] worth a try. I encouraged this family to tell their children their own stories now that they were older, and share with them why it is so important to be kind to people, because the hurt can last a lifetime.

Another professional in an agency serving children and youth talked about his conversation with a family regarding some confusion in the kinds of values they were trying to instill in their children:

They had always believed that it is important to never be critical. Dad had had his own bad experience with his own father being overly critical of him and he did not want to repeat this problem with his own son, and so he regularly offered encouragement and support, but his son was not succeeding in school, in sports, or with friends. In a frank discussion one day I helped Dad to recognize that perhaps he was rewarding his son in general ways for "trying" rather than giving him very specific feedback about what he was doing well, and encouraging him to succeed, not just try. He was always saying "good job" to his son, when what he needed to say was "I liked the way you studied so hard for your math test and did so much better than the last time. That shows that hard work pays off." Dad realized that maybe he was sending the wrong message to his son—that trying was more important than actually accomplishing some things he could be proud of. Dad realized that sometimes he needed to help his son to identify what he learned from his mistakes. When his son failed a test, he sat down with him and asked him what he thought the problem was. His son admitted he had goofed off, had not studied, and had been falling behind in his work. When Dad asked him what he learned from that, his son replied, "I guess I need to shape up and put more effort into it." Rather than offer to help his son, something he had done so often in the past, he gave him a vote of confidence: "That's the spirit, son! You're no quitter. I admire that. I had to struggle too sometimes when I was growing up, but didn't give up. It's so nice to see you have the same stuff."

It is never too late for families to examine what they are trying to transmit, to share real stories about their own lives, and to discuss with each other why some things are important to them. Transmitting good values from one generation to another is a primary function of families. Some families will need assistance to identify their values and examine whether or not they are transmitting the values they want to transmit to each other (Min, Silverstein, & Lendon, 2012).

## BUILDING SOCIAL SUPPORT

Everyone wants to have positive relationships with others, but sometimes, in families, giving attention to negative relationships takes up one's time and emotional energy. Spending too much time feeding in to others who regularly demand attention and help at the expense of spending time with those who are positive, self-sufficient, and supportive can be draining and defeat the point of having relationships with others.

Gable, Gonzaga, and Strachman (2006) propose a key question: "Will you be there for me when things go right?" Their research showed that being there for someone when they have good news is even more important than being there for them when they have bad news. Helping other people savour the moment when something good happens to them is what builds relationships. Referring to this as "active constructive responding," Gable states that it is one of the most positive things we can teach children about building relationships, and it is what fosters our own relationships with others.

Relationship killers are terse responses and hijacking conversations to make them about us rather than remaining "on topic" when someone has good news to share. A recent conversation that took place in a restaurant illustrated this. One woman was telling another how happy she was that she had just passed a difficult course. Instead of responding in a way that let the other woman know how happy she was for her, her "friend" said, "Yeah, feels good, doesn't it? I remember when I finished my master's program, how great it felt." She did not say a word of encouragement to her friend, and instead turned the conversation back to herself.

Some parents try too hard to help their children have friends. They organize elaborate parties and sleepovers when providing their children with good relationship-building and friendship-making skills is more important. Modelling good friendships and how to maintain closeness with others, as well as with family members, involves knowing how to solve problems, how to put oneself in another's shoes and see things from their perspective, returning conversation bids, and generally trying to be a decent person.

## COMMUNICATION BIDS

People regularly make bids to each other when they try to open the lines of communication with a "Good morning! It's a beautiful day isn't it?" or "You look so nice today!" Returning those bids with "Yes, it is beautiful, isn't it? I hope we both get out in the sunshine today" and "Why, thank you. That's so nice of you to notice" rather than a terse or non-existent reply helps to build relationships. Gottman (2001) refers to these as "bids for connection."

Returning communication bids in intimate relationships is even more important to maintaining long-term marriages and friendships. When a wife turned to her husband and said, "Honey, why don't we go away together this year?" and got nothing but a grunt from him as he was watching the game, she felt hurt and shut out. Later, when he tried to talk to her, she did not feel like talking, to which he said, "What the hell did I do now?" In the wife's view, she was trying to be romantic and suggest something the two of them enjoy, but her husband was more absorbed in the game on TV than in her, and she felt stung by that. His view of the situation may have been that she chose a bad time to talk about it. However, it is risky in relationships to ignore these kinds of communication bids because there is often something important behind them. In this case, the wife had been feeling neglected and wanted to try to solve the problem by suggesting quality time away with her husband. The problem was made worse for her when, once again, it seemed that he was ignoring her.

Children in families will model what they see their parents and older brothers and sisters do. Showing them how to build relationships is an important function of families. Returning communication bids is one of the best things families can teach children to help them have positive relationships in adulthood.

## SYMBOLIC COMMUNICATION

Symbolic communication occurs when behaviour sends a message that can be a metaphor for something else. Families regularly send messages about trust, love, rejection, abandonment, hope, and many other things to each other. If a parent is jealous or envious of someone else because the person has more money or has a skill they do not have, and feels bad about themselves for not having this but makes no effort to achieve something of their own, they are sending a metaphoric or symbolic message to children in the family that it is okay to envy what others have while not making an effort to set one's own goals and work toward them.

One former professional now teaching in a college had this to say about this process:

> I worked with this family, two parents, two kids, and a dog. The dog was a bit problematic because she was a bit aggressive at times with other dogs, and this worried the mother. Mom decided that they needed to give the dog up and this was causing some distress in the house. I sat down with Mom to try to help her see how her kids, and possibly her husband, might be interpreting how she intended to solve "the problem." Would she consider giving them away if their behaviour was not up to scratch? Did they consider the dog a part of the family? When she thought about it she realized that just getting rid of the dog would send the wrong message to everyone. She decided to get her husband and kids to join her in working with a professional trainer to help the dog overcome its aggressive tendencies. That went a long way to creating a sense of security and "we-ness" in the whole family. The message was "we solve our family's problems together"—a very good message to give to everyone.

Relationships are built on trust, shared good times, loyalty, and feelings of belonging. Helping family members to be able to trust each other, enjoy fun activities together, celebrate each other's successes, and promote a "we" feeling when confronting challenges or problems helps to strengthen their relationships with each other and others.

## STRENGTHS-BASED ASSESSMENT

Walsh (1993) was one of the first to point out that clinical perspectives concerning families tended to be deficit-based—where the inherent strengths, even in families that were confronting considerable challenges, were often ignored. Families were not considered a possible source of resilience and strength (Karpel, 1986). For a long time, this caused many professionals to search for possible sources of resilience and strength outside the family, in coaches, teachers, or other mentors (Walsh, 1996).

Walsh (1996, p. 9) points out that "resilience is that human potential to emerge from a shattering experience scarred, yet strengthened." She refers to a study done by Werner and Smith (1992) of "nearly 700 children born into hardship on the island of Kauai ... reared in poverty, with one third experiencing stress and [being] raised in families torn apart by fighting, divorce, alcoholism or mental illness," of which "many developed into 'fine human beings'" (Walsh, 1996, p. 4).

It appears that social influences and individual characteristics and temperament, as well as the family, all play a role in this. Significant individual characteristics that appear to contribute to resilience are having a reasonable level of self-esteem and self-efficacy as opposed to a sense of helplessness (Rutter, 1985); having an easygoing temperament and higher intelligence; and having good coping and problem-solving skills, all of which tend to invite more favourable responses from others (Walsh, 1996).

Kobasa (1979) found that resilient people tended to believe that they were able to influence events in their lives, often felt deeply committed to whatever they were involved with, and saw change as a challenge and learning experience rather than something to be feared.

With respect to a more cross-cultural perspective, Dugan and Coles (1989) found that "moral and spiritual sources of courage" tended to "lift individuals above hardship" (Walsh, 1996, p. 4).

The earlier deficit-based views of families have now been replaced with more of a focus on what strengths and abilities allow families to not only survive but thrive in spite of numerous challenges and stressors. What strengths allow families to flourish and overcome significant obstacles?

Focusing on family strengths requires a philosophical shift for professionals, where there is a recognition that families that "differ from the norm" tend to be "pathologized and presumed dysfunctional although their processes may be typical and even functional in their particular situation" (Walsh, 1996, p. 8). Over the years, numerous studies have been able to distinguish what causes a family to function irrespective of its form.

Some important questions are beginning to be asked about family functioning. For instance, especially in families that come from collectivist societies and varying cultural contexts, is being very highly cohesive a cause for concern about enmeshment, or is it important, especially during a major family crisis?

The ecological perspective takes into account multiple and overlapping cultural contexts in the lives of families. It incorporates as complete a view as possible of the complexities of family life—the constraints, the challenges, and the resources and protective factors in families that promote effective functioning. Family functioning is viewed "in context," and there is an understanding that "there are many pathways in resilience" (Walsh, 1996, p. 9).

In strengths-based assessment, professionals seek to answer the questions *Why is a family functioning as it is? What is adaptive and working for the family?*

One of the major tasks of a family is to raise children who can function well in the world. Four major factors that have been identified as critical for children to grow in a way that ensures that they can adapt readily to the world are the ability to form healthy attachments; the ability to self-regulate; the development of good communication and learning skills; and being able to establish and maintain relationships with others (Centre for Community Child Health, 2004). Helping families to identify strengths related to each of these factors offers a beginning point in strengths-based assessment.

The Centre for the Study of Social Policy (2013) has identified five protective factors as critical to healthy family functioning and development: parental resilience; social connections; concrete support in times of need; knowledge of parenting and child development; and children's social and emotional competence. Factors considered protective are those that may help children avoid mental health problems as they get older, because these factors help to offset adverse circumstances in their lives.

## PROTECTIVE FACTORS

The Centers for Disease Control and Prevention (2013) has also identified the following protective factors: "supportive family environment and social networks; nurturing parenting skills; stable family relationships; household rules and child monitoring; parental employment; adequate housing; access to health care and social services; caring adults outside the family who can serve as role models and mentors; communities that support parents and take responsibility for preventing abuse."

In 1998, Epstein and Sharma developed the Behavioral and Emotional Rating Scale (BERS), a standardized tool "for assessing and evaluating strengths." It is a 52-item scale that is intended to measure the "emotional and behavioral strengths of children and adolescents" across five domains: "interpersonal strength (emotional regulation in social settings), family involvement (quality of family relationships), intrapersonal strength (perception of the child's own competence and accomplishments), school functioning, and affective strength (the ability to express feelings and accept affection from others)" (Center for Effective Collaboration and Practice, 2013; see also Rudolph & Epstein, 2000).

There are numerous other assessment tools available. However, all have a problem in common—using them means that the professional sets the agenda and defines a family's strengths within particular domains or frameworks rather than the family determining what it considers most important. This robs the family of the opportunity to decide what the agenda should be in a discussion of its strengths, and forces it to fit into a framework. An open-ended strengths-based assessment is often much more empowering for families.

## SPECIFICS OF STRENGTHS-BASED PRACTICE

When professionals arrive, it is often the family's cue to begin talking about problems. The focus quickly becomes how the family is not working, and family members begin to feel angry, frustrated, and stuck. A professional using a strengths-based assessment within an empowerment framework will more likely open the discussion by saying, "Tell me all the things that are good about your family" (see Spindel, 2013). The family can then begin to define itself in a way that feels more positive. Many families feel negatively judged and defensive, and may believe that others see them as problematic. This does not provide a good base for positive changes to occur.

Questions that can be asked to encourage family members to begin identifying their strengths include *What are some of the things you have accomplished together? What are some of the ways that you have helped each other through hard times? In what ways do you think your family communicates effectively? Tell me about the friendships within your family—who are you close to and why? What do you like most about each other?* These kinds of questions encourage families to identify and discuss their own family culture. During these discussions, professionals will learn what is most important to the family and how family members see themselves and the family as a whole. They will also have the opportunity to observe family dynamics and what roles different family members play. By establishing the context for families to first identify and acknowledge their strengths and discuss what is most important to them, rather than forcing them to fit into a standardized assessment, professionals can help empower families by giving them the message that they are the experts in their own lives and that they know themselves best.

One professional described what happened using this approach with what had been identified as a multi-problem family by the local school and mental health centre. The family had emigrated from a war-torn country in the Middle East, and the consensus was that they were traumatized and suffering mental health problems as a result. Two of the children were acting out aggressively with other children, and the third child seemed withdrawn. When teachers tried to talk to the parents, they became very defensive and somewhat aggressive. The mother was said to appear depressed, and the father agitated and irritable with both the school and mental health centre staff.

In the professional's first meeting with the family, family members appeared suspicious due to their previous experiences with social services and the school system. However, she began by asking them to share what was good about their family. Their surprise was palpable, and at first they were silent. Then the mother responded by saying how proud she was that her children were going to school, something she had never been able to do. Her three children reacted by smiling shyly at each other and nudging each other playfully. Next, her husband said that he appreciated how his wife and children helped create a home that he felt good about, and that even though there were problems sometimes, he knew everyone cared about each other. When the children were asked, they said they liked when their parents played games with them, or they went on an outing together. It became clear before too long that the family's view of itself was not at all like the view prior professionals had of it. When the children were asked about friends and school, they said they had to fight at school because other kids were mean to them. The oldest child felt responsible for the younger ones, and admitted that he threatened some children who liked to pick on his younger brother and sister. They were able to tell this professional, who had a much more positive approach, what was happening from their perspective, and she developed a very different view of this family from the other professionals who were attempting, often unsuccessfully, to work with them.

In helping families to formulate ways that they would like to change, a framework may be helpful. Once families have spent some time identifying their strengths, the professional can move the discussion on to what they need. This may be a cue for family members to begin talking about what is wrong with their family. As they start identifying problems, it will be important to help them reframe these as needs.

For example, Philip and his wife, June, and their two children were going through a rough time. Philip did not like June's mother, who liked to come and visit June and the grandchildren. He felt that she was contemptuous of him, and they regularly got into screaming fights. June felt torn between her husband and her mother. The children tried to ease the tension by acting out, thereby shifting the focus away from their father and grandmother and onto them. June was almost at the end of her rope. Philip felt June's loyalty should be to him and that she should take his side against her mother. The ongoing battle was having a very negative effect on the family as a whole.

When Philip said that the problem in the family was that June's mother visited too often and did not respect him, his worker urged him to reframe it as a need of his. After thinking about it, Philip replied, "I guess I would prefer it if the children and June visited her on their own sometimes. And I would like June to tell her mother that when she is in our home, she needs to at least be civil to me." Reframing the "problem" in this way allowed both Philip and June to come up with a compromise that might work for the family.

When conducting a family assessment using a strengths-based model built on an empowerment practice framework, it is important to begin with strengths using open-ended questions until there is a nice, long list. Next, it is vital to help a family reframe problems as needs so that they can see a way forward rather than feeling stuck. Doing this can lay the groundwork for the family to identify goals that they would like to work on together.

## FOSTERING EMOTIONAL REGULATION

Serious issues arise in families when family members have difficulty controlling and managing strong feelings and emotions. One of these is the problem of catastrophizing. Knaus (2012) states that "worry, anxiety, stress, and panic are often the emotional expressions of catastrophic thinking." He defines catastrophizing as "an exaggerating, irrational style of thought where you painfully blow real or imagined disasters out of proportion" and as a "form of manufactured misery." This kind of thinking results in a sort of brain freeze where concentration becomes difficult and problem solving becomes almost impossible.

Dr. Anna Baranowsky of the Toronto Traumatology Institute stated during a workshop presentation that an "unanxious presence is the best gift that a professional can give to someone who is in distress." Teaching family members how to avoid catastrophizing and manage their strong emotions is another gift that professionals can give to families. Helping others to tolerate tension can help to address a host of difficulties that many families face. Knaus (2012) suggests a few ways to combat catastrophizing, the first being to see things as they actually are and not as one imagines them to be. This involves refusing to turn a "molehill … into a mountain" and distinguishing between "concerns, calamities, and catastrophe." Another helpful strategy is to identify what story is being told and determining what part of it is fact and what part is fiction. It is also beneficial to recognize that we sometimes have no control over events in our lives, but we do have control over how we react to them. Focusing on what one can do as opposed to worrying about what one cannot do is also helpful.

Burns (1989) has identified some of the core reasons for emotional dysregulation. These include all-or-nothing thinking; overgeneralization; disqualifying the positive; jumping to conclusions; magnification (or exaggeration); emotional reasoning (believing that negative thoughts reflect reality: "I feel it, so it must be true"); "should" statements (unrealistic expectations of self and others); labelling and mislabelling (emotionally loaded representations of self and others: "I'm a loser; he's a jerk"); and personalization (taking on blame for something that is not one's fault). Professionals can assist families in identifying these common pitfalls that cause or exacerbate emotional arousal and help them to manage what sometimes seem like overwhelming emotions.

Dialectical therapy—often used with those labelled with borderline personality disorder, a condition in which individuals have extreme difficulty managing their emotions—has laid out the process of emotional dysregulation as follows: A prompting event occurs, and the event is interpreted, resulting in a neuro-chemical brain change. This results in activation of the sympathetic (or arousing) nervous system. Physical changes then occur (muscles tense, heart rate goes up, breathing becomes more shallow, etc.), face and body language change, and behaviour (words or actions) occurs (Dialectic Therapy, 2010).

Burns (1989) has identified several "interpretations" that result in these kinds of brain changes and physical reactions. It is these interpretations that increase stress levels and often cause conflict in families. This is the point of intervention where professionals can be especially helpful—assisting families to reappraise a situation. This can greatly aid communication, a topic that will be covered more fully in chapter 4.

## LEARNING FROM MISTAKES

Individuals and families make mistakes. When the result is shame, guilt, and blame, a downward spiral can create family conflict. Mistakes, however, are actually opportunities for families to learn together, examining what went wrong and how it could be corrected without blame. Family members need to be encouraged to use "I" language when discussing mistakes. For example, "I would have preferred it if you had asked me if it was okay for your mom to visit" is better than "You never show me any consideration, about your mom visiting or anything else!" (Center for Parenting Education, 2014).

Helping families to learn from mistakes may involve addressing some of the negative attributions and interpretations outlined earlier in this chapter. In the statement "You never show me any consideration, about your mom visiting or anything else!" three things are happening. There is a blaming stance intended to invoke guilt; there is overgeneralization; and there is a negative attribution—the person was deliberately thoughtless. All of these need to be relabelled in a way that encourages learning.

Helping families to reframe mistakes as opportunities to learn a better way of handling things is an important intervention that professionals can make.

## HAVING FUN TOGETHER

Families who are stressed do not often have fun together. There is no play and few or no organized activities; many do not even cook or eat dinner together. Encouraging families to have a picnic in the park, with parents playing baseball with the kids after lunch, and making this a regular summer routine, does not cost money and encourages the family to play together. It is easy to find fun activities that families can participate in by checking a newspaper for weekend activities, or looking on the Internet for suggestions, or asking family members what kinds of things they like to do. Today, too many individuals in families engage in solitary activities such as computer games or texting that do nothing to increase their social skills or ability to form relationships with others. By encouraging family activities that everyone can engage in, professionals can help families to rediscover joy in each other's presence.

## CHAPTER SUMMARY

In this chapter, readers have been introduced to the concept of resilience and what promotes it in families. Examples of how values are transmitted in families have also been included. A case has also been made for the use of open-ended strengths-based assessment as opposed to assessment instruments. This allows families to set their own agenda and identify their culture on their own terms with professionals rather than being forced to respond within a particular framework. In addition to setting out a framework for engaging families in discussing their strengths, readers have also been encouraged to help families to reframe problems as needs to avoid becoming stuck or seeing situations as being unresolvable. The importance of building social skills through the use of communication tools, recognizing and responding to symbolic communication, and fostering emotional regulation are also included.

The next chapter will examine what developmental stages families experience and discuss how knowledge of these stages can be helpful for professionals.

## FURTHER READING

Alliance for Children and Youth of Waterloo Region. (n.d.). Strength based approaches. https://www.wellingtoncdsb.ca/strengthsineducation/strengths/aboutus/Documents/strengths_based_education.pdf

CanChild Centre for Childhood Disability Research. (2003). Identifying and building on parent and family strengths and resources. https://www.canchild.ca/system/tenon/assets/attachments/000/001/271/original/FCS6.pdf

Lee, M. Y. (2009, October). Utilizing family strengths and resilience: Integrative family and systems treatment with children and adolescents with severe emotional and behavioral problems. *Family Process*, *48*(3), 395–416. https://www.researchgate.net/publication/26763166_

Military One Source. (2018, November 11). Family resilience protective factors. https://www.militaryonesource.mil/family-relationships/family-life/keeping-your-family-strong/family-resilience-protective-factors

Walsh, F. (2012, October). Family resilience: Strengths forged through adversity. University of Chicago. https://www.researchgate.net/publication/232567591_Family_resilience_Strengths_forged_through_adversity

## CLASSROOM RESOURCES

*Changing season: On the Masumoto family farm.* (2014). NFB. https://www.nfb.ca/film/changing_season_on_the_masumoto_family_farm/

*Mystery of the secret room.* (2016). NFB. https://www.nfb.ca/film/mystery_of_the_secret_room/

## CLASSROOM ACTIVITIES

### A Strengths Family Tree (for smaller classes)

Ask students to draw a tree that contains their family's strengths. The tree may be drawn, or it may be a collage. Ask each student to describe what specific strengths their family possesses, how they acquired them, and what impact these strengths have had in their own lives.

### Gratitude Exercise

Ask each member of the class to write down what they feel grateful to their family for, and share with the group if they feel comfortable doing so.

Ask each member of the class to write down a particular struggle their family has had and how their family overcame it, again sharing with the group if they feel comfortable doing so.

## Social Support Exercise

Ask each member of the class to write the name of someone in their family who was a positive influence in their life, and write the strength they encouraged in them under their name. Remark on the importance of the people who encourage us in our lives and what a wealth of strengths they bring to us.

## QUESTIONS FOR REFLECTION

1. What values were you taught in your family?
2. In what ways do you believe your own family promotes resilience?
3. What has your own family taught you about emotional regulation?
4. How have your values and ability to regulate emotions helped or hindered you in your own practice with families?

## REFERENCES

American Psychological Association. (2013). The road to resilience. Retrieved from www.apa.org/helpcenter/road-resilience.aspx

Burns, D. D. (1989). *The feeling good handbook*. New York, NY: William Morrow.

Center for Effective Collaboration and Practice. (2013). BERS assessment. Retrieved from https://www.parinc.com/Products/Pkey/18

Center for Parenting Education. (2014). Healthy communication techniques: The skill of I messages—what to say when we are upset. Retrieved from http://centerforparentingeducation.org/library-of-articles/healthy-communication-techniques/the-skill-of-i-messages-what-to-say-when-we-are-upset/

Centers for Disease Control and Prevention. (2013). Child maltreatment: Risk and protective factors. Retrieved from www.cdc.gov/violenceprevention/childmaltreatment/riskprotectivefactors.html

Centre for Community Child Health. (2004). The underlying factors affecting child health and development and family functioning. Retrieved from www.rch.org.au/uploadedFiles/Main/Content/ccch/EY_UF_Summary.pdf

Centre for the Study of Social Policy. (2013). The Protective Factors Framework. Retrieved from www.cssp.org/reform/strengthening-families/the-basics/protective-factors

Dialectic Therapy. (2010). Model of emotions. Retrieved from www.dialectictherapy.com/tag/emotion-regulation/

Dugan, T., & Coles, R. (Eds.). (1989). *The child in our times: Studies in the development of resiliency.* New York, NY: Brunner/Mazel.

Epstein, M. H., & Sharma, J. M. (1998). *Behavioral and Emotional Rating Scale: A strength-based approach to assessment.* Austin, TX: Pro-Ed.

Extend-A-Family. (2019). Extend-A-Family mission. Retrieved from http://extendafamily.ca/

Gable, S. L., Gonzaga, G. C., & Strachman, A. (2006). Will you be there for me when things go right? Supportive responses to positive event disclosures. *Journal of Personality and Social Psychology, 91*(5), 904–917.

Gottman, J. M. (2001). *The relationship cure.* New York, NY: Three Rivers Press.

Grohol, J. M. (2014). What is catastrophizing? *Psych Central.* Retrieved from http://psychcentral.com/lib/what-is-catastrophizing/0001276

Jordan, R. (1994). *The fires of heaven.* New York, NY: Tor Books.

Karpel, M. A. (1986). *Family resources: The hidden partner in family therapy.* New York, NY: Guilford Press.

Knaus, B. (2012, November 28). Anxiety and exaggerations. *Psychology Today.* Retrieved from www.psychologytoday.com/blog/science-and-sensibility/201211/anxiety-and-exaggerations

Kobasa, S. (1979, January). Stressful life events, personality, and health: An inquiry into hardiness. *Journal of Personality and Social Psychology, 37*(1), 1–11.

Min, J., Silverstein, M. D., & Lendon, J. P. (2012, September). Intergenerational transmission of values over the family life course. Retrieved from https://experts.syr.edu/en/publications/intergenerational-transmission-of-values-over-the-family-life-cou

Rudolph, S. M., & Epstein, M. H. (2000). Empowering children and families through strength-based assessment. *Reclaiming Children and Youth, 8*(4), 207–209.

Rutter, M. (1985). Resilience in the face of adversity: Protective factors and resistance to psychiatric disorder. *British Journal of Psychiatry, 147*, 598–611.

Southwick, S. M., Litz, B. T., Charney, D., & Friedman, M. J. (2011). *Resilience and mental health: Challenges across the lifespan.* Cambridge, UK: Cambridge University Press. Retrieved from www.ocf.berkeley.edu/~eerlab/pdf/papers/2011_Troy_Resilience_in_the_face_of_stress.pdf

Spindel, P. (2013). *Case management from an empowerment perspective: A guide for health and human service professionals.* Toronto, ON: Spindel & Associates.

Walsh, F. (1993). Conceptualization of normal family processes. In F. Walsh (Ed.), *Normal family processes* (2nd ed.). New York, NY: Guilford Press.

Walsh, F. (1996, September). The concept of family resilience: Crisis and challenge. *Family Process, 35*(3), 261–281.

Werner, E., & Smith, R. S. (1992). *Overcoming the odds: High risk children from birth to adulthood.* Ithaca, NY: Cornell University Press.

## CHAPTER 3

# Developmental Stages in Families

*All that is valuable in human society depends upon the opportunity for development accorded the individual.*

　　—Albert Einstein

## CHAPTER OVERVIEW

Like individuals, families go through life stages. This chapter will list and provide a description of the joys and challenges of each stage of family development.

A number of authors have discussed family development theory (Mattessich & Hill, 1987; Rodgers & White, 1993). According to Mattessich and Hill (1987, p. 427), "Family development ... has uniquely pioneered the effort to describe and explain the processes of change in families. Family time—the sequence of stages precipitated internally by the demands of family members (e.g. biological, psychological, and social needs) and externally by the larger society (e.g. social expectations and ecological constraints)—is the most significant focal point of the family development perspective." Roles change as families mature, and there are different challenges that families must overcome at each stage of their development.

Five stages have been identified as part of the family life cycle. They are independence; coupling or marriage; parenting from infancy through adolescence;

launching adult children; and retirement or senior years. Families are challenged to master each of these stages and successfully move to the next. Failure to move successfully through each stage can create difficulties in relationships and lay the groundwork for rocky future transitions, whereas success in mastering each stage can create a firm foundation for the challenges to come.

## THE INDEPENDENCE STAGE

This is the life stage when young people leave home and establish themselves emotionally, financially, physically, and socially. It is a time when their adult personalities fully form, circles of friendship develop outside their family of origin, and decisions are made about how they want to live their lives and what form their lives will take. Hopes and dreams for the future are prominent in this stage as individuals begin deciding what type and level of education they wish to achieve, what kind of work they want to do, and what kind of family of their own they wish to establish and with whom. Establishing oneself physically and financially involves developing healthy eating and exercise habits, and finding ways of bringing in an income to support independent living.

This is also a time when young people learn a great deal about how to form and maintain relationships with others that will endure over the longer term. Individuals ask themselves what they may have in common with another and the nature and type of commitment they are seeking. Issues arise concerning interdependence and how to handle feelings and emotions within a relationship (HealthLink BC, 2013).

Forming an identity separate from one's family of origin is a critical aspect of this stage of development. Being able to truly connect with others while being one's own person becomes important. For those who are gay, lesbian, or transgender, this stage may include the additional challenge of "coming out" to one's family.

Many young people go through crises of confidence at this stage, especially if they have not had the opportunity to spread their wings and exercise their independence within their families of origin. Overprotection in earlier years, where parents hovered and did not allow children to make their own mistakes and learn from them, may now pose challenges as young people are required to deal with issues and problems without calling on their parents for help (HealthLink BC, 2013). This can become especially evident in educational settings where, often for the first time, young people are required to manage their time, meet assignment commitments, and learn additional academic skills, as well as learn how to relate to professors and other students in a positive way.

Young people who have been disadvantaged by too much parental involvement may find themselves challenged by the need to stand on their own and negotiate their own way through dilemmas and conflicts without parental intervention. It will be especially hard for young people who have not developed the personal discipline and time-management skills necessary to meet the challenges posed by this stage of development (Dixon, 2013).

Those young people who are going out to work for the first time will need to navigate employment expectations, workplace norms, and relationships with bosses and co-workers. If they have learned in their families of origin to work with others, get work done effectively, and problem solve, they will have no difficulty with this stage of their lives. However, if young people have not learned good relationship skills or have not had to meet earlier academic or other challenges without considerable help from their parents and others, they could face crises that challenge their coping abilities and, as a consequence, experience high levels of stress.

This is also the stage where serious mental health issues can first emerge. Conditions such as schizophrenia, bipolar disorder, and other mental health conditions generally arise when people are in their late teens or early twenties. This can cause a crisis in the life of the young person as well as their family (Centre for Addiction and Mental Health, 2012). Many mental health agencies have early psychosis intervention programs. Professionals can greatly help individuals and their families at this stage by locating these resources and helping people to link with them.

Young people may also find relationships with their parents strained at this time. Parents who have difficulty surrendering their parental responsibilities as their children grow up may expect the same kind of contact with their children as they have always had. However, their children may find this intrusive as they attempt to strike out on their own and establish their own identities.

In some cultures it is expected that children will stay home until they marry. Other families may arrange marriages for young people. In Canada and the United States, where children are more likely to have attended public schools, this can cause serious conflict, as some young people may want to find their own partners. This process of individuating from their families of origin can cause considerable family conflict.

## COUPLING STAGE

During the coupling stage, individuals seek to form a close and intimate relationship with another person. This involves trust and the ability to adapt to being part of a couple. This can present numerous challenges for those who have had difficulties with attachment in their early lives, or troubled family-of-origin relationships. This is the stage where these early difficulties may present themselves in the form of sometimes very emotional conflicts with romantic partners. All of the baggage that is brought to a new relationship from family-of-origin or earlier romantic relationships will now have to be resolved in some way. The challenge is to develop insight into one's own and a partner's behaviour and to have compassion for each other when trying to work through these sometimes painful issues (HealthLink BC, 2013).

Insecure early attachment may cause difficulties around commitment. Poor role modelling by parents—a father who had repeated affairs, a mother who withdrew when hurt, a father who refused to do his share of housework, a mother who escaped regularly from family life in external activities to avoid dealing with a marital relationship—can cause individuals to adopt maladaptive coping styles. These coping styles may now manifest in individuals as they attempt to function within a partnership and decide what kind of lifestyle they want; whether or not they want children; what kind of home they will build together; how close or distant they plan to be from their families of origin; who will manage the finances and how; what kind of wedding they will have if one is planned; who their friends will be; what they will spend money on; what kind of sex life they will have; how much autonomy each will have within the relationship; and how much closeness or distance will be acceptable to them both—all will need to be negotiated as intimate relationships begin to take shape (WebMD, 2013).

One important task that confronts the individual at this stage is the decision to make the one they love the most important person in their lives, above parents, siblings, or friends. Loyalty to the person that an individual plans to spend their life with is vital in this stage, yet conflicts may emerge. Parents may not approve of their child's choice of a life partner; however, if the individual is truly committed to making the relationship and possible marriage work, they will have to stand up to the displeasure of their parents and make it clear where their new loyalties lie. This can be very hard on a family of origin as a once-loyal son or daughter may say "Either you accept my partner, or you will have to do without me." Parents at this stage will need to reflect on how they can maintain a relationship with their son or daughter, and keep some degree of peace in the family, whether or not they accept the romantic choice their child has made. Failure to accept a son or daughter's choice of a mate can result in lifelong conflict and serious family schisms.

The coupling stage is also when two families may be asked to blend together. There can be great differences in the socioeconomic status of each family, or variations in their cultural, racial, or ethnic backgrounds. These can either pose problems or be a cause for celebration, depending upon how the couple and their families decide to treat them. This makes the coupling stage a very tricky one for a young couple to manoeuvre through—they are being asked to surrender or significantly change all their former relationships and ways of doing things, and have faith in the success of their new relationship. If family members are rigid or demanding, this can cause considerable stress on a young couple who are fearful of losing all they have held dear in favour of an unknown future with someone new. This can become unbearable, and some young people may sacrifice their partner to return to their families as they have not yet found the strength to fully take on the responsibilities and consequences of their new independence.

This is the stage where a new family system, consisting of two individuals, is formed. Both will need to make adjustments and accommodations in order for the relationship to work. Problems will result if one partner demands to always have their own way; so, too, if one partner is always giving in. For the relationship to be successful, both individuals will have to consider the other's needs and wishes. Sharing goals, putting another's needs above one's own, doing kind and considerate things for each other, and ensuring that there is passion and love in the relationship—these are tasks that will need to be mastered at this stage in a relationship (HealthLink BC, 2013).

This is also the stage where each person's personal boundaries will need to be clarified and respected by the other person. This and the other tasks inherent in this part of a family's development will require common goals and dreams, good interpersonal communication, the ability to confront problems together rather than seeing one another as the problem, and, often, having similar spiritual beliefs.

Problems not worked out at this stage in the family cycle will definitely surface later as significant sources of stress and conflict.

## PARENTING: FROM INFANCY THROUGH ADOLESCENCE

The third stage in the family life cycle often heralds the arrival of children. It is the most challenging but also potentially the most joyful and rewarding stage in the family life cycle, depending upon how the couple sees and responds to it.

Couples must decide whether and/or when to have their first child. In some cases, the decision is made for them in the form of an unexpected pregnancy. This need for quick adjustment and problem solving can create an emotional and financial crisis as the couple decides how to accommodate the new family member before they are ready (Hong, 2011). How the couple navigates this will determine whether or not the marriage or partnership survives, and if it does, what form it will take.

Galinsky (1987) has outlined six stages in the parenting process: the image-making stage (pregnancy, where individuals prepare for their own transformation into parents as well as fearing or embracing the new responsibilities they will have); the nurturing stage (birth to 18 months, where parents are balancing child care with other responsibilities in their lives); the authoritative stage (two to four years, where a couple is working out their parenting style and assessing its effectiveness); the interpretive stage (preschool through adolescence, where life lessons are taught and parents field questions about peers and relationships); the independent stage (adolescence, where parents help their children find their identity and ready them for independence); and, finally, the departure stage (where children prepare to leave home).

When a child is born, the identity of the couple changes from being that of romantic partners to being parents. Communication and problem-solving skills learned during the independence stage will serve a couple well at this stage. If these skills were not mastered, conflict may become more deeply embedded in the relationship, distorting the dynamics of the new family. If both partners were also able to resolve some of the baggage they brought from their families of origin during the independence phase, there is less of a chance that the more negative aspects of how their families of origin related to each other will be carried over into the next generation.

Even if a woman's pregnancy takes a relatively normal course, the couple will feel stressed about the changes to come; the stress only increases if complications arise. Health problems during pregnancy, and the worry these can cause, place considerable stress on a couple. If they are not able to talk about these stressors and support one another, harm can be done to the couple relationship. When a child is born, other stressors, such as lack of sleep and worries about the added responsibilities of a child, can lead to a breaking point in the relationship.

A child's healthy development requires parents who are able to integrate this new being into their relationship and work together to address the additional responsibilities inherent in having a new child. Both parents will need to adapt and to adopt new roles, transitioning from being individuals, to being a couple, to being parents.

Parenting infants and young children can be extremely challenging as well as very rewarding. There are some things that can make this stage much easier. The first is taking care of the couple relationship. Children feel more secure when their parents are at ease with and supportive of each other. The second is establishing routines, especially around meals, chores, and bedtimes. Routines create structure in a day that makes children feel safe and secure. Absence of routines can create a chaotic environment in which children feel upset and at loose ends.

The third is learning to set limits with children in a way that both parents can support. Parents, each of whom has a very different approach to child-rearing, can end up at odds with each other about how to set limits and discipline a child. This kind of friction and conflict is likely to have an upsetting effect on the child. Becoming educated about good child-rearing techniques and adopting strategies that both parents can support will be vital in creating a safe and secure environment for a child.

One of the skills that will be important during this stage is compromise. As couples purchase their first home and car, buy insurance, and decide on child-rearing strategies, compromise, which should have been learned during the independence phase, will become vital.

In-laws may become problematic during this phase, as grandparents wishing to spend time with the family and their new grandchild may begin making demands (HealthLink BC, 2013).

If both parents work, the stress of navigating and dealing with the day care and school systems will also begin. Now parents will have the stressors of work, caring for a child, dealing with in-laws, and possibly financial challenges, as well as outside stressors like day care and school. All of these require good communication skills, routines, and considerable organization.

Furthermore, it will be necessary for couples to take care of their relationship by ensuring that they get some time alone to reconnect. When parents focus too much on their children and not enough on each other, it can spell trouble in the form of distancing and/or extramarital affairs. Alternatively, if parents are able to navigate this period successfully through good communication, problem solving, and compromise, it can be one of the most rewarding and joyful periods of family life, as the family expands to include children and grandparents.

As children get older and turn into teens, a whole new set of challenges confronts a family. This is a time when caring and trust can be severely strained as adolescents test their own individuality and separateness from their parents. Being oppositional and challenging parents' belief systems and ways of doing things are vital for young adolescents as they begin to carve out an identity of their own.

In families where cultural beliefs are particularly strong, especially around dating practices and what is appropriate for young women and men within the family and outside it, conflict can become particularly acute.

For example, Aneesa is a good student, and a capable and caring young woman. She recently met a boy at school who is not Muslim, whom she likes very much. Since she is approaching her sixteenth birthday, she wants to be able to date him unchaperoned, but she knows this will cause enormous conflict in her family. Because of this, she decided to see this boy privately without informing her family, but her brother, who attends the same school, found out and told their parents. Since then the household has been in turmoil. Aneesa has been grounded and subjected to a strict curfew. She feels like a prisoner in her own house and has begun fighting and being very combative with her parents. Her mother fears that this conflict could escalate into violence since her father will not change his views on what he considers appropriate for a young girl.

This is an example of what can occur in families where a lack of flexibility exists. In cultures where parents arrange their children's marriages, this conflict can become especially acute as some children refuse to abide by cultural dictates and set out in search of their own mates.

Where families are able to negotiate compromises, the teenage stage can be much easier, but it is still not easy to deal with. It is important for parents at this stage to establish limits and boundaries for their teenage children while also helping them to explore their evolving selves within a society that is constantly changing and that presents challenges to each new generation (Monroe, 2018).

Teens need to have the opportunity to try out new ways of seeing the world, new behaviours, and, in some cases, new values. Maintaining a sense of balance—where some rules persist but others are negotiable, and a son or daughter is handed more and more responsibility as they get older and want more control over their lives—is a critical skill at this stage of a family's life cycle.

There are added stressors for gay or transgender youth at this stage, as they wish to begin exploring their sexuality. They may choose to either tell their parents about their sexual orientation or try to hide it from them. Coming out can be extremely difficult when a young person knows that their parents are unlikely to accept their sexual orientation or gender identity. This can cause extreme stress. In some cases the stress is so severe that it can increase the risk of suicide. Parents of gay and transgender teens will need to find ways to be supportive irrespective of what their own values are about homosexuality and gender identity. Their child's life may in some cases depend upon it (LaSala, 2011).

This is also a time in the family life cycle when parents in a couple's family of origin may be aging and have health problems of their own. Attempting to navigate the stressful teen years while dealing with the needs of aging parents can be extremely stressful. Couples in this situation are often referred to as being of the "sandwich generation," caught between the previous and the next generation's struggles and concerns.

Because of these demands, couples at this stage may be tempted to put their own needs last. The failure to balance their own need for "alone time" against the need to respond to the demands of others can be very damaging. The unrelenting stress can take its toll at this stage in the form of sleep deprivation, anxiety, depression, or even suicidal thoughts. This is a time when members of a couple may want to escape from the demands of their lives through drugs, alcohol, gambling, Internet addiction, or extramarital affairs. Some become sports fanatics, tied to the TV in order to avoid the stressors of everyday life. None of these help to effectively address the problems facing the family, and in most cases, they will make the problems worse. This means that this is a time when couples can reach a breaking point and end up separating and divorcing (Higginbotham, Henderson, & Skogrand, 2006).

The main cause of separation and divorce at this stage is the failure of couples to have effectively addressed the challenges of earlier stages—learning to solve problems and compromise, to balance their own needs against the needs and demands of others, to confront problems together rather than seeing each other as the problem, and to use appropriate coping strategies that ease stress.

Working on keeping a couple relationship strong is vital at this stage because it will take on a primary role in the next stage as couples get ready to launch their adult children into their own lives and into the world.

Mary and Bill's situation is a perfect illustration of this. Bill is a workaholic, and Mary is focused on her children to the point of being a "helicopter parent," constantly hovering over them and involving herself in every aspect of their lives. At 16 and 17 years of age, both children resent this, and there is considerable family conflict related to the children's push for more independence. Bill stays out of it, leaving much of this to his wife. He does not wish to incur her anger and deals with his own feelings by burying himself in his work. Bill and his wife have grown separate over the years, but Bill seems oblivious to this fact, choosing to take the path of least resistance and not talk about the real problems in their marriage—his distancing himself from her, her constant demands for his attention, and his current increase in drinking in order to try to cope. One child has now left home for college, and both Bill and Mary are developing health problems because of the constant stress in their lives. Mary has now confronted Bill and told him that if things don't change between them, she is leaving. Bill, who has denied any problems between them for years, is taken totally by surprise by this confrontation. He reacts angrily, telling her to "Go, then," and leaving the house to get drunk at the local bar.

This family's situation is illustrative of what can happen when the needs of the couple relationship are placed lower in priority than the need to focus on children and work. Bill and Mary are on the brink of divorce for failing to discuss each other's feelings and real needs in the relationship.

## LAUNCHING ADULT CHILDREN

Often referred to as the empty nest stage, this is the time when children finish high school and leave home to go to college or university, or to pursue a career. If parents have cared for their own relationship and have adequately prepared their children to enter the world by teaching them skills that will serve them well in higher education or in the job market, this can be a time of real freedom.

But if parents have built their lives around their children and have in some ways grown dependent on the role of parent, they may find it difficult to let their children go. This can cause conflict between the generations, and parents who have been overprotective or done too much for their children may find that their sons and daughters have difficulty establishing themselves in the world. Their children may lack a sense of purpose or direction, or the skills to find a good job or succeed academically without parents readily available to help with homework.

Some theorists, however, have contradicted this point by arguing that the launch phase may be different for various cultural communities. This is especially true where adult children remain at home until marriage and/or where there is an expectation that they maintain a high degree of closeness with parents as they establish lives of their own (Hong, 2011). Some may consider this behaviour "enmeshed," while others argue that this is where notions of the dominant culture clash with those of families from more collectivist cultures.

A modern phenomenon, perhaps the result of poor economic conditions in North America, has resulted in what are termed "boomerang children": those who return home because of their inability to find a job that pays enough for them to establish independent living arrangements or to be able to afford to get married (CBC News, 2012).

If a couple has neglected each other in favour of child-rearing and their lives have been out of balance in this regard for a long time, they may face real challenges in getting to know each other again and in coming together primarily as a married couple rather than just as parents. However, if couples have balanced their parenting and couple relationships, have continued to grow and develop on their own, and have helped their children to become independent, capable adults, this can be one of the most rewarding stages in the family life cycle. It is an opportunity to revisit career goals, travel, develop or return to old interests, make new friends and rekindle old friendships, explore new ideas and activities, do volunteer work, or simply enjoy the peace and quiet of an empty house and the luxury of time to oneself. This is also a stage where many begin to reflect on their life's journey—what they have learned from their mistakes and where and how they want to spend their remaining years.

Health issues may emerge at this time in the form of chronic conditions such as arthritis, diabetes, or heart disease. These can create limitations on how couples at this stage of life spend their time. Women are often coping with menopausal or post-menopausal symptoms, and they may need to explore a range of alternatives for dealing with these. Sexuality can also change at this time of life, and couple relationships can either deepen or partners may find that they do not have much in common anymore.

This is a stage where reorienting a previous relationship with children also becomes critical. Navigating a new kind of relationship with adult children, where the parental role makes way for an adult friendship, can be difficult for some who may want to continue to parent adult children and insert themselves into their decision-making process. Learning to be more of a hands-off parent at this stage involves re-examining beliefs and values and coming to terms with one's own life. Parents who have not taken the time to invest in their own growth and interests in previous life stages may find it hard not to focus on adult children, to let them go to live their own lives and make their own decisions and mistakes.

Some may also be caring for their aging parents at this stage and dealing with the grief and mourning associated with this (McGoldrick & Walsh, 2004). Having to witness the decline of a once robust and healthy parent can be a heart-breaking experience for many. And it raises the spectre of one's own mortality.

The tasks associated with this stage, therefore, are coming to terms with who one is as a person; rekindling or leaving a marital relationship; renegotiating a relationship with adult children; and dealing with the grief and sense of loss as parents age, become disabled, and/or die.

If families have mastered the stages that came before, this task is much easier. If not, the last stage of the family life cycle can be particularly taxing.

# RETIREMENT AND THE LAST STAGE OF THE FAMILY LIFE CYCLE

The last stage of the family life cycle can involve many changes, some joyful, some challenging. This is the stage where a new phase of family life can begin in the form of grandchildren. Many couples look forward to the arrival of a first grandchild, whom they can enjoy without having all the responsibilities of parenting.

Children are, by this time, usually well established, but they may have moved away or be travelling or very busy with lives of their own. If the tasks associated with the "launching" stage have not been addressed effectively, this can be a lonely time for some.

This is also a time when children may be getting divorced, so there may be some pain and strife in the family, and grandparents may be called on to help in times of crisis. This can place a real strain on individuals in this phase of their lives (HealthLink BC, 2013).

If elderly parents are still alive, there may be additional responsibilities in caring for them, or if placement in a long-term care home occurs, feelings of guilt and sadness. As close friends age and encounter health problems, there may also be stress, and grief may arise as friends and family members, especially older siblings and parents, die.

As people retire, there may be changes in how they manage their finances on a fixed or limited income. This can place some restrictions on their activities. However, if they have mastered the tasks of earlier stages and managed to save for retirement, this can be a wonderful stage of life, full of travel and new experiences.

Retirement can pose some real difficulties in some families where both partners may have once had considerable autonomy but now find themselves together much more frequently. This can either place a significant strain on relationships or, if each partner has found their own interests during the previous stage of the family life cycle, it can be a time where each person fully enjoys those interests as well as time together.

Couples in this stage may also experience some health problems, depending upon how well they have cared for their own physical and mental health during the previous stages. People who have maintained a healthy diet and exercise routine, and refrained from smoking and other unhealthy habits, may well enjoy very good health and a newfound vigour. But those who have neglected themselves and their own needs for a healthy and rewarding lifestyle, having put aside their needs to meet the needs of others, may now find that they are having to confront the fallout of those earlier decisions in the form of depression, physical illness, and loneliness.

Grief and mourning both the loss of one's own physical strengths and abilities, as well as the loss of significant others, can pose a real challenge during this phase of life. Feeling lost and abandoned and having fears of not being able to cope can be very real for some. Having a good social support system can help, but even this cannot replace a loved one. Each person has to pass through a period of significant mourning characterized by shock and numbness (disbelief that the person is actually gone); denial (talking and behaving as if the person is still there); anger (characterized by emotional outbursts—anger at the person for leaving and at oneself because of various regrets); bargaining (negotiating with God to reverse the loss); depression (feelings of helplessness and hopelessness, loss of interest in things the person once enjoyed, possible suicidal thoughts); and acceptance (a feeling of peace and recognition that life has changed and that there are new experiences and opportunities to be had) (Kubler-Ross, 1969).

For example, Martha always invested a lot in her children. As they were growing up, she was involved in every aspect of their lives—school, hockey games, family activities, dance classes. Her life was a whirlwind of activity, all focused on her husband and children. Once her children left home to establish their own lives, she found it difficult and insisted on calling them every day to chat. Her children found this oppressive, and their relationship with her deteriorated. She saw and heard less and less of them. When her husband had a stroke and later died, she found herself in a very difficult situation. She had neglected making and maintaining friends of her own earlier in life when she had put all her emphasis on her family. She also had not taken care of her own health but, instead, had focused on the needs of others. Now in her seventies, she has lost her husband, and her children find her difficult to deal with. She has almost no friends and spends much of her time feeling very lonely.

Martha's story is indicative of what can happen when individuals fail to master the tasks required of them in earlier stages of the family life cycle. Balance is always the key. Parents who invest too much in their children's lives and who are in some ways overinvolved with them may find that their children resent this as they get older and want to live more independent lives. This can cause real pain and hurt in families for both the children who are attempting to be mature adults and for the parents who have not developed other friendships and interests.

Marie and Fred, for instance, had the opposite problem. With three young children, they would have liked a bit of help from their parents, but that help was not available. Once Marie and Fred married, their parents saw this as an opportunity to finally travel, go to cultural events, pursue their own interests and friendships apart from their families, and experience the freedom not having so many responsibilities entailed. They were rarely available to help babysit, and spent months in warmer climates away from their children and grandchildren. This left Fred and Marie feeling abandoned and hurt that their parents were not taking the interest they once had in their lives.

This stage of the family life cycle holds both great promise and great pain. As with all the other stages, it is a journey—one that is either embraced or feared. Professionals working with individuals during this stage of life will need to listen with compassion to the feelings and needs of families. As with other stages in the family life cycle, it will be important to use good communication and problem-solving skills to address the issues that can arise.

## THE SPECIAL CHALLENGES AND OPPORTUNITIES IN AGING FAMILIES

A great deal has been said and written about the challenges of our aging population. Less has been said about the significant contributions that older adults make to each other and to younger family members. As Mitchell (2006) points out, "It is argued that this negative view of the 'overburdened' aging family is based on 'apocalyptic' or 'voodoo' demographic thinking that is more ideological than factual (Gee & Gutman, 2000). In other words, it is asserted that the notion that recent changes in family life invariably have catastrophic consequences for youth, society, and intergenerational relations has been 'oversold'" (p. 157).

It is argued that during a time when children may be staying at home longer or returning home, with three and possibly four generations living in one house, there is a special opportunity to share the knowledge, perspective, and skills of older generations with younger ones. Many grandchildren have particular warmth for their aging grandparents and great-grandparents, and may in fact listen to them more readily than to their own parents. This can create conflict, but it can sometimes also solve problems. Where older family members have acquired considerable wisdom, this can often be applied to the problems and concerns of the young.

Martin-Matthews (2001) has pointed out that "the world of elderly people is a world of women" (p. 3), and says that this is because women, on average, live seven years longer than men do, although this has begun to change. A problem that she identifies is that many older women have remained childless, and are therefore without family support as they age—something that may or may not be problematic.

> One way in which the current cohorts of very elderly persons, the "old old", differ from the cohort now entering old age is in their high rate of childlessness. Canadian women born in the first two decades of this century had unusually high rates of childlessness and low rates of fertility.... By contrast, those now entering old age and those in their early- to mid-70s (the "young" old) are the parents of the baby boom. Thus the "oldest old" are rather different from the "young old" in their intergenerational family structure. For example, for those now very elderly women whose one child was a son, it is quite likely that many of those mothers outlived their child. Thus, substantial proportions of very old people do not have any living children. While there is some evidence of higher rates of institutionalization amongst childless and single elderly persons, overall elderly people without children are not seen to be especially disadvantaged in later life. (Martin-Matthews, 2001, p. 4)

She also says that families across Canada are getting older, and so "smaller families will be supporting larger numbers of aged family members" (Martin-Matthews, 2001, p. 3). This can place considerable strain on family relationships or it can cause families to pull together. Much will depend upon the nature of these relationships prior to an older family member becoming disabled. Where there has been warmth and nurturing between the generations, this is likely to continue. But where there has been rancour, resentment, and disappointment, this too is likely to continue.

For example, Bertha, at 82, had a beautiful halo of white hair and sparkling blue eyes, as well as a great sense of humour. She also had a tendency to play her two daughters against each other, usually about money. This caused a lot of competition and feelings of resentment between the daughters, especially since one daughter was very involved with Bertha while the other was not around much. Bertha's tendency to favour the one who was not around as much, and to give her money and other things, annoyed her closer daughter no end and drove a wedge between the two sisters. However, after she had to have surgery, Bertha went to live with her eldest daughter, with whom she had not had much contact. Eventually she returned home, but as soon as she did, the younger daughter placed her in a nursing home, sold her own house, and moved into Bertha's. The eldest daughter only came to see Bertha every few months while the youngest was there every day. In the end, when Bertha died, the eldest daughter got a lump sum from her will, but the youngest daughter inherited everything else. The two daughters never spoke to each other again.

Sibling rivalry and competition have no age limit. The dynamics that are present when children are young tend to continue, often into old age. The conflicts that can occur when a parent is aging, is becoming disabled and needing care, or has died can leave scars that last a lifetime.

It is therefore very important that professionals working with families try to help family members understand that they are each going through their own grieving processes, and that they need to support one another as well as their aging parent, who is also experiencing considerable loss. Siblings, because of extended lifetimes, will have many years to live once their parents die. Healing sibling bonds may therefore become very important since siblings may be one another's few supports as they themselves age.

Anyone who has ever lost a parent knows how difficult the time prior to and after the loss can be. For those adult "orphaned children" who have lost both parents, the impact can be even greater. There is now a sense that nothing is standing between them and eternity, and many come face to face with their own mortality at this time.

Older spouses also face particular challenges. Because of the lack of community support options that maintain people in their own homes, one or both spouses may be institutionalized in nursing homes or other long-term care facilities. This is a particular problem for individuals who have been together for 50, 60, or 70 years. Losing one's life partner to death or institutionalization can be particularly devastating, and depression is common among older people. In fact, older men have the highest risk of suicide.

Martin-Matthews (2001, pp. 5–6) points out the following:

For those who remain married into old age, increased longevity means that the potential for long-term marriage has increased. Moreover, due to changes in fertility behaviour (such as closer spacing and smaller numbers of children), combined with increased longevity, these couples will have an earlier and significantly longer "empty-nest" phase of family life....

Associated with this change comes also the expansion of the period of time when one spouse may be required to provide assistance and additional care in response to a partner's increasing frailty or ill health. For many older women in particular, the last years of their married lives are likely to be spent in what are called "caregiving" roles to an increasingly frail spouse. While most men live out their last years as husbands cared for by their spouse, most women live out their last years as widows. If and when they become dependent and in need of assistance and "care", it is usually provided by adult children, friends and other relatives.

Although most women spend their last years in widowhood while most men spend their last years in marriage, there have been some changes to this pattern in recent years. Partly due to reductions in the mortality rates of older men, more older women and men today are married and fewer are widowed than was the case 30 years ago.

Providing caregiving to a husband or wife can be an act of love if the marriage has been a good one, or it can be cause for resentment if the marriage was not. Similar dynamics can occur between parents and children where caregiving is required. And the lack of support to families with members who require care makes this problem even worse.

The challenges at this stage of a family's life cycle can be many and as diverse as the families that experience them.

There have been several criticisms of developmental theory in families. Some theorists have argued that men's and women's experiences of family life at each stage is not the same (Cheal, 1991). Others have said that these life-cycle stages tend to apply more to nuclear families than to single-parent or gay- and lesbian-led families. McGoldrick (1988) tried to address this issue by adding developmental stages for families where divorce occurred, arguing that developmental theory can help in providing a framework for professionals seeking to understand the experiences of families with whom they are working.

## CHAPTER SUMMARY

This chapter contains an outline of the life stages families experience and has shown how at each stage families are required to master specific tasks that will help them through the stages that follow (Havighurst, 1952). It has also demonstrated how failure to master tasks in earlier stages of a family's life cycle can create conflict, strain, and challenge in the next stages. It is as if, at each stage, families are given another chance to work out and master the tasks required. Professionals with a strong knowledge of the life challenges at each stage can be helpful to families by posing important questions, helping families to explore options, and listening carefully to hear and understand what issues families are presenting at each stage.

## FURTHER READING

Martin, T. F. (2018, February 26). Family development theory thirty years later. Retrieved from https://onlinelibrary.wiley.com/doi/10.1111/jftr.12237

Trask, B. S. (2018, April 30). Integrating life course, globalization, and the study of racial and ethnic families. https://onlinelibrary.wiley.com/doi/10.1111/jftr.12259

## CLASSROOM ACTIVITIES

### Families across the Lifespan

Internet resource: University of Nebraska, http://extensionpublications.unl.edu/assets/pdf/g2124.pdf

Lead a class discussion about the life stage of students' families and what the challenges and rewards are of this stage of development.

### Socratic Questioning Exercise

1. What stage of your family's development was most difficult and what factors caused these difficulties?
2. Did you or your family members make any assumptions that added to these difficulties? How did these assumptions impact your family's development?

## QUESTIONS FOR REFLECTION

1. What questions might be useful at each stage of the family life cycle to help families come to terms with the tasks they must master?

2.   What are some options that families have at each stage of the family life cycle for managing the challenges and taking advantage of the opportunities that can arise?

3.   What new insights have you gained about how your family mastered or failed to master tasks at each stage? How has this affected your own family life?

4.   Is the developmental approach to looking at families a reasonable one, or should it be replaced, as some have suggested, with a more flexible way of looking at how families function?

## REFERENCES

CBC News. (2012, September 19). Boomerang kids trend returns in latest Canadian census. Retrieved from www.cbc.ca/news/canada/boomerang-kids-trend-returns-in-latest-canadian-census-1.1162383

Centre for Addiction and Mental Health. (2012). Mental illness and addiction statistics. Retrieved from www.camh.ca/en/hospital/about_camh/newsroom/for_reporters/pages/addictionmentalhealthstatistics.aspx

Cheal, D. (1991). *Family and the state of theory.* Toronto, ON: University of Toronto Press.

Dixon, H. (2013). "Helicopter parents" creating a generation incapable of accepting failure. Retrieved from www.telegraph.co.uk/education/10277505/Helicopter-parents-creating-a-generation-incapable-of-accepting-failure.html

Galinsky, E. (1987). *The six stages of parenthood.* Boston, MA: Da Capo Press.

Gee, E. M., & Gutman, G. M. (2000). *The overselling of population aging: Apocalyptic demography, intergenerational challenges, and social policy.* Toronto, ON: Oxford University Press.

Havighurst, R. I. (1952). *Developmental tasks and education* (2nd ed.). New York, NY: Longmans, Green and Co.

HealthLink BC. (2013). Family life cycle. Retrieved from www.healthlinkbc.ca/kb/content/special/ty6171.html

Higginbotham, B., Henderson, K., & Skogrand, L. (2006). Marital transitions and the sandwich generation: The implications of divorce and remarriage. *Family Resources.* Utah State University. Retrieved from http://extension.usu.edu/files/publications/publication/FR_Marriage_2006-02.pdf

Hong, G. K. (2011, Spring). Exploring the family life cycle: Families with children. *The Family Psychologist.* Retrieved from https://bacigalupe.files.wordpress.com/2010/03/tfp-spring-2011-272.pdf

Kubler-Ross, E. (1969). *On death and dying.* New York, NY: Scribner.

LaSala, M. C. (2011). Transgender youth and their parents. *Psychology Today*. Retrieved from https://www.psychologytoday.com/ca/blog/gay-and-lesbian-well-being/ 201102/transgender-youth-and-their-parents

Martin-Matthews, A. (2001). The ties that bind aging families. *Contemporary Family Trends*. Retrieved from http://catalogue.iugm.qc.ca/GEIDEFile/17622. PDF?Archive=194733591291&File=17622_PDF

Mattessich, P., & Hill, R. (1987). Life cycle and family development. In M. B. Sussman & S. K. Steinmetz (Eds.), *Handbook of marriage and the family* (pp. 437–470). New York, NY: Plenum Press.

McGoldrick, M. (1988). Women and the family life cycle. In B. Carter and M. McGoldrick (Eds.), *The changing family life cycle: A framework for family therapy* (2nd ed.). New York, NY: Gardner Press.

McGoldrick, M., Carter, B., & Garcia-Preto, N. (2011). *The expanded family life cycle: Individual, family, and social perspectives* (4th ed.). Boston, MA: Allyn & Bacon.

McGoldrick, M., & Walsh, F. (2004). A time to mourn: Death and the family life cycle. In F. Walsh & M. McGoldrick (Eds.), *Living beyond loss: Death in the family* (2nd ed., pp. 27–46). New York, NY: W.W. Norton.

Mitchell, B. A. (2006). The boomerang age from childhood to adulthood: Emerging trends and issues for aging families. *Canadian Studies in Population*, *33*(2), 155–178. Retrieved from http://ejournals.library.ualberta.ca/index.php/csp/article/ viewFile/15959/12764

Monroe, H. S. (2018, February 2). Why boundaries matter: Teens, authentic connection, and positive relationships. Retrieved from https://www .newportacademy.com/resources/mental-health/teens-health-boundaries/

Rodgers, R. H., & White, J. M. (1993). *Sourcebook of family theories and methods*. New York, NY: Springer.

WebMD. (2013). The importance of family ties. Retrieved from www.webmd.com/ children/tc/family-life-cycle-coupling-stage

## CHAPTER 4

# Family Communication Styles and Couple Dynamics

*Communication is at the heart of intimate human relationships—it is literally the foundation on which all else is built.*

   —D. Olson & J. De Frain (2003)

## CHAPTER OVERVIEW

In this chapter, readers will learn about the importance of healthy communication in families—what is helpful and what is not. Special attention is paid to couple relationships and the part communication styles play in building strong bonds or in causing conflict and distress.

Epstein, Bishop, Ryan, Miller, and Keitner (1993) have defined family communication as the "exchange of verbal and non-verbal information." In fact, it is much more than this. It is how families exchange the thoughts and feelings that lead to particular interpretations. It is fraught with assumptions, especially those that developed from a couple's families of origin. It is subject to intergenerational transmission: unless there is a conscious effort to overcome it, the way one's parents communicated can become the way children communicate in their future relationships. It is therefore important that families try to create healthy and effective means of communicating.

## PRINCIPLES OF COMMUNICATION

All communication is two-way. The sender needs to pay attention to the response of others to their message, while the receiver needs to accurately assess the sender's intent. Each is affected by beliefs, attributions, family scripts and history, personal experience, temperament, and many other factors.

Communication in families conveys beliefs, needs, feelings, wants, and concerns, as well as love and affection, or negative emotions such as disgust or contempt. This is the "process" side of communication. It tends to be non-verbal, conveys information about the relationship, and is subtle (Matsumoto, Frank, & Hwang, 2013). It is conveyed through tone, facial expression, posture, gestures, and eye contact. All family communication is either affective, where emotions are shared, or instrumental, where information is shared (Burleson, Kunkel, Samter, & Werking, 1996).

The content of a message conveys information. It is verbal and obvious. Both content and process are important in decoding communication. Content refers to the topic contained in the communication, whereas process refers to the way in which the content is delivered. For example, when someone says "I have a bad headache today," the content is the information that they have a headache, but the process may involve the person's feelings about the communication—their tone of voice, facial expression, and body language related to the context in which the comment occurs. If the person is telling a workmate this, it may mean they are asking for help, but if they are telling a spouse this, it may mean that they are not interested in sexual contact. It is impossible not to communicate. Whether silent or speaking, we are always communicating.

For example, Phil and Jen have been married for five years. Jen has noticed that Phil does not want to discuss issues that come up for either of them in their relationship. When Jen tries to talk to Phil about anything that is troubling her, he grows silent. If she continues, he walks away. Phil learned in his family of origin that discussions like this always lead to very bad fights. His intent is to try to avoid the discussion completely if he can, not understanding that this leaves Jen frustrated, rejected, and unheard. Jen believes that if you don't talk about things, you can't work them out. She sees Phil as evading his responsibility to her as a partner.

It is easy to see from this dynamic that Phil and Jen are headed for trouble even though Phil has said nothing. His silence is killing the relationship. From his perspective, Jen's constant desire to discuss issues that will lead to fights will destroy the relationship.

When communication is healthy, families function well. Healthy communication is clear and direct, and co-operative rather than competitive. Both Phil and Jen need to be direct with each other. They need to work co-operatively to move from a position of seeing each other as the problem to acknowledge and confront the bad communication that is occurring in their relationship.

Self-disclosure is an important aspect of good communication. Knowing when and how to self-disclose—to reveal personal information about oneself—is an important skill in good communication. Self-disclosure helps to build relationships. The more someone discloses to another, the more likely the recipient will also disclose, thereby deepening their intimate knowledge of each other (Olson, Olson-Sigg, & Larson, 2008). Of course it is much easier to self-disclose to someone who is accepting and a good listener rather than to someone who tends to be judgmental and who wants to assert their own beliefs and positions rather than accepting differences.

Being a good recipient of self-disclosure depends on a person's willingness to listen. Listening while preparing to make a counter-argument or listening with a view to moving a conversation in a certain direction is not really listening. However, listening while suspending judgment, and not deciding if what someone is saying is right or wrong, is a critical skill in building strong relationships. When people feel accepted and understood by others, they feel closer to them, and this builds trust and intimacy. Listening with a view to hearing another's story, unmediated by wanting to influence it in any way, encouraging someone to speak and allowing them to get to the heart of what they want to say and then acknowledging it, is an advanced communication skill. This comes from sincerely wanting to know another person and understand their story, the reasons why they feel as they do and believe what they do, and how they came to believe it. This is known as attunement (Spindel, 2013). To truly understand someone, attunement is required. Being known to another is one of the core elements of intimacy and one that is missing in too many couples and families. Helping families learn to really listen to each other, without attempting to inject their own agendas into conversations, can go a long way toward easing family conflict.

Having said that, some communication styles make listening much easier. For example, assertive communication is considered to be the easiest to listen to. It usually begins with "I" messages—"I feel good about our relationship because we confront problems together" or "I feel bad sometimes when you tell me that I am not a very good listener. I want to be a better one." Essentially, assertive communication allows someone to be themselves without denying another person the same right (Mayo Clinic, 2013).

Passive communication usually involves withholding; that is, being unwilling to say what is on one's mind or in one's heart for fear of being rejected or offending another. Where assertive communication reinforces good feelings about oneself, passive communication tends to reinforce poor self-esteem and increase personal anxieties. It is a major factor in distancing from others because it causes others to not really know us (Mayo Clinic, 2013).

Aggressive communication also creates distancing but mostly because of fear—fear of being hurt, rejected, put down, or criticized. Aggressive communication generally leads to all of these. The goal of aggressive communication is to hurt or control another person. It is intended to make the aggressor feel better at another's expense, but seldom actually achieves that. Instead, it often fuels angry feelings and is self-perpetuating. Aggressive communication can lead to hurtful and unsatisfying interactions between partners and in families (Mayo Clinic, 2013). And as poet Maya Angelou (2014) said, "I've learned that people will forget what you said, people will forget what you did, but people will never forget how you made them feel."

Perhaps one of the most damaging forms of communication is passive-aggressive. Passive-aggressiveness is "a deliberate and masked way of expressing covert feelings of anger" (Long, Long, & Whitson, 2008).

## PASSIVE-AGGRESSIVE COMMUNICATION

Whitson (2010) has identified several phrases that are hallmarks of passive-aggressive communication. Each bespeaks a certain aspect of passive-aggressive behaviour and communication. The first, "I'm not mad," denies any anger when in fact there is plenty; the second, "Fine, whatever!" usually heralds sulking or the silent treatment and results from a person feeling that the honest expression of their feelings will only result in punishment or other negative consequences; the third, "I'm coming!" usually occurs because the speaker verbally complies with someone's request but resents having to and delays its completion; the fourth, "I didn't know you meant now," usually involves procrastination; the fifth, "You're such a perfectionist," accuses another when in fact the speaker has done a substandard job on something; the sixth, "I thought you knew," involves not sharing information and then claiming ignorance while taking pleasure in the other's anguish, upset, or trouble; the seventh, "I was only joking," is often delivered sarcastically, leaving the other person feeling hurt but also open to blame because they "can't take a joke"; and, finally, the last, "Why are you getting so upset?" allows the passive-aggressive communicator to take pleasure in others finally blowing up because of their frustration, and then blaming them for being upset, thereby causing more anger and resentment (Braiker, 2004). In these ways, passive-aggressive communication can destroy relationships and leave wounds that never heal. Both people are left unhappy, not understanding what they can do to change it.

For instance, James feels a lot of anger toward his wife, Anita, who is highly accomplished and makes more money than he does. Whenever Anita asks James for anything, he has a range of passive-aggressive ways of resisting her requests. He "forgets" to do things, acts like he misunderstands what she is saying, ignores her, or constantly offers reasons for why something simply cannot be done. This frustrates Anita to no end. She knows James is capable and smart, but he repeatedly does not live up to his abilities and seems instead to focus on appearing to be both incapable and obtuse. Anita has not figured out yet that James's behaviour is passive-aggressive. It is rooted in a deeply felt sense of failure and personal inadequacy that started in his childhood and that is made worse by having to witness his wife's success. Until James and Anita deal with the root of the problem in their marriage—James's resentment of her, and her lack of understanding of his feelings of inadequacy—this passive-aggressive pattern will likely continue and possibly lead to separation or divorce.

Calling someone on their passive-aggressive behaviour is not easy, but it is necessary if a relationship is to survive. Being unwilling to accept it, removing oneself from it, and, if it continues, suggesting counselling are reasonable ways to confront this problem. Also effective is discussing why and how this type of communication developed with the person, during a quieter period, and giving them permission to say when they are angry without having to fear consequences.

## POOR COMMUNICATION AND DISTORTED FAMILY DYNAMICS

Poor communication can create distortions and dynamics that greatly impede a family's functioning or even pose a threat to the family's continued existence as a unit.

Four types of communication have been identified, all of which contribute to particular family dynamics. First, clear and direct communication occurs when both the message and the person for whom the message is intended are made clear. This is considered the healthiest kind of communication: "John, I would have appreciated it had you done the dishes last night when I was tired." Second, clear and indirect communication happens when a message is obvious, but the intended recipient of the message is not: "It would have been nice if someone had done the dishes last night when I was tired." Third, masked and direct communication occurs when the intended recipient is identified, but the message is not clear: "John, wouldn't it be nice if the dishes had gotten done when I came home tired?" And fourth, masked and indirect communication occurs when neither the recipient nor the message is clear: "Wouldn't it be nice if people were more considerate around here!?" (Epstein et al., 1993).

Good communication tends to be positive and affirming, clear and concise, and delivered in a warm tone. Poor communication tends to be indirect, negative, critical, contemptuous, dismissive, unclear, and delivered in an angry or frustrated tone. The latter leads to conflict, confusion, resentment, anger, ineffective problem solving, insecurity among family members, lack of intimacy and emotional bonding, distancing, and at times scapegoating, and can, in its most extreme form, lead to violence, separation, and divorce.

For example, in Vahe's family, he and his brother resent their sister, Harpreet. They feel that she is a princess, spoiled by their parents, and that they are not seen as being as important. Rather than tell their parents how they feel, both boys indirectly communicate with their parents and Harpreet. For instance, they will often say that they were unable to get homework done because Harpreet was playing her music. Or they will make jokes about boys being better than girls. When Harpreet gets upset and cries, they call her a baby and tease her. Harpreet, at age 12, is beginning to develop mental health problems. She is depressed and often stays in her room. The boys make fun of her, telling her that she is crazy. Harpreet's parents are at their wit's end with their boys, repeatedly punishing them for their behaviour, thereby making things worse and adding to the boys' resentment. Unless this family gets to the root of the problem—the boys' sense that their sister gets preferential treatment from their parents—this problem will not be resolved.

There can also be communication twists and turns in the form of mixed messages and double binds. A mixed message occurs when there is a discrepancy between what is said and what is conveyed non-verbally. This creates dissonance in the receiver of the message between what they are hearing and what they are feeling.

A double bind occurs when one person puts another in the position of being damned if they do and damned if they don't. For example, Marie and Julie are in a lesbian relationship. They have decided to have a child together and require a male donor. Julie wants to get pregnant, and Marie does want a child; however, Marie has told Julie that she is uncomfortable with her having a child from either a known or unknown male donor. Since Julie is unable to get pregnant any other way, she is in a double bind. If she does not use a male donor, she and Marie will not have a child. If she does, Marie will be uncomfortable with it, while admitting "it's not rational." Neither she nor Marie wants to adopt. Their relationship is currently in a stalemate over this question.

Generally, the resolution of a double-bind situation involves discussing the reasons behind it. This is called meta-communication and it will lead to possible compromises. If Julie can talk about how important it is to her to have a child and why, and Marie can talk about why having a male donor makes her so uncomfortable, both may be able to show compassion for the other and together reach a compromise. Could this cause more conflict and possibly end the relationship? Yes. This is the difficulty with a double bind—engaging in a discussion about why someone is communicating something can further inflame passions and lead to the end of the relationship. However, not communicating and allowing the double bind to continue will likely lead to the same outcome.

Gender, too, seems to play a role in communication. While males and females are not uniformly homogenous in their communication styles, some features seem to be true of each. Males often communicate in a competitive way, seeking dominance or control of the communication. The goal appears to be that of achieving independence and, perhaps, respect. The female style tends to be more affiliative, coming across as less dominant and as seeking connection. It leans toward developing relationship and/or intimacy (Glass, 1993). The task when men and women are communicating is to seek a balance between separateness and togetherness, intimacy and independence, so that both can feel comfortable within the relationship.

Culture also plays a significant role in communication. Some cultures are more non-verbal, preferring to express themselves by hugging, bowing, and either averting their eyes or making eye contact. Other cultures are much more verbal.

Irrespective of style and type of communication, some conflict is inevitable in families. How it is handled is critical. Helping families to communicate in positive and effective ways can ease many of the dynamics that occur and help to keep them intact and functioning well. However, this often begins with the parent or parents. How parents communicate with each other or how a single parent communicates with their children sets the stage for how children will communicate in future relationships.

## COUPLE COMMUNICATION

Because children learn how to communicate from their parents, helping couples to communicate well is vital. Some studies have found that several factors are present in couples who are happiest in their relationships. These include satisfaction with the way they communicate; the ability to be honest with each other about their true feelings; refraining from negative comments about each other; and feeling understood and listened to (Olson et al., 2008).

Keeping communication clear, direct, co-operative, and positive is always helpful to a family. However, there are some issues that regularly surface for couples that can seriously skew family dynamics.

## RETURNING BIDS

When two people communicate, they are constantly "making bids" to each other for a response. Hopefully it will be the kind of response that feels good. But sometimes bids are rejected or ignored, or the response is not what someone expected (Gottman, 2001), as in this example:

"Good morning, darling! How are you today?"

Response: "You're awfully cheerful. What are you so happy about?"

This apparently friendly bid got returned with an implied accusation or criticism that the bid sender was not expecting. This may mean that the receiver is feeling something that they are not being clear or direct about.

"You look so nice today!"

Response: "Thanks" (unenthusiastic response).

That is also not the response the sender of the message was expecting. Again, the receiver is clearly feeling something but not conveying what it is.

"Think maybe we could go and see my parents this weekend?"

No response.

This is a bid that was completely rejected with no answer at all. The message here may be "I want to avoid this topic." The receiver is saying nothing, possibly in an effort to avoid an uncomfortable discussion.

When one partner in a couple makes a communication bid, it is usually a good idea for the other to return the bid in the same tone and manner. Then, if there is something else on the recipient's mind, they can discuss it after, hopefully in a positive and co-operative way.

"Good morning, darling! How are you today?"

Response: "I'm fine, hon. What are your plans today? You look so nice. Are you going somewhere special?"

Now we can begin to sense what may be going on. Still, there is no accusation, only a question. Is he worried that his partner is so cheerful because she is seeing someone special today, someone of whom he is jealous? Perhaps. But it is best to respond to this bid with a non-accusatory question in case that is not what is planned.

One of the main challenges facing couples today in their communications is finding the time to actually focus on each other. The demands of children, parents, neighbours, friends, and electronic communications all impede the ability of couples to just be together without distraction in order to talk about important things in their relationship. Couples these days often need to make appointments with each other and keep them if they are to talk without distractions. This means turning off the phone, computer, and TV and possibly going out on their own in order to work out issues in their relationship (Shimberg, 1999).

Some ways that couples can begin to deal with issues in their relationship is to have some communication rules. If someone is a "yeller," meet in a public place where the person will be uncomfortable doing so. If people interrupt each other, make a rule that there will be no interrupting until each person is finished speaking. Couples need to look at and listen to each other and acknowledge what the other is saying whether or not they agree. For example, "Yes, I can see that you have always been close to your mother and want to spend time with her. Let's work something out whereby you get to spend time with her but I don't always have to be there, because my relationship with her is not as strong as yours is."

## COMMON RELATIONSHIP ISSUES

A big problem in a relationship is when neither or only one partner sees the relationship as a priority. This situation, coupled with taking each other for granted, can sometimes signal the death of a relationship or pave the way for an affair. Relationships take time and effort. Making sure that there is enough time alone together; ensuring that each says positive things to the other and regularly compliments them; going out to places the couple went when dating, regularly talking about intimate things known only to the couple; setting limits with children, parents, friends, and others to let them know the relationship comes first—all can help to send the message that the relationship is special and a priority.

Sex is a big issue in many marriages. How much, how often, what type? All are questions that couples argue about. A lack of sexual relations can often be a symptom of a larger problem with couples—that of who has power in the relationship. If a husband feels his wife is withholding sex, he may feel she is exerting power over him and he will try to resist. A wife, however, may feel that her husband should not have automatic access to her body if she does not feel like having sex. This can cause a stalemate. Again meta-communication may be the answer. Perhaps the couple needs to discuss why either having or not having sex is so important, thereby developing more intimacy and a deeper understanding of each other's feelings and the reasons for them.

Task sharing is another cause for friction in couple relationships. When one partner does a lot more around the house than the other, resentment can grow. Both parties may need to take on tasks and write them down so that there is clarity about who does what. Or, if neither likes to clean the house, perhaps they could each chip in some money and hire someone else to do it.

Perhaps one of the most serious issues, and the one that most likely will lead to divorce, is finances (Winter, 2013). When two people have very different spending habits—one is a spender, the other a saver—it can cause big problems. These types of arguments seem to last longer and be more intense than arguments about children or sex. Setting priorities together about where money needs to be spent and ensuring that each partner has some disposable cash for themselves, can greatly help. "Financial infidelity"—hiding information about finances—can cause major problems in a marriage that may be deep and long-lasting. Coming up with a budget together with all financial cards on the table is critical to resolving financial issues in a marriage. Partners seeing finances as a problem that needs to be confronted together, rather than seeing each other as the problem, can be helpful.

Some argue that these issues are only the tip of the iceberg, and that the real issues underlying them involve power and control, and feelings of neglect (Sanford, 2010). Recognizing that a partner may feel neglected or that their autonomy is being threatened can help couples begin to discuss what underlies their most frequent conflicts. Fear of real intimacy or of being engulfed by another can lead to distancing behaviour, but feeling too distant can lead to fear of rejection. The key is finding a balance, and this may be the real challenge couples face. We bring many of our feelings concerning intimacy and fear of rejection with us as we enter romantic relationships. They are present in our families of origin. Recognizing some of these fears and where they originate, and discussing them with our intimate partner, can help in working out these issues.

Conflict and arguments are inevitable in every relationship, but taking on a victim or aggressor role are not. Blaming, accusing, and finger pointing tend to escalate conflict. In any conflict it is important to try to focus on a solution achieved through understanding each other's point of view, and not on "winning." Defensiveness will not solve a conflict. Listening and acknowledging, then stating one's own views and feelings, is generally more constructive.

Explanations and apologies can also go a long way. Sometimes it is not clear to a partner why someone did what they did or feels the way they do. It is important to explain why. And if a partner knows they are wrong, it is better to say so instead of trying to defend an indefensible position in order to win the argument. Respect grows between partners when they can explain themselves to each other and apologize if they are wrong.

It is vital that each partner be aware of how the receiver of a message is taking it. Sensitivity to another's feelings is important in attempting to resolve situations. Ignoring someone's feelings will only cause conflict to escalate. Acknowledging the feelings behind what someone is saying can help to strengthen a relationship.

Boundaries are also very important in relationships. Respecting a person's privacy and setting limits—"I don't want to discuss this now. Can we please talk about this tomorrow?"—are vital to maintaining a healthy relationship. If someone is saying no, the answer is no. Barging in on someone without knocking, interrupting them when they are speaking, taking over tasks they were already doing, breaking a confidence—all of these are boundary violations that can damage relationships.

Sometimes a sense of humour can be a saving grace. Learning to laugh at things can ease tensions in a relationship. Humour restores perspective and teaches us not to take ourselves too seriously.

Perhaps the most important lesson that couples can learn is that they cannot be all things to each other. Trying to do so places a great deal of strain on relationships. It is very important that each member of a couple has some down time away from the relationship, where they can just do as they please without having to please someone else. Each member of a couple needs to get away alone at times, to spend time with their own friends or engage in activities that they really enjoy. This can revitalize a relationship and allow each re-energized partner to bring resources back in to nourish it.

## CHAPTER SUMMARY

This chapter has examined various forms of communication and the impact they have on couple and family dynamics. Common issues that arise in families and in relationships in general have also been discussed.

## FURTHER READING

Heidari, M., Mortezaee, H., Masomi, H., & Raji, A. R. (2016). The relationship between family communication patterns and mental health in adolescents. *International Journal of Humanities and Cultural Studies.* www.ijhcs.com/index.php/ijhcs/article/download/754/666

Sheet on alternative communication patterns. https://depts.washington.edu/hcsats/PDF/TF-%20CBT/pages/9%20General%20Skills/Family%20Communication%20Patterns%20handout.pdf

Young, J. (2014). Thesis on family communication patterns, parental modeling, and the intergenerational transmission of confirmation to romantic relationships. https://repository.tcu.edu/bitstream/handle/116099117/4560/Young_tcu_0229M_10502.pdf?sequence=1&isAllowed=y

## CLASSROOM RESOURCE

*Secrets of body language.* (2008). Top Documentary Films. https://topdocumentaryfilms.com/secrets-of-body-language/

## CLASSROOM ACTIVITIES

### Affirmation Role Play

Form triads that include two people interacting and a third observing.

Ask the dyad to begin discussing their family's communication styles. Ask the observer to give feedback on what they observed regarding each person's communication style.

Now ask each person to replay the conversation, but this time, ask each person to acknowledge what the other is saying before moving on to the next topic and identify what difference occurs in the communication.

## Brainstorming Exercise

Ask the group, having completed the affirmation role play, what they identified that they do that is not ideal communication. Write it on a board or flipchart. Then go through each comment and ask what should replace this style of communication.

## QUESTIONS FOR REFLECTION

1.  What issues seem to come up most often in your own relationships? Why do you think this is the case?
2.  What types of communications did you learn in your family that you now realize you need to change to make future relationships work better?
3.  What are three things that you believe you can do to begin to alter the way you communicate?
4.  Can you identify some of the communication styles of friends and family members? How do you plan to address these now that you know what they are?

## REFERENCES

Angelou, M. (2014, May 29). May Angelou quotes: 15 of the best. *Guardian*. Retrieved from http://www.theguardian.com/books/2014/may/28/maya-angelou-in-fifteen-quotes

Bailey, S. J. (2009). Positive family communication. Montana State University. Retrieved from http://msuextension.org/publications/HomeHealthandFamily/MT200916HR.pdf

Braiker, H. B. (2004). *Who's pulling your strings?* New York, NY: McGraw-Hill.

Burleson, B. R., Kunkel, A. W., Samter, W., & Werking, K. (1996). Men's and women's evaluations of communication skills in personal relationships: When sex differences make a difference and when they don't. *Journal of Social and Personal Relationships*, *13*, 201–202.

Epstein, N. B., Bishop, D., Ryan, C., Miller, I., & Keitner, G. (1993). The McMaster Model view of healthy family functioning. In F. Walsh (Ed.), *Normal family processes* (pp. 138–160). New York, NY/London, UK: The Guilford Press.

Fitzpatrick, M. (2005). Family communication patterns theory: Observations on its development and application. *The Journal of Family Communications*, *4*(3/4), 167–179.

Glass, L. (1993). *He says, she says: Closing the communication gap between the sexes*. New York, NY: Putnam.

Gottman, J. M. (2001). *The relationship cure: A five step guide to strengthening your marriage, family, and friendships*. New York, NY: Three Rivers Press.

Koesten, J., & Anderson, K. (2004). Exploring the influences of family communication patterns, cognitive complexity, and interpersonal competence on adolescent risk behaviors. *The Journal of Family Communication, 4*(2), 99–121.

Long, J. E., Long, N. J., & Whitson, S. (2008). *The angry smile: The psychology of passive-aggressive behavior in families, schools, and workplaces* (2nd ed.). Austin, TX: Pro-Ed.

Markman, H. J. (1981). Prediction of marital distress: A 5-year follow-up. *Journal of Consulting and Clinical Psychology, 49*, 760–762.

Matsumoto, D., Frank, M. G., & Hwang, H. S. (Eds.). (2013). *Nonverbal communication: Science and applications*. Thousand Oaks, CA: Sage.

Mayo Clinic. (2013). Being assertive: Reduce stress, communicate better. Retrieved from www.mayoclinic.com/health/assertive/SR00042

Noller, P., & Fitzpatrick, M. A. (1990). Marital communication in the eighties. *Journal of Marriage and the Family, 52*, 832–843.

Olson, D., & De Frain, J. (2003). *Marriages and families: Intimacy, diversity, and strengths* (4th ed.). New York, NY: McGraw Hill.

Olson, D. H., Olson-Sigg, A., & Larson, P. J. (2008). *The couple check-up: Finding your relationship strengths*. Nashville, TN: Thomas Nelson.

Sanford, K. (2010, June). Perceived threat and perceived neglect: Couples' underlying concerns during conflict. *Psychological Assessment, 22*(2), 288–297.

Schrodt, P. (2005). Family communication schemata and the circumplex model of family functioning. *Western Journal of Communication, 69*(4), 359–376.

Shimberg, E. F. (1999). *Blending families*. New York, NY: Berkeley Trade.

Spindel, P. (2013) *Case management from an empowerment perspective*. Toronto, ON: Spindel & Associates.

Whitson, S. (2010, November 23). 10 common passive aggressive phrases to avoid. *Psychology Today*. Retrieved from http://www.psychologytoday.com/blog/passive-aggressive-diaries/201011/10-common-passive-aggressive-phrases-avoid

Winter, K. (2013). Arguing about money could spell disaster for your marriage. *Mail Online*. Retrieved from dailymail.co.uk/femail/article-2373463/Couples-row-finances-likely-divorce-argue-children-sex.html

# CHAPTER 5

# Family Roles, Diversity, and Gender Issues

*We all should know that diversity makes for a rich tapestry and we must understand that all the threads of the tapestry are equal in value no matter what their color.*

    —Maya Angelou

## CHAPTER OVERVIEW

This chapter will explore the varying and diverse challenges confronting families led by immigrants and refugees, Indigenous people, single parents, and members of the LGBTQ (lesbian, gay, bisexual, transgender, and queer) community. All struggle with the impact of social stress, but for various reasons and in varying degrees. Because of this, each requires a unique response from the professionals who are working with them.

North American families today are much more diverse than the families of yesteryear. Social, demographic, and economic changes have created shifts in family structure and roles. The changing roles of women; a declining economy that now requires both parents to work; increased levels of immigration; and more acceptance of single parenthood, gay and lesbian relationships, and the premarital birth of children have all had an impact on how families have changed over the last three decades. While there was some ethnic diversity decades ago, it does not compare to the racial, cultural, and ethnic diversity of today's families.

## FAMILY ROLES

Family roles and many other aspects of family life continue to be defined, at least to some degree, by ethnic and cultural background, and by gender. Van Hook (2014, p. 109) says that "cultural messages shape the meaning systems (the paradigms and schemas) that affect how family members perceive life events and potential solutions, the organizational patterns of families, the ways in which family members communicate, the characteristics of the support system (the nature of the extended family and other external resources that are available), the nature of appropriate problem-solving strategies, and the type of situations facing families." What this means is that families are affected by their culture, their life experiences, and their roles, and also by how they deal with each other and how much social and family support is available to them.

In most families, who completes which tasks is usually mutually agreed upon. But in families where this is determined by religious beliefs and cultural standards, family roles are decided externally. The father may be expected to be the "leader of the family" and to make the major decisions. The eldest daughter may be expected to help care for younger children. In some families, the wife must acquiesce to her mother-in-law. In some cultural or religious traditions, women are revered as life-givers; in others, they are prescribed inferior roles.

Roles are often ascribed to gender. Often, though not always, it is the mother who takes time off to be with a sick child. In many families, household tasks are not evenly distributed between husband and wife even when both work. According to Statistics Canada (2013), "Women generally reported a higher number of hours per week than men [on unpaid child care in the home]. In 2010, women spent an average of 50.1 hours per week on child care, more than double the average time (24.4 hours) spent by men." It is still rare, although becoming more common, for fathers to be stay-at-home parents.

Gender roles in families continue to pass from one generation to the next through parents' direct communication with their children; through instruction: mom may teach her daughters how to cook; and through guidance: dad may help his son understand the importance of treating women with respect (Eccles, 1994). Lytton and Romney (1991) have argued that parents may encourage their children's involvement in what are considered to be gender-specific stereotypical activities—the daughter who is encouraged to take up ballet, the son who is encouraged to take up hockey. Collins and Russell (1991) have pointed out that children are socialized according to their gender through parents' modelling of stereotypic male and female behaviour. However, Martin, Ruble, and Szkrybalo

(2002) found that youth may develop their attitudes to gender through external contexts as well as through family transmission. Other authors have found that parents with higher educational attainment and income express more egalitarian gender-role orientations (Crompton & Lyonette, 2005).

Interestingly, where traditional family roles dominate, there tends to be more, not less, family conflict (Marks, Bun, & McHale, 2009). These authors identified three types of familial patterns: "egalitarian parents and children, traditional parents and children, and a divergent pattern, with parents more traditional and children more egalitarian" (p. 221). It was only in the traditional group that family conflict dominated.

## CHILDREN OF IMMIGRANTS

Rumbaut (2005), has stated the following:

> A familiar story in the American national narrative and a major theme in the psychology of the second generation is that children of immigrants perceive that they are a main if not the main reason for the immigration of their parents, who often stake all of their hopes for the future on their children's success. Perceiving the sacrifices made by their parents, ostensibly on their behalf, not a small amount of guilt tinges the children's sense of obligation toward their parents and spurs their motivation to achieve—a dynamic that, in turn, can give immigrant parents a degree of psychological leverage over their children. (p. 1)

He also says that to some degree this can be offset by "embarrassment, marginality and role reversals [that] prevail in the relationship between immigrant parents and their more acculturated U.S. raised children" (Rumbaut, 2005, p. 1), which can undermine the authority of parents and provide children with some leverage in their dealings with them. The biggest fear that parents have is that their children will lose their culture of origin as they begin to assimilate while struggling to "fit in." Predictably, this can cause considerable conflict in the family.

But conflict outside the family also affects children of immigrants. Ethnocultural gangs in high schools create a dangerous environment for some immigrant children. Rumbaut (2005, p. 34), in a study he conducted in the United States, found that "three out of ten students (29.5 percent) reported a high degree of unsafe and disruptive conditions at their school. In particular, four out of ten perceived that there were many gangs at their school (39 percent) and frequent fights between racial-ethnic groups (42 percent)." As well, approximately 25 percent of immigrant children reported being approached by drug dealers. About the same number of boys reported being involved in fights, while only 7 percent of immigrant girls reported this. Fights at school often led to suspensions.

So how at-risk are immigrant children for joining gangs or becoming involved in criminal activity? Roy (2012) quotes Dr. Anthony Hutchinson: "Children of immigrants or immigrant children themselves face a greater risk of falling through the cracks because of a number of reasons, the most important among them being a loss of identity." Children of newcomers can have a tough time fitting in. If they are young and do not speak English, it can be difficult for them to communicate, and this can lead to conflict. If they are older, because their beliefs and values and/ or appearance may be different, they may face bullying and discrimination, both of which can have a negative impact on their identity formation. Seeing their parents struggle to establish themselves may make this worse, especially if parents who enjoyed high status in their countries of origin now find themselves underemployed. Add to this the fact that Canada's education system is very different, with consequences for lack of school attendance, missed classes, and late assignments, and more stress is felt.

However, because children of immigrants tend to value education, they are more likely to complete homework and attend school. Only 24 percent reported spending an excessive amount of time in front of the TV (Rumbaut, 2005, p. 9). Asian and West Indian children are more likely to be engaged in their schools than other immigrant children, and Asian children tend to spend twice as much time on homework. Clearly family values related to education have a considerable impact in this regard. An interesting outcome of Rumbaut's (2005) study is that girls, on average, score higher in the realm of educational goals than boys: "girls aim much higher than males, with half of the females (49 percent) expecting to earn advanced degrees, compared to 39 percent of the males" (p. 42).

## RISK AND PROTECTIVE FACTORS

Culture can also provide specific risk and protective factors that influence family functioning and greatly affect family structure. For example, the family itself is more important in some cultures than in others. Single parenthood is variously scorned or accepted. Whether or not it is acceptable for extended family to live together in the same house; whether or not children can leave home before marriage; how families confront discrimination and oppression; and the level of a family's engagement with the outer world—all are often features of culture. This chapter will describe the risk factors and protective factors related to culture that are often seen in families.

Some of the risk factors faced by immigrants and refugees include poverty, discrimination, fear of deportation, lack of culturally sensitive services and supports, stigma and lack of cultural awareness in the rest of the population, lack of awareness within cultural communities related especially to mental health, substance abuse issues, authoritarianism in families, rigid roles related to parenting and domestic chores, school failure and/or low educational levels, as well as bullying. Acculturative stress, trauma, especially in refugee populations, and parental conflict related to all of the above may be present as risk factors (Van Hook, 2014).

However, protective factors that may mitigate risk are also present in many immigrant and refugee families. These include strong family bonds; ethnic and cultural pride; coping ability related to cultural mores; supportive mentors in a cultural community; neighbourhood support; educational programs related to history and culture; religious rites, rituals, and festivals; culturally sensitive services and supports; role flexibility among family members, including extended family; family rituals and routines; a sense of family honour; affectionate personal relationships; active parental involvement in school programs; higher education achievement; a sense of hope for the future; good health; being able to speak English; positive role models within the culture; and peer support (Van Hook, 2014). All of these can help immigrant and refugee families to not only survive but thrive, and this has implications for how professionals work with them. Helping families to increase protective factors and reduce risk factors will help them in functioning well. This means that professionals focusing on family strengths will emphasize the protective factors that they see in families and help them to redefine the risk factors as needs—issues that the family can confront together.

For instance, Farah, 16, is the eldest daughter in a Somali family living in Toronto. The family has very rigid ideas about child-rearing and each family member's role. Farah lives with her mother, father, six brothers and sisters, and her parents' parents. She is expected to wear the hijab and refrain from fraternizing with boys from other cultures. Nevertheless, she has made friends with a young Southeast Asian boy, and they spend considerable time together at school. She would like to be able to go out with him unchaperoned, but her parents have strictly forbidden this. She has begun seeing him secretly.

By contrast, Aasiya, also 16, who lives with her parents, five brothers and sisters, and two grandmothers, is part of an Iranian family where roles and expectations are less rigid. When she first became friends with a young Christian boy from Kenya, her parents invited him to dinner. Aasiya has also been invited to dinner at his parents' home. The families have now become friends and take delight in sharing different aspects of each other's cultures and religious beliefs.

Each of these scenarios points to how flexibility in relation to family roles can be either problematic or protective. In the second example, the family is able to incorporate a cultural change, whereas in the first, the family is not able to do so. Both illustrate earlier points about an authoritarian style in families, which has been shown to increase family conflict.

Helping families to explore alternative options for confronting family issues and to examine the functionality of current beliefs and roles can sometimes help to prevent conflict. Where conflict does occur, it can be helpful for the family to share stories of how and why things have been done this way in the family, perhaps for centuries.

Helping family members listen to one another and try to understand their differing viewpoints and motivations, as well as stressing the need for flexibility when it comes to roles, can be critical. Parents who adhere to very strict beliefs and attempt to force their children to do so as well are likely to end up in painful situations that create downward spirals within the family. Helping parents to understand that becoming more flexible leaders of a family, leaders who are able to share stories and the reasons for their own beliefs, while also respecting that their children live in a different world with which they must contend, can help families to reach some degree of rapprochement.

## OTHER ISSUES IN NEWCOMER FAMILIES

Newcomer families are essentially splintered families. Generally, only a part of a family emigrates, leaving other family members behind. Sometimes attempts are made at "family reunification," meaning that the family member(s) that emigrated may try to bring relatives left behind to their new chosen country. This type of immigration can be especially hard when a breadwinner emigrates and their spouse and children are left behind.

Separation can be painful for the partner who has moved to the new country and who may also be confronting culture shock, discrimination, and the effects of dislocation, possibly with little to no support system. It can be somewhat easier for the spouse left behind who does not have to contend with these issues, but separation itself can mean loneliness and feelings of anxiety.

In some cases the spouse who has moved may seek comfort and support from new people, and this can result in affairs and the establishment of a new set of relationships separate from the spouse left behind. This can lead to permanent separation and divorce and to children and a former spouse feeling abandoned.

Canada's immigration policies make it difficult for families to reunite quickly once one person emigrates. As Tate (2011) points out, "Rather than being linear and finite, with reunification as the end point, FSR [family separation and reunification] is now commonly marked by long separations, aggravated by a globalized economy with widely dispersed employment opportunities. At the same time, technology enables more frequent and varied forms of contact over great geographical distances (e.g., telephone, email, occasional visits, etc.). Some families have become 'transnational,' retaining intense social and economic relationships while being spatially dispersed across nation states on an ongoing basis, sometimes permanently" (p. 1; see also Bernhard, Goldring, Landolt, & CERIS, 2005).

Newcomer families with children who came from a more collectivist culture are often shocked at the lack of familial support in Canada, which is an individualistic society. Hui (1986, p. 225) defined collectivism as "(1) concern by a person about the effects of actions or decisions on others, (2) sharing of material benefits, (3) sharing of nonmaterial resources, (4) willingness of the person to accept the opinions and views of others, (5) concern about self-presentation and loss of face, (6) belief in the correspondence of own outcomes with the outcomes of others, and (7) feeling of involvement in and contribution to the lives of others. Individualists show less concern, sharing, and so on than collectivists." In our individualistic society, families tend to be more encapsulated, living lives separate from others—even, in some cases, from their own extended families. Even within families there is at times not much communication, interaction, or support. Whereas collectivist families tend to rely on extended family and others in their communities for interaction and support, individualistic families tend to consider child-rearing and family life to be private and personal. It can be a real challenge for individuals from highly collectivist cultures who believe it takes a village to raise a child to immigrate to a country that considers the raising of children to be solely the responsibility of the child's parents.

## REFUGEE FAMILIES

Refugee families may face considerable strain if parents and children have been traumatized by war, natural disasters, torture, violence, and dislocation. Their decision to flee their countries of origin often comes quickly and sometimes without warning. This can have a very damaging effect.

Refugee families are often contending with trauma—the stressful impact on family relations of war, natural disasters, oppressive political regimes, extreme violence, and physical, emotional, and sexual abuse (Catherall, 2004). Secondary traumatization is often present in children whose parents are haunted by wartime experiences or the effects of extreme violence, torture, and natural disasters (Figley, 2005). Children exposed to parents who are experiencing disruptive symptoms may develop symptoms themselves. A good example of this is the impact of the Holocaust on second-generation survivors. Kluger (2010) informs us that, apart from PTSD symptoms being acquired through learning, they may also be acquired genetically.

> Over the years, a large body of work has been devoted to studying PTSD symptoms in second-generation survivors, and it has found signs of the condition in their behavior and even their blood—with higher levels of the stress hormone cortisol for example. The assumption—a perfectly reasonable one—was always that these symptoms were essentially learned. Grow up with parents afflicted with mood swings, irritability, jumpiness, and hyper vigilance typical of PTSD and you are likely to wind up stressed and high strung yourself. Now a new paper adds another dimension to the science, suggesting that it's not just a second generation's emotional profile that can be affected by a parent's trauma; it may be their genes too.

It is important to understand that many refugees and children of refugees can also have positive symptoms related to the trauma they have experienced. According to Leventhal and Ontell (quoted in Kaplan, 2012), "Holocaust survivors may actually be more task-oriented, cope more actively, and express more favorable attitudes toward family, friends, and work." These favourable traits can be found in refugees of many cultures and racial groups. It is important for professionals to not only attempt to assist individuals with the symptoms of trauma, but also to help them to identify the strengths and resilience that they also demonstrate as a result of the trauma they have suffered.

A great deal will depend upon whether or not trauma survivors and their children can find alternative sources of reassurance and comfort through strong connections, either with other family members, with friends, or in the communities in which they live (Walsh, 2006). Recovering from trauma can be a transformative and growth-producing process, especially if professionals working with refugee families focus on their strengths, promote their resilience, and respond "compassionately to symptoms of distress and memories of pain, helplessness, and loss ... [while] identify[ing] and affirm[ing] strengths and resources in active, initiative, recovery and adaptation" (p. 290).

The impact of trauma on those fleeing war, natural disasters, and highly oppressive regimes can be significant, but as Walsh (2006, p. 290) states, "Forged in the cauldron of crisis and challenge, new strengths, untapped potential, creative expression, and innovative solutions can emerge as we reach more deeply within ourselves and reach out to connect with others."

This has implications for how professionals work with families experiencing the effects of trauma. It is important to help them discuss openly the reality of the traumatic event that led to them fleeing their country of origin and sharing their feelings about this experience of tremendous loss. It can also be helpful to, as a group, discuss coping strategies—ways of handling emotions and making sense of what has happened, perhaps within the realm of spirituality. Often families will need to reorganize by changing their roles and setting about to rebuild their lives. This can be a process of hope and transformation if they can be urged to help one another (Walsh, 2006).

Cultural and spiritual values involving transcendence can lead to forgiveness and create meaning where previously there was none. They can help to rebuild a sense of hope and purpose. Assisting families to rediscover the strength they might find in meditation, prayer, and the sharing of positive memories and stories; in memorializing lost loved ones, engaging in vigils and remembrances, and helping family members to reaffirm their family identity through these and the celebration of special holidays and birthdays; and in engaging in creative pursuits such as music, art, and writing—all can be helpful in promoting healing as a family. As Walsh (2006, p. 296) reminds us, "Recovery is a journey of the heart and spirit, bringing survivors back to the fullness of life."

For many immigrant and refugee families, the mobilization of any kin they may have in their new country, as well as any other social or community networks, can be very helpful in promoting recovery. Helping people to feel that they are part of a larger social network can create a connectedness that aids healing (Speck, 2003).

Moreover, helping these families to navigate financial and support systems and to access resources in their communities can help them to get back on their feet. It is critical that any professional working with immigrant and refugee families have a good resource network and access to specially trained trauma counsellors and, where necessary, to medical help in order to make referrals. In this way, professionals can be especially helpful in assisting families to get on a more solid financial and emotional footing.

## INDIGENOUS FAMILIES

Indigenous people in Canada are not homogenous; therefore, it is not possible to describe a common culture or tradition. Different cultural practices and belief systems arose from each First Nation's experience of the land and each other; however, there is a strong connection to the spirit world in all Indigenous cultures (First Nations Pedagogy Online, 2019). Relationship to all of creation has given rise to "oral teachings, prayer, music, dance, spiritual and social ceremonies, rites of passage, housing, even clothing, adornment, art, tools, and object creation" (First Nations Pedagogy Online, 2019). Indigenous people and, hence, Indigenous families, are strongly connected to the natural world and there is an underlying belief in the interconnectedness of all things and that all things are filled with spiritual power.

Rituals are an important part of life, and they mark the seasons, turning points in individuals' lives and community. Important rituals include birth and naming rituals; solitary experience rituals that occur in adolescence in order to find a life direction and to be accepted into adult society; the sacred pipe ceremony, a powerful spiritual ritual wherein the pipe is the symbol of unity and harmony, and the need for truth and balance; smudging, a holy act where "sacred herbs are burned in a shell or earthen bowl and the smoke is brushed over participants" in order to purify people or places; and the sweat lodge, intended to purify mind, body, and spirit and bring the relationship with self, others, and the Creator into balance (Canadian Aboriginal, 2019).

Throughout the year, celebrations and festivals occur at specific times. Some communities hold sun dances in summer, a harvest feast in fall, and powwows to renew and restore "right relationships and healing of all creation" (Canadian Aboriginal, 2019). On June 21 of each year Canadians celebrate National Indigenous Peoples Day and recognize the culture and contributions made by First Nations, Inuit, and Métis in Canada.

No discussion of Indigenous families would be complete without an acknowledgement of the impact of colonialism; misguided attempts at assimilation, especially in residential schools, and the lateral violence that resulted; as well as current attempts at reconciliation and decolonization.

Colonialism is "a practice of domination, which involves the subjugation of one people to another" (Stanford Encyclopedia of Philosophy, 2017). Assimilation, in this context, refers to "the absorption and integration of people, ideas, or culture into a wider society or culture" (Assimilation, n.d.).

Residential schools were "an extensive school system set up by the Canadian government and administered by churches that had the nominal objective of educating Aboriginal children but also the more damaging and equally explicit objectives of indoctrinating them into Euro-Canadian and Christian ways of living and assimilating them into mainstream Canadian society" (Indigenous Foundations, UBC, 2009). Residential schools were a means of committing cultural genocide against Indigenous people in Canada. Cultural genocide is described in the Truth and Reconciliation report as "the destruction of those structures and practices that allow the group to continue as a group" (Truth and Reconciliation Commission, 2015, p. 1).

Lateral violence is negative and damaging behaviour that occurs when oppressed people turn on each other, and can include gossip, shaming, blaming, putting others down, feuds and estrangement within families, rage, violence, anger, frustration, jealousy, envy, and many other negative emotions and actions (Equay-wuk, n.d.).

The Indian Residential School Settlement Agreement established the largest class-action suit settlement in Canadian history. It created the Truth and Reconciliation Commission, which produced a massive historical record of the residential school system, now located at the University of Manitoba. From 2007 to 2015, the Commission held hearings resulting in a six-volume final report detailing the horrific history and legacy of residential schools in Canada (Government of Canada, 2019).

Reconciliation refers to restoring friendship or harmony (Reconciliation, n.d.). However, reconciliation may mean two different things to Indigenous and non-Indigenous Canadians. Indigenous Canadians may consider achieving self-government and control over economic activity in their communities to be a primary goal of reconciliation, while non-Indigenous Canadians appear to see Indigenous people moving away from dependence on government funding and systems to be more important. There is alignment between Indigenous and non-Indigenous Canadians on many other issues, including "the value of acknowledging the unique contributions of Indigenous Peoples to Canadian society, as well as providing for greater opportunity and equality for Indigenous Peoples. The two populations are further aligned on taking steps towards the necessary institutional reform and individual changes required to move reconciliation forward" (Reconciliation Canada, n.d.).

Decolonization refers to "restoring an Indigenous world view, cultural and traditional ways, and replacing Western interpretations of history with Indigenous perspectives of history" (Indigenous Corporate Training, 2019). It involves shifting the ways both Indigenous and non-Indigenous people have viewed themselves.

Refugees are not the only traumatized population suffering intergenerational transmission of trauma. The lingering effects of Canada's attempts to assimilate Indigenous people can be seen in the after-effects and impact on individuals and communities. Canada systemically produced trauma in Indigenous children who were forcibly removed from their parents and taken to residential schools, where many were neglected and subject to physical, emotional, and sexual abuse. Not being raised by their natural parents had a negative impact on their own abilities to parent as adults, and the results of this can be seen in the number of Indigenous children taken into the care of child protection agencies.

In Ontario, "Aboriginal children are greatly overrepresented with 22 percent of all Crown Wards being Aboriginal" (Ontario Association of Children's Aid Societies, 2011). Understanding this number requires knowledge of the tragic history that led to it. As previously discussed, the history of Indigenous Peoples in Canada is one of colonialization, oppression, and attempted assimilation, formally legislated under the Indian Act. For almost 150 years, the Government of Canada endeavoured to suppress traditional Indigenous ways and encourage the assimilation of Indigenous people into settler Canadian ways (Aboriginal Affairs and Northern Development Canada, n.d.). One of the methods used was that of residential schools, wherein Indigenous children were removed from their families and raised in what were often religious schools, in an attempt to divorce them from their culture. Children were forced to abandon their traditional lifestyle—their language, dress, and religion. To achieve this, "a vast network of 132 residential schools was established across Canada by the Catholic, United, Anglican, and Presbyterian churches in partnership with the federal government. More than 150,000 Aboriginal children attended residential schools between 1857 and 1996" (Aboriginal Affairs and Northern Development Canada, n.d.).

In some schools, 50% of the children died from starvation and disease, with more dying within six months of leaving school (Milloy, 1999). They also endured physical, sexual, spiritual, and emotional abuse. Those who survived were impacted by the traumas resulting from their own victimization, the witnessing of others' victimization, the loss of parenting and attachment, disconnection to the land, loss of traditional teachings, loss of language, and loss of identity. As parents stood helpless to protect their children, many turned to alcohol and drugs to numb their pain and shame. The result of these multiple traumas provides the foundation for current Aboriginal experience, identity and relationships. (Best Start Resource Centre, 2012, p. 7)

The horrible trauma suffered by residential school survivors is only part of what Indigenous people struggle with today. The Royal Commission on Aboriginal Peoples (RCAP, 1996) reported that, historically, "in some communities, disease killed 85% of the population, hitting the young and old the hardest. Relocation programs took a toll on Indigenous life by eliminating natural sources of food and creating a dependence on non-traditional items such as flour and sugar. This laid the foundation for the current health issues faced by Indigenous people today, such as diabetes, high blood pressure, and obesity" (Best Start Resource Centre, 2012, p. 7).

Even though efforts have since been made to alter the damaging effects of this early history—including a historic formal apology on June 11, 2008, to all former residents of residential schools for the suffering they endured—the legacy of the residential schools and the attempted assimilation of Indigenous people continues to have a negative impact on Indigenous family life. The legacy of abuse perpetrated in the residential schools continues to run throughout Indigenous families, resulting in high rates of placement in child welfare.

Prior to these attempts at assimilation, children were raised in a culture where elders passed down values and traditions considered to be gifts from the Creator to one generation after another. Indigenous society was defined by sacred traditions, rituals, songs, dances, festivals, and a rich oral history. Indigenous children "learned how the world came into being and that they were a part of the whole of creation. People gave thanks to everything in nature, upon which they depended for survival and development as individuals and as members of their communities. First Nations treated all objects in their environment—whether animate or inanimate—with the utmost respect" (Aboriginal Affairs and Northern Development Canada, n.d.). Indigenous values promoted "wisdom, love, respect, bravery, honesty, humility, and truth" and considered these to "enable people to live in a way that promotes harmony and balance with everyone and everything in creation" (Aboriginal Affairs and Northern Development Canada, n.d.).

In 2003, the Aboriginal Healing Foundation completed a landmark study that set out the dynamics and reasons for the high prevalence of domestic violence in Indigenous families. It described this violence as a "multi-factorial social syndrome and not simply an undesirable behavior" and as residing "within Indigenous individuals, families, and community relationships [and] manifesting itself as a regimen of domination that is established and enforced by one person over one or more others through violence, fear, and a variety of abuse strategies" (p. ix). The Foundation reported the problem as widespread and subject to intergenerational transmission and as "almost always linked to the need for healing from trauma" (p. ix). The Foundation links the continuation of domestic violence to "the presence of enabling community dynamics, which, as a general pattern, constitute a serious breach of trust between the victims of violence and abuse and the whole community" (p. ix), and states that the "entire syndrome has its roots in Aboriginal historical experience, which must be adequately understood in order to be able to restore wholeness, trust, and safety to the Aboriginal family and community life" (p. ix).

The impact of domestic violence, substance abuse, and the physical, sexual, and emotional abuse and neglect of children in Indigenous families is similar to that experienced by children of any family where this kind of abuse is prevalent. All are forms of lateral violence. Children of these families can be expected to experience school failure and have difficulty forming and sustaining relationships, to exhibit signs and symptoms of trauma, and to feel desolate and lonely in their ongoing struggles to survive. Special attention needs to be paid to children who appear to be suicidal. Safeguards need to be put into place to assist them and to encourage them to talk with others, especially elders in their own communities.

The Canadian Press (2011) reported that there are more Indigenous children in care now than there were when residential schools were active.

> Instead of being at home with their parents, brothers and sisters, tens of thousands of First Nations children are in foster homes, staying with distant relatives or living in institutions.... A disheartening mix of poverty, addiction, history and politics has conspired to separate First Nations children from their parents. Researchers aren't certain how many native kids are no longer living with their parents. A major study in 2005 pegged the number at 27,500. Since then, provincial and federal data as well as empirical reports suggest the numbers have risen.

The Canadian Press also reports that, according to the Auditor General of Canada, Indigenous children are eight times more likely to end up in the care of child protection agencies. In provinces such as British Columbia, almost half of the children in CAS care are Indigenous, in spite of Indigenous people composing only 8 percent of the population. Because children in Indigenous families are so highly at risk of placement, professionals working with Indigenous families need to have significant skills related to trauma, addiction, and family violence, and considerable knowledge of Indigenous cultural values.

John's family is a perfect example of the kinds of issues that can surface in Indigenous families struggling to deal with the consequences of the residential school system and intergenerational trauma. At 8, John was placed in foster care. His father was in jail. His mother had serious substance abuse issues, and he and his four siblings were all separated and placed in different foster homes. At 12, John and two of his siblings were reunited with their mother, who was getting help for substance abuse. Unfortunately, she had repeated relapses, during which she would disappear with a variety of partners and abandon the children. John often took care of his two younger siblings during his mother's "absences," which would last anywhere from days to over a week. At 14, John was picked up by police for shoplifting and also charged with possession of drugs. He ended up in youth detention. By 16, discharged from youth detention, he ended up on the street. His life went into a downward spiral until a social worker from an Indigenous housing agency intervened and helped him to obtain housing and a job. The worker also arranged for counselling for his addictions from an Indigenous Elder who had himself struggled with similar issues at one time and had overcome them. He took a special interest in John, and together they sought healing for the pain of years of abandonment and heartbreak. Today John helps other young people struggling with similar issues. His familiarity with the system and the struggles that many young Indigenous people experience give him the knowledge and strength to help them.

Indigenous women are at an increased risk of violence. LeBlanc (2014) tells us the following:

Indigenous women suffer from much greater levels of violence than other women in Canada, leaving them more vulnerable to murder and brutality at the hands of their spouses, family members and acquaintances, an RCMP report has found. For the first time, a series of numbers and statistics over three decades have been produced to illustrate the extent to which aboriginal women suffer disproportionately from violence in Canada. The contrast with the situation of other women in the country is stark, as aboriginal women are not benefiting from a long-term decrease in homicide numbers.... Overall, the RCMP said 1,017 aboriginal women were murdered from 1980 to 2012, while another 164 of them had gone missing. Aboriginals represent 4.3 per cent of Canada's population, but aboriginal women represented 16 per cent of all

female victims of homicide in Canada, and 11 per cent of missing women.…
Overall, women were most frequently killed by their spouses, but aboriginal
women face greater threats among other members of their immediate circle.

Years of attempting to address the issue of violence against women and children in Indigenous communities have not yielded effective measures to reduce the
violence. Part of the problem is that many Indigenous communities, in particular
reserves, are isolated; therefore, enforcing legal remedies such as restraining orders
can be difficult. Bigger problems include the failure to apply resources to what has
been long documented as a serious problem. And the absence of culturally appropriate and sensitive services to help victims and perpetrators alike has meant that
many Indigenous families are not getting the assistance they need from within
their own communities or from external organizations.

Professionals working with Indigenous families need to familiarize themselves
with positive Indigenous cultural values that were in place prior to colonization; be
aware of spiritual beliefs that may be able to aid in healing; and be familiar with
rituals, routines, ceremonies, art, and dance that can help families to reclaim a rich
cultural heritage. Paramount among these is understanding the importance of the
"Medicine Wheel."

> The medicine wheel is the foundation for many teachings. Some cultures
> recognize the four directions (North, East, South and West) and others,
> seven directions (North, East, South, West, Above, Below and Here). First
> Nations culture is based on connection and cycles of life. There is a medicine
> wheel for the aspects of self: physical, emotional, spiritual and mental. There
> is a medicine wheel for the stages of life, from baby to Elder. There are circles
> to represent one's place in community. At the core is the understanding
> of balance, connection and relationship.… The Medicine Wheel is a
> representation of traditional theology, philosophy, and psychology. For
> Indigenous people it represents the teachings of the Creator about all aspects
> of life. (Best Start Resource Centre, 2012, p. 6)

All practice with Indigenous families needs to be culturally competent.
Repeating the history of forcing non-Indigenous treatments and interventions on
Indigenous families will not be helpful. These families require a different kind
of healing, steeped in a rich culture and tradition with which they can become
reacquainted. As with all families, helping members to understand and become
acquainted with their roots, and to understand what may have been a tragic family
history and how to come to terms with it, can be helpful in aiding healing.

## THE IMPACT OF DIVORCE AND SEPARATION

Single-parent families, who are an ever-increasing part of the community fabric of North America, also face special challenges. Divorce can have a significant impact on children, especially where custody disputes have been particularly bitter (Arkowitz & Lilienfeld, 2013). It can be an especially lengthy and emotionally painful experience. In fact, emotional divorce—where "positive feelings of love and affection are displaced by increasing feelings of anger, frustration, hurt, resentment, dislike, or hatred, and the perception that the positive feelings are gone forever" (North Carolina State University, n.d.)—exposes children to the negative feelings experienced by both of their parents. While mediation services are now more widely available and there is more of a focus on the rights of children during divorce, children still suffer ill effects.

Fortunately, divorce rates are on the decline in Canada, and the majority of divorces are uncontested. According to Statistics Canada (2012), "in 2010/2011, civil courts in the seven reporting provinces and territories handled just over 921,000 cases. About two-thirds (65 percent) of cases were general civil cases, while one-third (35 percent) involved family law. Of the total civil court cases, almost 494,000 were new cases initiated in the seven provinces and territories, representing a 5 percent decline from the year before."

Marital separation does tend to reduce income and may also have a negative impact on social networks. It is also true that "compared with children growing up in intact families, outcomes across a range of measures are poorer for children who experience family breakdown, and some of these persist into adulthood. For example, they are less likely to gain educational qualifications, and more likely to leave home and become a parent at a younger age. The differences, however, are comparatively small, with many children not affected, and most children are not adversely affected in the long term" (Mooney, Oliver, & Smith, 2009, p. 21).

Fraley and Heffernan (2013) found that parental divorce, especially when children are young, may lead to relationship problems between them and their parents once they are grown up. However, other studies, such as that of Arkowitz and Lilienfeld (2013), have found not much difference between the ability of children of divorced parents and those whose families remained intact. It appears that children bounce back fairly quickly in many cases after divorce.

More focus, however, needs to be placed on the strengths of children growing up in homes where there may be an absent father, since much of the research has studied only the negatives. For example, Sigle-Rushton and McLanahan (2004) have found that, "although children raised in a home where a father is present graduate from high school and attend college at much higher rates than children raised in a fatherless home, nearly 70 percent of children from fatherless homes do graduate from high school and 50 percent of them attend college" (Barajas, 2011, p. 13).

Nevertheless, children in single-parent households do face more challenges than those in relatively healthy two-parent homes. Rayner (2013) reports that "family structure was associated with a greater number of activity limiting days and decreased odds of mothers reporting that their child's general health was very good or excellent. In addition, the longitudinal analyses revealed that on average, children spending any time in a single-parent family had lower odds of being reported in excellent or very good health. These relationships were partially explained by factors exacerbated in single-parent families such as increased poverty, maternal distress and lower social support."

It would also appear that males exhibit more overt behavioural issues related to divorce. McLanahan and Sandefur (1994) have pointed out that boys are more overt in their expression of emotional pain than girls, largely by being defiant, whereas girls tend to turn their pain inward and become depressed.

Single parents can be very good parents to their children. However, if they are faced with the challenges of having to work at two jobs to make ends meet, they cannot possibly provide adequate supervision and attention to children who may feel lost without ongoing parental support. Poverty continues to be a major issue for many single parents, and it is more likely that single parents will have a lower socioeconomic status than do families with two working parents.

Given the lack of adequate daycare, single parents may have to rely on friends, family, or in some cases substandard and unregulated daycare providers. The presence of a wide and positive circle of family and friends can have a protective influence on a single-parent family. But where a single parent is stressed because of financial concerns, feels lonely because of a lack of family or community support, and feels overwhelmed attempting to raise children alone, the impact on growing children can be considerable. Children who do not feel adequately protected, who feel lost and believe they do not belong, and who have nowhere to go after school when parents are not home to be with them are particularly susceptible to gang recruitment. Lohmann (2010) has identified the need for protection, the need to belong, and the need to have somewhere to hang out and something to do as three reasons teenagers join gangs. She also points out that gang membership for both boys and girls is on the increase. This does not mean that children of single parents are the only ones who join gangs; it is only that the children of single parents who suffer a lack of parental supervision as a result of additional stresses may be more susceptible to gang recruitment strategies.

It is important to recognize that much of the research on single-parent families has focused on Caucasian families, with little attention to different cultural groups (Barajas, 2011). Much more needs to be done to identify both the risk and protective factors present in single-parent homes.

## LGBTQ FAMILIES

The number of LGBTQ (lesbian, gay, bisexual, transgender, and queer) families in Canada has risen significantly. Since Canada legalized same-sex marriage in 2005, there has been a 42 percent increase, to 64,575 LGBTQ families as of 2011 (Statistics Canada, 2011).

According to International Spectrum (2016), the formerly derogatory term *queer* is now an umbrella term sometimes used by LGBTQ people to refer to the entire LGBTQ community. Some people are now reclaiming it as a statement of empowerment. The term itself is controversial, with some people embracing it because they wish to avoid the sometimes rigid categorizations that come with the usual "straight" and "gay" characterizations. Others still consider the term to be derogatory because it implies "deviance." It is, however, always best to ask individuals how they wish to self-identify.

When any person from a minority group, including the LGBTQ community, finds themselves in conflict with larger societal values concerning marriage, family, and raising children, it can cause considerable stress and feelings of alienation from social institutions—schools, courts, churches, governments—because the norms of society do not reflect the values and beliefs of the minority group (Pearlin, 1982). Furthermore, Moss (1973) has pointed out that health can be compromised when an individual's interactions with society leads to information that is incongruent with their own view and experience of the world.

Repeated studies have shown a higher incidence of mental health issues in LGBTQ populations, which appear to be related to stigma and social stress. LGBTQ populations are said to suffer more from substance use disorders, affective disorders, and suicide (Cochran, 2001; Sandfort, de Graaf, Bijl, & Schnabel, 2001). Meyer (2003, p. 675) has said, "If LGBTQ people are indeed at risk for excess mental distress and disorders due to social stress, it is important to understand this risk, as well as factors that ameliorate stress and contribute to mental health. Only with such understanding can psychologists, public health professionals, and public policy makers work toward designing effective prevention and intervention programs." (Chapter 11 will examine ways to help families where a parent is experiencing mental health or substance abuse issues.)

Many same-sex couples are raising children. According to the Vanier Institute (2013, p. 2), in figures compiled by Statistics Canada, "the proportion of same sex couples with children in the home rose from 9% in 2006 to 9.4% in 2011."

Of these, 80 percent are female-led families. These children may be in the home as a result of adoption, surrogacy, or as part of a blended family after divorce or separation. Studies have shown that children of same-sex couples do not differ from children growing up in heterosexual homes except in their experience of social discrimination (Dufur, McKune, Hoffmann, & Bahr, 2007; Short, Riggs, Perlesz, Brown, & Kane, 2007).

Breashears and Braithwaite (2013) have found that "children of gay parents overcame stigmatization through suppressing negative messages and using positive language when speaking of their family dynamics.... The researchers identified four common pathways that were used to marginalize negative messaging: Emphasizing opposing views as ignorant; highlighting flaws of religious views; stressing others' lack of authority to judge; and emphasizing the precedence of love. The most common way of overcoming negative messaging was to emphasize opposing views as ignorant."

But what happens in families when a parent comes out as being transgender? Little research has been done concerning transgender issues in families; however, we do now know that a "significant number of transgender people have children" and of these families more trans women than trans men have children (Motmans, Dierckx, & Mortelmans, 2017). Because of heteronormative expectations in our society, trans families, like gay families, tend to be socially stigmatized. "Families of transgender people are often confronted with feelings such as loss, shame, grief, betrayal, guilt, fear and anger and, at the same time, can be confronted with rejection and social stigmatisation in their social surroundings" (Motmans et al., 2017).

Children witnessing the social gender transition of a parent may require help throughout the process, and this is supported by most transgender parents (Davies et al., 2013). The transgender parent may wish to move quickly, whereas other family members may be more reluctant and need more time to process what is occurring. What is most important for children is that both parents agree on the process and are able to support children through it. The reaction of a cisgender parent can have a significant impact on how children react (Hines, 2006). The implications for clinical practice with transgender families are clear. Professionals need to be attuned to the varying needs of family members throughout the transition process, and be sensitive to the stigmatization by extended family, friends, and the larger society that they are experiencing. Family members who are most closely involved may be deeply concerned about possible treatment outcomes and be wrestling with their own feelings of shame and fear of rejection and what family life will be like in the future (Motmans et al., 2017). Where social support groups are available, professionals should make families aware of this resource.

## CHAPTER SUMMARY

This chapter has examined the diversity present in today's families by discussing the issues facing immigrants and refugees, Indigenous families, single parents, and LGBTQ families. It has presented information on how history and social stigma can negatively affect families, and identified some protective factors that can be emphasized and/or created to assist them.

## FURTHER READING

### Roles in Families

Virginia Cooperative Extension. (2009). Families first—keys to successful family functioning: Family roles. https://www.pubs.ext.vt.edu/350/350-093/350-093.html

### Immigrant Families

Caring for Kids New to Canada. (2018). An overview of immigrants and refugees in Canada. https://www.kidsnewtocanada.ca/care/overview

Psych Central. (2017). New immigrant families face many challenges. https://psychcentral.com/news/2017/10/27/canadian-study-new-immigrant-families-face-many-challenges/127987.html

Statistics Canada. (2019). The wealth of immigrant families in Canada. https://www150.statcan.gc.ca/n1/en/catalogue/11F0019M2019010

### Indigenous Families

Government of Canada. (2018). Improving child and family services in First Nations communities: Engagement. https://www.sac-isc.gc.ca/eng/1478808657410/1533314955002

Government of Canada. (2019). Reducing the number of Indigenous children in care. https://www.sac-isc.gc.ca/eng/1541187352297/1541187392851

Ontario Centre of Excellence for Child and Youth Mental Health. (n.d.). Working with Indigenous families: An engagement bundle for child and youth mental health agencies. www.excellenceforchildandyouth.ca/file/9101/download?token=m0kjO6_P

Truth and Reconciliation Commission Reports. http://www.trc.ca/

Vanier Institute for the Family. (2017). Indigenous families in Canada. https://vanierinstitute.ca/indigenous-families-canada/

## Divorce and Separation

Canadian Counselling and Psychotherapy Association. (2014). The psychological effects of divorce. https://www.ccpa-accp.ca/the-psychological-effects-of-divorce/

Government of Canada, Department of Justice. (2004). High conflict separation and divorce: Options for consideration. https://www.justice.gc.ca/eng/rp-pr/fl-lf/divorce/2004_1/p2.html

Ontario Women's Justice Network/METRAC Action on Violence. (2016). Introduction to divorce and separation in Canada. http://owjn.org/2016/07/introduction-to-divorce-and-separation-in-canada/

## Gay and Transgender Families

Brill, S. A., & Kenney, L. (2016). *The transgender teen: A handbook for parents and professionals supporting transgender and non-binary teens.* San Francisco, CA: Cleis Press.

Human Rights Campaign. Resources for people with transgender family members. https://www.hrc.org/resources/resources-for-people-with-transgender-family-members

Lev, A. I. (2004). Transgender emergence: Therapeutic guidelines for working with gender-variant people and their families. New York, NY: Haworth Press.

Motmans, J., Dierckx, M., & Mortelmans, D. (2017). Transgender families. In W. P. Bouman & J. Arcelus (Eds.), *The transgender handbook: A guide for transgender patients, their families and professionals* (pp. 81–90). Nova Science. https://www.researchgate.net/publication/316220915_Transgender_Families

---

## CLASSROOM RESOURCES

*Baggage.* (2017). NFB. https://www.nfb.ca/film/baggage_en/

*Life on Victor Street.* (2012). NFB. https://www.nfb.ca/film/life_on_victor_street/

*Love makes a family.* (1991). Fanlight Productions. http://fanlight.com/catalog/films/116_lmaf.php

*Sisters and brothers.* (2015). NFB. https://www.nfb.ca/film/sisters_brothers/

*Welcome to Canada.* (2016). NFB. https://www.nfb.ca/film/welcome_to_canada_campus/

---

## CLASSROOM ACTIVITY

### Questions for Small-Group Discussion

1. Do your parents or grandparents have a history of trauma (dislocation, slavery, fleeing their country, attending residential schools, surviving natural events, etc.)

that you believe affects your own view of the world? If so, what effects do you believe it has had? What strengths do you believe you have developed as a consequence of your family history?

2. Did you grow up in a single-parent family? If so, what struggles do you believe your family had that two-parent families may not have had? What strengths have you developed as a result of growing up in a single-parent family?

## QUESTIONS FOR REFLECTION

1. Who determines what roles people play in your family? Do culture or gender have anything to do with it?
2. Are you the son or daughter of an immigrant? If so, how has this affected your life?
3. What cultural and spiritual values did you receive from your family that you believe guide you in your life?
4. Did you grow up in a single-parent family? What challenges and opportunities did this present, and how has it affected your life?
5. What are your views on same-sex marriage? Have they been affected by reading this chapter, and if so, how?

## REFERENCES

Aboriginal Affairs and Northern Development Canada. (n.d.). First Nations in Canada. Retrieved from www.aadnc-aandc.gc.ca/eng/1307460755710/1307460872523#chp3

Aboriginal Healing Foundation. (2003). Aboriginal domestic violence in Canada. Retrieved from www.ahf.ca/downloads/domestic-violence.pdf

Arkowitz, H., & Lilienfeld, S. O. (2013, March 19). Is divorce bad for children? *Scientific American*. Retrieved from www.scientificamerican.com/article. cfm?id=is-divorce-bad-for-children

Assimilation. (n.d.). In *Oxford Dictionary*. Retrieved from https://en.oxforddictionaries. com/definition/assimilation

Barajas, M. S. (2011). Academic achievement of children in single parent homes: A critical review. *The Hilltop Review*, 5(1), 12–21. Retrieved from http://scholarworks. wmich.edu/cgi/viewcontent.cgi?article=1044&context=hilltopreview

Bernhard, J. K., Goldring, L., Landolt, P., & CERIS. (2005). *Transnational, multi-local motherhood: Experiences of separation and reunification among Latin American families in Canada*. Toronto, ON: CERIS.

Best Start Resource Centre. (2012). *Supporting the sacred journey: From preconception to parenting for First Nations families in Ontario.* Toronto, ON: Author.

Breashears, D., & Braithwaite, D. O. (2013). What is family? Study explores how children of gay parents overcome stigma. University of Nebraska. Retrieved from http://newsroom.unl.edu/releases/2013/08/08/What+is+family%3F+Study+explores+how+children+of+gay+parents+overcome+stig

Canadian Aboriginal. (2019). Rituals, worship and festivals. Retrieved from https://canadianaboriginal.weebly.com/rituals-worship-and-festivals.html

Canadian Press. (2011). First Nations children still taken from parents. CBC News. Retrieved from www.cbc.ca/news/politics/first-nations-children-still-taken-from-parents-1.1065255

Catherall, D. R. (2004). *Handbook of stress, trauma, and the family.* New York, NY: Brunner-Routledge.

Cochran, S. D. (2001). Emerging issues in research on lesbians' and gay men's mental health: Does sexual orientation really matter? *American Psychologist, 56,* 931–947.

Collins, W. A., & Russell, G. (1991). Mother-child and father-child relationships in middle childhood and adolescence: A developmental analysis. *Developmental Review, 11,* 99–136.

Crompton, R., & Lyonette, C. (2005). The new gender essentialism—domestic and family "choices" and their relation to attitudes. *The British Journal of Sociology, 56,* 601–620.

Davies, A., Bouman, W. P., Richards, C., Barrett, J., Ahmad, S., Baker, K., … Stradins, L. (2013). Patient satisfaction with gender identity clinic services in the United Kingdom. *Sexual and Relationship Therapy, 28*(4), 400–418. doi:10.1080/14681994.2013.834321

Dufur, M., McKune, B. A., Hoffmann, J. P., & Bahr, S. I. (2007). *Adolescent outcomes in single parent, heterosexual couple, and homosexual couple families: Findings from a national survey.* Paper presented at the annual meeting of the American Sociological Association, New York.

Eccles, J. S. (1994). Understanding women's educational and occupational choices: Applying the Eccles et al. model of achievement-related choices. *Psychology of Women Quarterly, 18,* 585–609.

Equay-wuk. (n.d.). What is lateral violence? Retrieved from http://www.equaywuk.ca/HFHNDVT/WhatIsLateralViolence.pdf

Figley, C. R. (2005). Strangers at home: A commentary on the secondary traumatization in partners and parents of Dutch peacekeeping soldiers. *Journal of Family Psychology, 19*(2), 227–229.

First Nations Pedagogy Online. (2019). Culture. Retrieved from https://firstnationspedagogy.ca/culture.html

Fraley, R. C., & Heffernan, M. E. (2013). Attachment and parental divorce: A test of the diffusion and sensitive period hypotheses. *Personality and Social Psychology Bulletin*, *39*, 1199–1213.

Government of Canada. (2019). Truth and Reconciliation Commission of Canada. Retrieved from https://www.rcaanc-cirnac.gc.ca/eng/1450124405592/1529106060525

Hines, S. (2006). Intimate transitions: Transgender practices of partnering and parenting. *Sociology*, *40*(2), 353–371. doi:10.1177/0038038506062037

Hui, C. H. (1986). Individualism-collectivism: A study on cross-cultural researchers. *Journal of Cross-Cultural Psychology*, *17*(2), 225–248.

Indigenous Corporate Training. (2019). A brief definition of decolonization and indigenization. Retrieved from https://www.ictinc.ca/blog/a-brief-definition-of-decolonization-and-indigenization

Indigenous Foundations, UBC. (2009). The residential school system. Retrieved from https://indigenousfoundations.arts.ubc.ca/the_residential_school_system/

International Spectrum. (2016). LGBT terms and definitions. Retrieved from https://stlukesuccindep.org/mt-content/uploads/2017/07/lgbt-terms-and-definitions-_-international-spectrum.pdf

Kaplan, F. (2012). Holocaust survivors and their children: A search for positive effects. American Academy of Experts in Traumatic Stress. Retrieved from http://www.aaets.org/article96.htm

Kluger, J. (2010, September 9). Genetic scars of the holocaust: Children suffer too. *Time*. Retrieved from http://content.time.com/time/health/article/0,8599,2016824,00.html

LeBlanc, D. (2014, May 16). Aboriginal women suffer disproportionately from violence: RCMP. *Globe and Mail*. Retrieved from www.theglobeandmail.com/news/politics/aboriginal-women-suffering-disproportionately-from-violence-rcmp-finds/article18714014/

Leventhal, G., & Ontell, M. K. (1989). A descriptive demographic and personality study of second-generation Jewish Holocaust survivors. *Psychological Reports*, *64*(3), 1067–1074.

Lohmann, R. C. (2010, October 11). Teen gangstas. *Psychology Today*. Retrieved from www.psychologytoday.com/blog/teen-angst/201010/teen-gangstas

Lytton, H., & Romney, D. M. (1991). Parents' differential socialization of boys and girls: A meta-analysis. *Psychological Bulletin*, *109*, 267–296.

Marks, J., Bun, L. C., & McHale, S. M. (2009, August). Family patterns of gender role attitudes. *Sex Roles, 61*(3/4), 221–234. Retrieved from www.ncbi.nlm.nih.gov/pmc/articles/PMC3270818/#R22

Martin, C. L., Ruble, D. N., & Szkrybalo, J. (2002). Cognitive theories of early gender development. *Psychological Bulletin, 128*, 903–933.

McLanahan, S., & Sandefur, G. (1994). *Growing up with a single parent: What helps, what hurts.* Cambridge, MA: Harvard University Press.

Meyer, I. H. (2003). Prejudice, social stress, and mental health in lesbian, gay, and bisexual populations: Conceptual issues and research evidence. *Psychological Bulletin, 129*(5), 674–697.

Milloy, J. S. (1999). *A national crime: The Canadian government and the residential school system, 1879 to 1986.* Winnipeg, MB: University of Manitoba Press.

Mooney, A., Oliver, C., & Smith, M. (2009). Impact of family breakdown on children's well being: Evidence review. Retrieved from http://dera.ioe.ac.uk/11165/1/DCSF-RR113.pdf

Moss, G. E. (1973). *Illness, immunity, and social interaction.* New York, NY: Wiley.

Motmans, J., Dierckx, M., & Mortelmans, D. (2017, January). Transgender families. Retrieved from https://www.researchgate.net/publication/316220915_Transgender_Families

North Carolina State University. (n.d.). Long term effects of divorce on children. Retrieved from http://www.carneyandgood.com/uploads/1435155507_long-term-effects-of-divorce-on-children.pdf

Ontario Association of Children's Aid Societies. (2011). *Children's well-being: The Ontario perspective, Child welfare report 2011.* Toronto, ON: Author.

Pearlin, L. I. (1982). The social context of stress. In L. Goldberger & S. Breznitz (Eds.), *Handbook of stress: Theoretical and clinical aspects* (pp. 367–379). New York, NY: Academic Press.

Rayner, J. L. (2013). Differentials in physical health outcomes among children in single-parent and dual-parent families. Paper 1085. Western Libraries. *University of Western Ontario—Electronic Thesis and Dissertation Repository.* Retrieved from http://ir.lib.uwo.ca/etd/1085

Reconciliation. (n.d.). In *Merriam Webster Dictionary.* Retrieved from https://www.merriam-webster.com/dictionary/reconcile

Reconciliation Canada. (n.d.). *The Canadian reconciliation landscape: Current perspectives of Indigenous peoples and non-Indigenous Canadians.* Vancouver, BC: Author.

Roy, B. (2012). 6 strategies to keep newcomer youth safe. *Canadian Immigrant.* Retrieved from http://canadianimmigrant.ca/family/6-strategies-to-keep-newcomer-youth-safe

Royal Commission on Aboriginal Peoples. (1996). *Looking forward looking back.* Indian and Northern Affairs Canada. Retrieved from http://www .reconciliationgroup.ca/wp-content/uploads/2018/05/RCAP-V1-1-Looking-Forward-Looking-Back.pdf

Rumbaut, R. G. (2005). Children of immigrants and their achievement: The role of family, acculturation, social class, gender, ethnicity, and school contexts. Retrieved from https://papers.ssrn.com/sol3/papers.cfm?abstract_id=1878129

Sandfort, T. G., de Graaf, R., Bijl, R. V., & Schnabel, P. (2001). Same-sex sexual behavior and psychiatric disorders: Findings from the Netherlands Mental Health Survey and Incidence Study (NEMESIS). *Archives of General Psychiatry, 58*, 85–91.

Short, E., Riggs, D. W., Perlesz, A., Brown, R., & Kane, G. (2007). Lesbian, gay, bi-sexual and transgender parented families: A literature review prepared for the Australian Psychological Society. Retrieved from https://www.psychology.org .au/getmedia/47196902-158d-4cbb-86e6-2f3f1c71ffd1/LGBT-families-literature-review.pdf

Sigle-Rushton, W., & McLanahan, S. (2004). Father absence and child well-being: A critical review. In D. Moynihan, T. Smeeding, & L. Rainwater (Eds.), *The future of the family.* New York, NY: Russell Sage Foundation.

Speck, R. (2003). Social network intervention. In G. P. Sholevar & L. D. Schwoen (Eds.), *Textbook of family and couples therapy.* Washington, DC: American Psychiatric Press.

Stanford Encyclopedia of Philosophy. (n.d.). Colonialism. Retrieved from https://plato .stanford.edu/entries/colonialism/

Statistics Canada. (2011). Portrait of families and living arrangements in Canada. Catalogue no. 98-312-X-2011-001. Retrieved from www12.statcan.ca/census-recensement/2011/as-sa/98-312-x/98-312-x2011001-eng.cfm

Statistics Canada. (2012). Divorce cases in civil court, 2010/2011. Retrieved from www. statcan.gc.ca/pub/85-002-x/2012001/article/11634-eng.htm#a2

Statistics Canada. (2013). Families, living arrangements, and unpaid work. Retrieved from www.statcan.gc.ca/pub/89-503-x/2010001/article/11546-eng.htm#a12

Tate, E. (2011). Family separation and reunification of newcomers in Toronto: What does the literature say? Toronto Public Health. Retrieved from https://pdfs. semanticscholar.org/c64d/dad31a370ddbd9a6fa25ce2fe7056f4380e7.pdf

Truth and Reconciliation Commission. (2015). Honoring the truth, reconciling for the future. Retrieved from http://nctr.ca/assets/reports/Final%20Reports/Executive_ Summary_English_Web.pdf

Van Hook, M. O. (2014). *Social work practice with families*. Chicago, IL: Lyceum Books.

Vanier Institute of the Family. (2013, March). Same sex families raising children. Retrieved from https://vanierinstitute.ca/wp-content/uploads/2015/11/FFAM_2013-03-00_Same-Sex-families-raising-children.pdf

Walsh, F. (2006). *Strengthening family resilience* (2nd ed.). New York, NY: The Guilford Press.

## CHAPTER 6

# Family Scripts, Myths, Beliefs, Secrets, and Legacies

*Beliefs are the lenses through which we view the world. Beliefs are the bedrock of our behavior and the essence of our affect. Beliefs are the blueprints for which we construct our lives and intermingle them with the lives of others.*

    —L. M. Wright, W. L. Watson, and J. M. Bell (1996)

## CHAPTER OVERVIEW

At the heart of every family is a family belief system. It is present in the stories we tell about our families and in the stories we tell ourselves about who we are. These stories are shaped by our family's beliefs, scripts, myths, and legends, and by our interactions with family members at the earliest stages of our lives. The stories we tell ourselves and each other lead to the legacies we pass on from one generation to another.

## FAMILY SCRIPTS AND MYTHS

Byng-Hall (1999) defines a family script as "the family's shared expectations of how family roles are to be performed within various contexts (including that of attachment/caregiving)" (p. 626). Scripts can be identified in what are typical family interactions that occur repeatedly, especially if related to important tasks or events in family life. They occur at what Byng-Hall says are "decisive moments" in a family's history. Each script will have a context, often involving a task of some kind, a plot that includes family members' motives, and an outcome, which involves the consequences of having acted out the script. Families may either attempt to change or collaborate in the re-enactment of a script.

When family scenarios are repeated again and again, they can be said to be operating according to a script. How families confront common life challenges—someone becoming ill, a child leaving home, a family member getting into trouble with the law, family members dying, weddings, the birth of a child—often play out the same way over generations in a family. There are generally routines associated with these scripts, as well as implied instructions on what family members are to do or say in particular situations. These arise from family stories about what should be avoided or emulated. These stories are told and passed on from generation to generation. How and when did Grandma get married? What did she wear? Who was there? What was involved in Grandpa's courtship of her? Did their families approve of the match? What about our parents? Similar questions get asked, and stories get told.

Sandra's mother and grandmother both became pregnant and married young. Sandra had a different plan. She decided to go to college, and at 17 entered her first year of a social work program. While at college she met a young man, Jackson, whose ambition was also to enter social work. He was one of the few males in her class. They began seeing each other, and by the end of her first year, Sandra realized that she was pregnant. She and Jackson made quick plans to have a civil marriage ceremony over the summer. When the baby arrived, Sandra planned to take a leave of absence from college for a year, but return as soon as she could work out daycare. But in sorting out their expenses, it became impossible for her to return to school; she worked full time until her baby was born, and she and Jackson moved in with his parents. In the end, Jackson graduated, but Sandra remained at home with the baby, doing occasional contract work when Jackson's parents were able to provide child care. The power of her family script was so strong that she unwittingly repeated it and became the third generation of women in her family to become pregnant and marry young. Neither her mother nor her grandmother had graduated from college, and both had had hastily arranged civil ceremonies, giving birth before the age of 20. The parallels were stunning. However, Sandra and Jackson did deviate from the script in one respect: they agreed that as soon as Jackson got a good job and daycare could be arranged for their daughter, Sandra would return to finish her diploma.

In this case study, we see the power of scripts that are acted out unconsciously. In spite of Sandra's desire to complete a college diploma, her unconscious drive to fulfill the script written by her mother and grandmother was so strong that it overtook her conscious ambitions. It takes a great deal to consciously violate earlier family scripts, and it will often take considerable insight and resolve to do so. Parents are often advised that children will copy what they do, not what they say. In this case, in spite of Sandra's mother's support and urging that she go to college and graduate, Sandra unconsciously fulfilled her mother's and grandmother's script.

Where routines are firmly embedded in particular scripts, a paradox may occur. Family members may actually feel secure enough in the knowledge of what is expected that they are able to improvise—to try variations on the theme (Byng-Hall, 1996). But many times family scripts are rooted in belief systems that suggest that families behave in particular ways to solve problems in order to avoid an even worse one. As such, there can be scripts related to almost any challenge a family faces, including parenting, grieving, caring and distancing, control, and identification, among others. Where family breakup occurs, there is likely to be a disrupted script underlying it. Some examples of scripts can be found in the daughter in a family becoming pregnant before the age of 20, as happened to Sandra, or the eldest son joining the military in every generation. Or there may have been conflict between parents and children wishing to marry outside their social circumstances, race, culture, or class in every generation.

## BELIEFS AND MYTHS

Individuals can believe certain things, even when there is little truth to support them. This may be indicative of a family script operating according to a family myth—a story the family has told itself over and over again as if it were true. Kradin (2009, p. 217) defines a family myth as representing "an imaginal narrative that emphasizes the importance of the family's founders, its collective values, and its position with respect to 'outsiders.'"

For example, Grandma used particular remedies to address certain ailments. A grandson or granddaughter may continue to use these remedies, even though they appear to have no effect, and Grandma's reputation as a family healer remains unchanged. Belief in ghosts or other supernatural phenomena is often passed from one generation to another. Some observances have some aspect of truth while others may be purely fictional. Nevertheless, family members will recount instances of even fictional ghost visitations as if they were true. Great Aunt Mary was able to commune with spirits, and hence sensitivity to supernatural phenomena runs in the family.

Rituals, symbols, and metaphors are often used in family mythology to create shared meanings about events and people (Anderson & Bagarozzi, 1983). In this way families create common understandings known only to them. Where no guideposts exist in the form of family stories, family myths may take their place in an effort to provide guidance to the next generation.

Sometimes beliefs that arise from family scripts can be quite constraining and prevent families from seeing and exploring other options. Wright and Nagy (1993, p. 123) have said, "Constraining beliefs arise from social, interactional, and cultural contexts. Constraining beliefs inhibit the autonomy of the individual and family by restricting options for alternate solutions to problems." Refusing to deviate from how things have always been done in a family can be highly problematic and prevent families from embracing new scripts that might be healthier and more positive in their outcomes.

For instance, Sue, a woman in her forties, became gravely ill with a chronic disease that would require a liver transplant. She had, during her lifetime, sometimes made some unfortunate choices that had led her to abuse drugs. Her family was quite judgmental about this, and she was treated as the family scapegoat and often blamed for the family's problems. If it weren't for Sue, the family would be fine. Sue had a 14-year-old son whom she had raised quite well. He was a nice young man who had not shown any propensity for the problems that had plagued his mother. When Sue's condition suddenly became worse and she was hospitalized, the family did nothing to help her. Instead of advocating for her to be moved to the hospital where her doctor was, and where she may have had a life-saving liver transplant, she was left to suffer and die in a hospital where her condition was basically left untreated. She had begged to at least be allowed to return home, but her mother would not hear of it. Years later, when her mother was dying of cancer, her remaining children did the same to her. They abandoned her in a nursing home, far from her friends and support system, where she later died.

This is an example of a particularly noxious family script about what happens to family members when they become very ill. At the heart of it is a belief system that, once people begin to fail physically, they should be abandoned to their fate.

In this case the possibility of having to care for an ill or injured family member in one's own home may be seen as worse than leaving them to die. Or the script may be based on a belief that dying sooner rather than later is more humane. Beliefs can be shaped by many things—religion, life experience, the influence of others, and a family's history.

> Ivan's family, for example, lived through the Holocaust and maintained a strong belief that marrying outside of Judaism was taboo. When Ivan found himself falling in love with a non-Jewish girl, it caused a family crisis. He was terribly conflicted. His loyalty to his family was being tested against his loyalty to the young woman he loved. In the end, he decided not to continue his relationship with the young woman, and maintained, at least for a while, his family tradition of not marrying outside their religion.
>
> This belief was strongly rooted in the family's history and ethnic, cultural, and religious identification. With so many members of his family having been killed in concentration camps, his remaining family felt duty- and honour-bound to remain true to their memories by not marrying outside their religion, thereby helping to keep Judaism alive in the face of those who would destroy it.

This belief system is very strong in many families, irrespective of race, culture, or ethnicity. Remaining true to one's family history by honouring it with the same traditions as came before is a very strong script, founded on a belief system that arose early in a family's history.

Scripts can also be based upon family myths, which Byng-Hall (1979, p. 103) defines as "false or edited beliefs about the present which may be coupled with family legends which support those beliefs." These can take the form of yarns (where liberties can be taken with the way the tale is elaborated), or outright lies (which are presented as true), or legends (which may well be true but have been altered in the telling and retelling). Lewis, Beavers, Gossett, and Phillips (1976) believe that "healthy myths ... fill in gaps of observation, and provide a matrix of shared meaning. What is more they are not rigid but can be changed. They are gentle and humorous, thus allowing for human frailty and not demanding that people live up to (or down to) stereotyped images" (Byng-Hall, 1979, p. 105).

Family myths serve important purposes in maintaining homeostasis, or family stability (Ferreira, 1963). They can serve as defences against overwhelming truths, such as someone having died of a horrible terminal illness; they can mask deep sadness in families to prevent others from seeing it. They can be useful distractions to avoid taboo themes in families, such as the presence of abuse, alcoholism, or extramarital affairs (Byng-Hall, 1996). For example, focusing on Grandpa as a hero of some sort may help to mask the fact that he also molested children in the family. Seeing Mother as a competent businesswoman may mask the fact that she is also an alcoholic. Byng-Hall (1979) refers to this as a paradox—a story that is both true and false at the same time.

Family stories, myths, and legends establish a foundation that allows each new generation to launch novel responses from a secure base. They make the rules of family behaviour real to each new generation. Having a historical framework that sets out how a family functions helps to allow experimentation and introduces change in a new generation.

## REPLICATION OR ERADICATION OF FAMILY BELIEF SYSTEMS

Families may deal with their stories, beliefs, and histories by either replicating them or attempting to eradicate them. Byng-Hall (1996) sees neither of these as being particularly adaptive, the first because it may create a self-fulfilling prophecy, and the second because unconscious knowledge of family history may still be recreated irrespective of how hard a family tries not to do so.

Let's first examine replication. Joan became pregnant at the age of 16 like her mother. Grandma Marge had predicted that Joan's daughter would also become pregnant at this age, and that is exactly what happened. Did Grandma, by making this prediction, cause the event? Possibly, by having this expectation, she may have created a Pygmalion effect, or a self-fulfilling prophecy.

Now let's examine eradication. A mother and father attempted to shield their children from the past by not talking about it. Unfortunately, this had a harrowing effect in that their children assumed that terrible things had happened to the family. Their son struggled his whole life with depression, believing that his grandparents had likely been killed in some horrible way since he had no contact with them and his parents refused to discuss them. Their daughter travelled the world, possibly looking for answers, and contracted a serious illness from which she later died. The children may have unconsciously and inadvertently acted out the actual history of their family—mental illness and premature death—that their parents did not want to discuss.

## HELPING TO REWRITE NEGATIVE FAMILY SCRIPTS

Professionals working with families can help by acquainting them with authentic stories from their pasts and guiding them in seeing the influence these stories have on the present. Also helpful is allowing families to see that they can alter these stories somewhat without having to fully eradicate or deny them.

To illustrate this, let's look at the Grundy family. The father grew up in a violent home in which his brother and his own father beat his mother and sister. His mother consequently became an alcoholic. The father had to intervene to save his mother and sister from his violent brother on at least one occasion. In his own marriage, he did not beat his wife, although he often became very angry with her. Instead he beat his child, thereby displacing his anger onto her, in a completely maladaptive attempt to change his family story. By not beating his wife, he was trying not to repeat his father's actions. But by beating his child instead, he was creating a situation that was just as bad or worse. The challenge for the professional in working with this family would be to help this man channel and transform his justifiable anger about his family of origin so that he no longer feels the need to beat anyone.

## GENOGRAMS

Sometimes it is helpful to use genograms to incorporate the stories of ancestors and to demonstrate how responses have changed through the generations. A genogram is "a diagram outlining the history of the behavior patterns (as of divorce, abortion or suicide) of a family over several generations" (Genogram, 2013). As the genogram is created and the stories of each ancestor are shared, it becomes possible to see similarities, but also differences, in how family dilemmas, challenges, and conflicts have been handled. Perhaps one ancestor left home forever to escape a violent family. Perhaps another in the next generation left for a time and returned but limited his association with the family. Perhaps a daughter became pregnant without being married and gave her child up, while a daughter in the next generation kept her child when she found herself in the same predicament. These different responses can provide guideposts for the next generation. It may also be possible to help families to reframe some of their history. Did the first son abandon the family by leaving a violent home? Or did he, instead, have the courage to build a new life apart from his family? Both describe the same event, but the tone and feeling of each viewpoint are very different.

## FAMILY BELIEF SYSTEMS

The stories told over and over again in families help create family belief systems. These, in turn, may fuel the scripts that families follow from one generation to another. The emotional, social, financial, physical, and spiritual legacies that are passed down from one generation to another are recreated in each family. The legacy of public service, where each family member in the previous generation served in some way, tends to be recreated in the next generation, in which individuals also gravitate to public service. Military families are composed of individuals who, throughout the generations, have fought wars on behalf of their countries. In some cases, the way that individuals handled specific challenges can become legacies for those in subsequent generations. For example, where there is unresolved grief over a lost love in one generation, there may also be yearning for a lost love in the next as a similar scenario is acted out. Where someone married a person because of social pressure rather than love, but maintained an affair with the person they did love, this too may be re-enacted in the next generation.

> For example, Ella thought she had lost the love of her life in the Second World War. When the war was over, she waited for two years in the hopes that he would come home. When he did not, she reluctantly agreed to marry another man whom she did not love as strongly. Two days after her marriage, her first love came home but never spoke to her again because she had not waited for him. This scenario was replayed in the life of her daughter, who fell in love with a man of a different social class and ethnicity. When he could not marry her, she married another man but always longed for her first love. In this way, the legacy of unrequited love was handed down from one generation to the next.

Belief systems create thoughts that create feelings that, in turn, create behaviour (Snyder, 1984). Once family members embrace a particular family belief system, they can be expected to think about things in a similar fashion, feel the emotions that their ancestors felt, and act in accordance with these. In this way, the family belief system is turned into a cognitive, emotional, and behavioural legacy that is passed from one generation to another.

It is vital that professionals working with families uncover specific belief systems. These can often be traced back by using questions designed to bring the underlying beliefs to light. For example:

"Melissa, how were you feeling when you undertook an affair with Charles?"

"I was feeling distraught, unloved, and uncared for by my husband."

"Do you recall your mother ever having said that she felt similarly?"

"Yes, actually she did."

"And how did she handle this?"

"I believe, but am not sure, that she may have had an affair with someone named Victor."

"So would it be fair to say that, in your family, when women feel distraught, unloved, and uncared for, they are vulnerable to having affairs?"

"Yes, I guess that's true!"

This dialogue sets the stage for Melissa to begin to question her family's, and specifically her mother's, belief system that may well have been passed down to her. It is now possible to ask her if it is reasonable to handle feelings of neglect in this way or if there are other options for handling such difficult feelings.

A sense of duty was the underlying belief system in John's family. No matter what, once a task or obligation was undertaken, the men in the family were expected to unfailingly see it through. One of John's favourite expressions in response to his children was "You made your bed, now lie in it." John himself was lying in a bed of pain created by his loveless marriage. He and his wife's indifference to each other negatively affected their two sons, both of whom were showing signs of depression. One was not doing well in school, was sick a lot, and at times found it hard to get out of bed or feel motivated to do anything. The other acted out, often tormenting the girls in his class. Both sons were displaying symptoms of having been hurt by their parents' pain. Might things have been better for all concerned if John and his wife had been able to seek counselling to determine whether or not their marriage could be saved or improved? Rather than simply feeling that he had made his bed by marrying his wife and he now needed to lie in it, could breaking from the family belief system that had become a script possibly free John to explore other alternatives that might help him, his wife, and children?

Professionals working with families like these can help by first uncovering the belief systems underlying the repetitive scripts that are being played out to determine if these beliefs are still functional and serving the family well. Helping families to identify and determine the functionality of the scripts they are repeating, and possibly helping them to rewrite them, can also assist them in adopting different ways of relating to each other.

It may also be useful to help families recognize that the myths within their family systems could provide important life lessons or guidelines for children, thereby freeing them to transform them into fables (Byng-Hall, 1979).

## FAMILY SECRETS

Every family has secrets, things that are too taboo, horrible, or shameful to talk about. Kuhn (2002, p. 1) has said, "Although we take stories of childhood and family literally, I think our recourse to this past is a way of reaching for myth, for the story that is deep enough to express the profound feelings we have in the present." Dad abused his eldest daughter. Mother did unspeakable things when she drank. The oldest son was a coward who went AWOL during the war. The youngest daughter became pregnant by a man not of her race and culture, who abandoned her, and she aborted the baby. These are the kind of secrets that families regularly keep because they cannot be discussed openly. They create distancing, and unnamed and sometimes unconscious hurts in family members.

For example, the Timmins family had always only gathered together for special occasions, and when they did, there was often tension and conflict. The father of this family had been an alcoholic; the mother, emotionally cruel, especially to her two daughters; and the two sons both had emotional problems—one with control and the other with abdication of responsibility. The father had divorced the mother and gone off with another woman, whom he later married. He had little contact with his children and did not have a child with his second wife. The eldest daughter had been sexually abused by her father, very likely with the mother's knowledge. The mother had failed to protect her own child, and the father had simply used her, and showed no regard for the impact of his behaviour. Whenever this family got together, the eldest daughter was criticized and scapegoated by the other siblings. Her mother afforded her special treatment, of which she took advantage, doing her laundry at her mother's house and accepting gifts of money. Her mother's second husband was not happy with the situation, but said little to nothing about it. The other siblings, however, seethed with resentment.

Eventually, as the eldest daughter lay in hospital dying of a serious illness caused by her use of drugs, likely in an effort to cope with her abusive history, the family decided to have a meeting to decide what to do about her and her 14-year-old son. As the family meeting progressed, the two brothers broke down in tears, practically acknowledging that they knew their father had abused their eldest sister. The younger sister remained cold and behaved much like her mother, insisting that they limit the discussion to the arrangements that needed to be made. This same sister later refused to aid her dying sister, abandoning her to die in the hospital and failing to contact her sister's specialist for help. The wife of the eldest brother, a nurse, also remained cold like the mother, who remained silent throughout the exchange, not looking at any of her children. Both constantly blamed the eldest daughter for her own situation. The family secret had been revealed, but even so, the eldest daughter, who had been a victim of her father's abuse and her mother's failure to protect her, was left to die. The family was willing to allow the dark family secret to die with her.

In this way, family secrets are extremely destructive to a family's well-being, resulting in distancing, resentment, envy, anger, shame, and deep pain. Revealing a family secret, however, is a tricky matter. Having a family member reveal a secret can lead to shunning, shame, legal consequences, and, as in the case above, even death (Bradshaw, 2013).

A family member may discover, in seeking his baptismal certificate, that he is not Catholic, but Jewish (Muller-Paisner, 2005); someone else may find out that his father is not who he thought he was; another may discover that his grandfather collaborated with the enemy during the war; still another may learn that he is adopted. Such is the stuff of family secrets. As Bradshaw (2013) says of such secrets, "Their potency builds with time. There is no turning back, no closing the lid. The truth explodes reality, the truth demands accounting." However, this needs to be done carefully and with great sensitivity.

The revealing of family secrets can change everything, and the possible consequences need to be explored prior to anyone discussing a secret that they have guarded for a long time—the parent who has to tell her children that they have an older brother or sister who was given up for adoption before they were born; the parents who have to tell their other children that they gave away their sister to an asylum when she was very young because she had severe disabilities; the father who does not want to reveal that he was terribly abused by a Scout master. The impact of these kinds of secrets can be considerable, and a great deal of discussion and preparation with a family member is required concerning possible consequences and likely reactions before they can be revealed.

## CHAPTER SUMMARY

This chapter has examined family belief systems and how they can, unbeknownst to family members, often create scripts that get repeated. It has also outlined the usefulness of family myths and how these can be used to teach life lessons and values to the next generation. Taken together, family belief systems, the scripts they help to create, family myths, and even family secrets can create an intergenerational legacy that may or may not be in the best interests of a family. Helping families to examine all of these can be a positive way of promoting change.

## FURTHER READING

Boss, P. (2002). Family values and belief systems: Influences on family stress management. In *Family stress management: A contextual approach* (pp. 135–148). Thousand Oaks, CA: Sage Knowledge.

## CLASSROOM RESOURCES

*Birth of a family.* (2016). NFB. https://www.nfb.ca/film/birth_of_a_family/
*Family secrets.* (1984). Half Pint Productions, NBC. https://www.amazon.com/Family-Secrets-Stefanie-Powers-Stefania/dp/B000JJJONG
*Hidden family secrets.* (2018). Stargazer Films. https://www.moviefone.com/movie/hidden-family-secrets/NR3o7WJxgTS950Rvd1KkB3/main/

## CLASSROOM ACTIVITY

For the next week, ask students to spend a few moments each night journalling some of their family's history: its beliefs and the actions these beliefs create, its myths, its scripts, and its secrets. At the end of the week, students should summarize what impact all of these have had in their own lives, and should be prepared to report some of their findings in class.

## QUESTIONS FOR REFLECTION

1. What are some of the key beliefs in your own family?
2. How do you feel these beliefs may contribute to family scripts that are regularly repeated in various interactions and behaviours?

3.  What myths do you think may be occurring in your family? What function do you think these myths may have in teaching specific values or beliefs to the next generation?

4.  If you had the opportunity, what family scripts might you yourself rewrite? How would you change them?

## REFERENCES

Anderson, S. A., & Bagarozzi, D. A. (1983). The use of family myths as an aid to strategic therapy. *Journal of Family Therapy, 5*(2), 145–154.

Bradshaw, G. A. (2013, November 12). Family secrets. *Psychology Today.* Retrieved from www.psychologytoday.com/blog/bear-in-mind/201311/family-secrets

Byng-Hall, J. (1979). Re-editing family mythology during family therapy. *Journal of Family Therapy, 1,* 103–116.

Byng-Hall, J. (1996). *Rewriting family scripts.* New York, NY: The Guilford Press.

Byng-Hall, J. (1999). Family and couple therapy: Toward greater security. In J. Cassidy and P. R. Shaver (Eds.), *Handbook of attachment: Theory, research, and clinical applications* (pp. 625–645). New York, NY: The Guilford Press.

Ferreira, A. J. (1963). Family myth and homelessness. *Archives of General Psychiatry, 9,* 457–467.

Genogram. (2013). In *Merriam Webster Dictionary.* Retrieved from www.merriam-webster.com/dictionary/genogram

Kradin, R. (2009, April). The family myth: Its deconstruction and replacement with a balanced humanized narrative. *Journal of Analytical Psychology, 54*(2), 217–232.

Kuhn, A. (2002). *Family secrets: Acts of memory and imagination.* Brooklyn, NY: Verso Books.

Lewis, M. J., Beavers, W. R., Gossett, J. T., & Phillips, V. A. (1976). *No single thread: Psychological health in family systems.* New York, NY: Brunner/Mazel.

Muller-Paisner, V. (2005). Broken chain: Catholics uncover the Holocaust's hidden legacy and discover Jewish roots [Print catalogue entry]. Retrieved from www.pitchstonebooks.com/catalog/broken-chain?rq=broken%20chain

Snyder, M. (1984). When belief creates reality. *Advances in Experimental Social Psychology, 18,* 247–305.

Wright, L. M., & Nagy, J. (1993). Death: The most troublesome family secret of all. In E. Imber Black (Ed.), *Secrets in families and family therapy.* New York, NY: W.W. Norton.

Wright, L. M., Watson, W. L., & Bell, J. M. (1996). *Beliefs: The heart of healing in families and illness.* New York, NY: Basic Books.

## CHAPTER 7

# Family Functioning, Scapegoating, and Attachment Issues

*[Perfectionistic parents] put the burden of stability on the child to avoid facing the fact that they, as parents, cannot provide it. The child fails and becomes the scapegoat for family problems. Once again, the child is saddled with the blame.*

   —S. Forward (2002)

## CHAPTER OVERVIEW

In this chapter, various ways that families attempt to maintain homeostasis, both positive and negative, will be discussed. The impact of negative attempts to maintain homeostasis, such as through scapegoating and abuse of power, and their impact on children's early attachment are also examined.

Even though families consist of individuals, they tend to function as a system. And like most systems, they tend toward maintaining homeostasis, or stability. This requires balance and some degree of predictability in the relationships between individuals in a family (Janzen, Harris, Jordon, & Franklin, 2006). Where these relationships are healthy, family goals are met, growth is encouraged, and a positive state of homeostasis is achieved. However, in some families, homeostasis is achieved only at the expense of one or more family members. In this case, destructive interactions may occur that are designed to harm one or more family members, and a negative state of homeostasis is achieved.

## SCAPEGOATING

Families in which one or both parents regularly battle for position, with one or the other threatening to leave, can have a devastating effect on children. Their fear of losing one or both parents may cause them to "act out" in an attempt to shift the parents' focus away from each other and onto themselves, thereby stopping the parents' fighting and keeping them together. The child may get into trouble at school or with peers, or be disruptive, violent, or destructive at home. Children in this situation are often scapegoated—the family blames them for all of its problems, thereby easing the anxiety of the rest of the family members. Mook (1985, p. 1) defined scapegoating as "a dysfunctional interactional process where unintentionally a scapegoat role is attributed to one member who is then held responsible for being the sole agent of all the family's problems." As long as the scapegoated child can be blamed, it is unnecessary for the other family members to examine their behaviour toward each other, and the core issue in the family, the parents' relationship, does not need to be examined (Janzen et al., 2006).

Scapegoating tends to occur in any family where there is a high degree of anxiety, anger, and pain, and/or where maltreatment occurs. It happens for many different reasons, but the family member who is scapegoated carries the anxieties of the whole family system. They often behave in disruptive or dysfunctional ways, thereby allowing the rest of the family to continue to see them as the problem. Pillari (1991) describes scapegoating as an intergenerational phenomenon wherein individuals are chosen to bear the family's anxiety, anger, and pain. Hamilton-Giachritsis and Browne (2005, p. 619) point out that where there is a scapegoated child in abusive families, there is often risk to all siblings: "In 44% of families (valid cases), the index child was scapegoated, in 37% maltreatment was nonspecific to all siblings, and in 20% maltreatment was specifically directed at some but not all siblings. Scapegoated children were more likely to be older and to experience physical or sexual abuse, whereas younger children and index child referrals for neglect, emotional abuse, or mixed abuse were associated with risk to some or all siblings." When working with children and teens who are depressed or who act out, it is wise to look more deeply at the family system to determine if the child is playing the role of the scapegoat. Helping to ease family anxiety related to other issues may also alter the child's role as family scapegoat.

For instance, Leslie was the eldest child in her family. Her father was an alcoholic, and her mother was embittered because of his drinking and lack of attention to her. Leslie's mother resented having to have sex with her husband and began ignoring the fact that her husband appeared to very much favour Leslie. Leslie was eventually sexually abused by her father, who finally left the family in a drunken rage after a particularly angry confrontation with his wife. The other three children in the family were also affected in various ways by their father's drinking, and the second-oldest child, a brother, and the youngest, also a brother, had some inkling that Leslie was being abused and felt terrible guilt about it. This was a family with a high degree of anxiety, and Leslie became the scapegoat for the family's pain. At a young age, she took up with a man and moved west. She thereafter became pregnant. During her delivery, she was given tainted blood and developed hepatitis C. She also developed a drinking and drug problem to cope with her early abuse. She struggled with both alcoholism and heroin addiction for years, and eventually returned to the city where her family lived, after years of separation. Her mother, who was by then in a new relationship, was both indulgent and resentful of Leslie—indulgent because of her own guilt in not protecting her, and resentful because Leslie took advantage of her guilt to extract cash and other amenities from her. Leslie's three siblings hated her, as did the oldest brother's wife. They repeatedly criticized her and blamed her for the family's problems. Leslie made a good scapegoat. Her drinking and drug use made it easy for her siblings to blame her for everything, and she took on the burden of being the family's safety valve.

As Hollingsworth, Glass, and Heisler (2007) have pointed out, this is symptomatic of "empathy deficits" developed by other children in the family when a family member is scapegoated. "In many families, siblings identify with the parent, joining in blaming the victim for the caretaker's abuse of that child. They demonstrate empathy deficits, which may protect them from the effects of witnessing the process" (Hollingsworth et al., 2007, p. 69). As is so often the case in families where a parent is an alcoholic, this family functioned in complete denial of the very negative patterns and family scripts that were being acted out and the children took on both parents' lack of empathy for the scapegoated child.

## CLOSENESS AND DISTANCING

Families must find ways to balance separateness and togetherness. Where there is too much separation, there is distancing, with family members feeling unconnected to each other. Where there is too much togetherness, enmeshment often occurs, leaving family members feeling engulfed or smothered and unable to maintain their own independence (Janzen et al., 2006). Janzen and colleagues describe it this way:

> The ways in which family members want to be together and the ways they want to be apart are reflected in the family's patterns of behavior. Some families develop around an excessive need for emotional closeness, while other families place great emphasis on separateness. If the need for closeness is too great, fusion within family relationships is likely to result.... Family members will not be able to express themselves in a manner other than what is preferred by the family. If the drive for individuality and self-determination exceeds all other interests, the ability of family members to be close and supportive in relationships with one another is lessened. Extremes in either case contribute to family dysfunction. (Janzen et al., 2006, pp. 18, 19)

## FAMILY DISTANCING

Scharp and Hall (2018) have outlined four types of distancing behaviour in families. The first is pulling away, where usually one member of the family creates distance from the family by putting geographic distance between themselves and the family, interacting very infrequently, or directly informing the family that they are cutting off contact with them. The second is mutual distancing, where family members agree that where there seems to be irresolvable conflict, not getting together for traditional holidays or other "family" events and little contact may be best. The third is a form of involuntary distancing, where a family member is pushed out by other family members. This is a person who is usually labelled a "black sheep" and is excluded from family events. The fourth is third-party removal, where an authority of some sort such as child welfare removes a child, where a family member is incarcerated, or, in the case of refugee families, where they may become separated during wars or natural disasters. Scharp and Hall (2018) argue that where there is mutual agreement that distancing is best for a family, it need not be considered to be a negative outcome.

Where families have difficulty maintaining appropriate levels of either closeness or separateness, the problem likely began in the couples' own families of origin. One way that family members may attempt to address tension and anxiety associated with imbalanced systems of closeness or distancing is to form triangles, where a third person or issue, such as work, sports, or finances, enters the picture.

## TRIANGULATION

Triangulation is a way that families attempt to remain viable. Triangulation can be between three people, or two people and an issue. Janzen et al. (2006, p. 14) have said that "the two person system has difficulty maintaining its stability under the pressure of anxiety and tension. When this system experiences intolerable frustration, it triangulates a third person or an issue in the hope of reducing the level of tension." Guerin, Fogarty, Fay, and Kautto (1996, p. 8) have also commented that "it is the instability of dyads that produces relationship triangles."

Murray Bowen's theories suggest the following:

A triangle is a three-person relationship system. It is considered the building block or "molecule" of larger emotional systems because a triangle is the smallest stable relationship system. A two-person system is unstable because it tolerates little tension before involving a third person. A triangle can contain much more tension without involving another person because the tension can shift around three relationships. If the tension is too high for one triangle to contain, it spreads to a series of "interlocking" triangles. Spreading the tension can stabilize a system, but nothing gets resolved. People's actions in a triangle reflect their efforts to ensure their emotional attachments to important others, their reactions to too much intensity in the attachments, and their taking sides in the conflicts of others. (Bowen Center, 2014)

The problem with triangulation is that, as Bowen suggests, it creates an "odd one out"—something that is very difficult for a third party to tolerate, unless they are used to playing this role in a family of origin.

For example, Lisa is having an emotional affair with Charles, who is married to Mary. She is not happy that Charles is remaining married to Mary and he often reminds Lisa that his family is the most important thing in his life. Lisa, however, tolerates the three-way relationship because it mirrors the relationship that she had in her own family of origin. While Lisa's mother was jealous of her relationship with her father (much as Charles's wife is jealous of his relationship with Lisa), her father would not stand up for himself or for her (much as Charles will not stand up for himself or her in his relationship with his wife). Charles is not really happy with his wife but tends to deny it, seeking comfort in his regular talks with Lisa. He will not deal with the problems in his own relationship, but instead seeks to downplay issues and avoid confrontations—much as Lisa's father did. So while Lisa is not comfortable in the relationship, her own loneliness and her affection for Charles cause her to stay in this uncomfortable arrangement.

As Bowen (Bowen Center, 2014) has illustrated, in a triangle, the odd person out is always trying to get closer to one of the other people in the triangle while the "insiders ... actively exclude the outsider."

Someone is always uncomfortable in a triangle and pushing for change. The insiders solidify their bond by choosing each other in preference to the less desirable outsider. Someone choosing another person over oneself arouses particularly intense feelings of rejection. If mild to moderate tension develops between the insiders, the most uncomfortable one will move closer to the outsider. One of the original insiders now becomes the new outsider and the original outsider is now an insider. The new outsider will make predictable moves to restore closeness with one of the insiders. (Bowen Center, 2014)

It is easy to see how this might work in an affair, whether it is sexual or emotional. Whoever is pulling the strings of the other potential outsiders maintains an uneasy control in the relationship. This provides a rather dysfunctional way for the one in control to try to maintain harmony—at least in two sides of the triangle. The Bowen Center (2014) describes it this way:

At moderate levels of tension, triangles usually have one side in conflict and two sides in harmony. The conflict is not inherent in the relationship in which it exists but reflects the overall functioning of the triangle. At a high level of tension, the outside position becomes the most desirable. If severe conflict erupts between the insiders, one insider opts for the outside position by getting the current outsider fighting with the other insider. If the maneuvering insider is successful, he gains the more comfortable position of watching the other two people fight. When the tension and conflict subside, the outsider will try to regain an inside position.

All of this can cause real problems for the people involved in triangulated relationships. When an insider is pushed to an outside position, they can become depressed or even physically ill. Interestingly, in the case of Charles, Lisa, and Mary, all have developed physical problems due to being positioned as outsiders at one point or another and have felt extreme and ongoing stress and anxiety because of it.

Bowen suggested that all of this is driven by what he termed "anxious attachment," in which "a blurring of boundaries occurs between two people wherein the transmission of anxiety is so intense that both people become convinced that they can't survive without the other." This is manifested in "cycles of closeness and distance" (Guerin et al., 1996, p. 11).

For example, Sue and Fred have long had an unsettling relationship. Sue can be quite demanding of Fred, something he generally tries to cope with but at times has difficulty handling. Sue considers Fred to be evasive and not engaged enough with her. They have two children, both teenage boys. One is quite immature, while the other is quite savvy and street-smart, and tends to sometimes get into trouble at school. In this family, both boys alternate being in the triangulated position. One or both will ally themselves with one of the parents whenever anxiety, anger, or pain increases in the family, thereby creating a three-on-one situation. When Sue and Fred are in conflict, one or the other of the boys will act out in particular ways that draws their attention away from each other. Fred spends inordinate amounts of time with his sons and other family members, thereby avoiding his wife. One son, who is not close to his mother, triangulates to video games and friends at school. The other son tends to be more clingy with his mother. From time to time, when the son who is clingy is not present, the mother feels abandoned within the family. Now that the eldest son is leaving for college, the younger son is alone at home with his parents. He has begun to experience some conflict with his father. Fred has become very friendly with a female co-worker recently in what is likely an unconscious attempt to take the pressure off his relationships with both his wife and his remaining son.

Here we see repeated triangulation that has become a family script, which can be destructive to the family as a unit. This family needs to learn to balance closeness and distancing to reduce its level of anxiety, the disappointment each member feels toward the others, and the resulting emotional pain.

# RIGID FAMILY STRUCTURE AND ROLES

Another issue facing families is the extent to which the family structure, roles, and culture are rigid or flexible. Janzen et al. (2006, p. 21) state that the family structure "should not be so rigid as to prohibit variability and change.... It should be sufficiently stable so that members can experience the family as dependable and predictable enough to provide some guidelines by which the individual members can be clear about what role and behavior is expected ... [but] it should also not be so changeable as to be chaotic with no clearly defined roles or rules for behavior ... and no sense of leadership or control."

In any family it is necessary for there to be clear roles, a sense of boundaries, and guidance or rules about what is or is not acceptable behaviour. However, when boundaries, rules, and roles are so fixed that they do not allow for change when it is necessary, this can become problematic in a family. Family crises occur from time to time, and these may demand role flexibility and a variety of adaptive coping mechanisms. Families whose roles are too rigid often have difficulty coping with crises. If the father, who is considered the leader and decision-maker in the family, becomes ill and unable to perform his role, his wife must be able to take over. If she has never had to make decisions, handle finances, or drive a car, the family's crisis may be much worse than if she had shared these duties and roles with her husband. A woman who handles all the household tasks in a rigid domestic routine, based on the belief that it is the man who brings home the money and the woman who takes care of the home, may find herself in a difficult situation if something happens to her husband. Similarly, a man may find himself in a problematic situation if he has no basic knowledge of how to keep the household running when something happens to his wife. A family's task is always about finding the balance between creating just enough guidance and stability and role flexibility, with room for individuals to grow and explore other options and alternatives in their lives.

In families with children, the family's main role is to create and sustain an environment that is safe, stimulating, and nurturing, where family members protect, help, and love each other. How families function has a significant impact on how securely attached children will be to their parents and ultimately to others as they go out into the world. How children attach to or bond with their original caregivers is vital because it has implications for their relationships and how well they are able to function throughout their lives.

## INTERGENERATIONAL TRANSMISSION

Parents raising children will often repeat the patterns and attitudes of their own parents, and may struggle with core beliefs that they acquired through their own attachment experiences. These can be either positive or negative. Both are transmitted from one generation to the next. In the case of negative core beliefs, helping family members to identify and change these can be an important process in impeding the intergenerational transmission of belief systems that cause pain and dysfunction. Similarly, helping family members to identify belief systems that are positive and adaptive and that promote resilience can also be useful in assisting families to build on their strengths.

## ATTACHMENT ISSUES

To begin our discussion, it may be helpful to look at the four characteristics governing attachment outlined by Bowlby (1979, 1988): proximity maintenance, where we want to be near the people to whom we are attached; safe haven, where we return to the people to whom we are attached for comfort and safety in the face of danger; secure base, where we feel sure enough of those who care for us that we can explore the surrounding environment knowing that we can return; and, finally, separation distress, which is what children experience when an attachment figure is either absent or unavailable physically and/or emotionally.

Ainsworth, Blehar, Waters, and Wall (1978) built on Bowlby's earlier thoughts on attachment by identifying three specific types of attachment: secure attachment, ambivalent-insecure attachment, and avoidant-insecure attachment, with a fourth type added later by Main and Solomon (1986), that of disorganized-insecure attachment.

We can now examine what constitutes a securely attached child and how they came to be securely attached in their relationship with caregivers and within their family of origin. Securely attached children feel comfortable and confident in their dealings with the world. They have gone through their early stages of development successfully and have learned to be trusting, to master life tasks, and to form intimate relationships with others and to maintain them. They tend to be more optimistic and positive in their approach to life and have reasonable problem-solving skills. They have parents who respond to their needs in ways that cause them to be secure in the knowledge that they will be able to get their needs met in other relationships as well.

Cassidy and Berlin (1994) refer to infants with ambivalent-insecure or ambivalent-resistant patterns of attachment as a very small percentage of the population, approximately 7 to 15 percent of all infants, who show high degrees of distress when a parent departs but are not soothed by their parent's return. These children are described as vacillating "abruptly between angry, frustrated resistance to contact ... and clinging, dependent, contact-maintaining behavior" upon reunion with their parent (Cassidy & Berlin, 1994, p. 971). These infants are "characterized by their preoccupation with, as well as their ambivalence toward, their parent" (p. 971).

Brotherson (2005) describes children considered to have an avoidant-insecure attachment style as those who "avoid or ignore a parent's presence, show little response when parents are close by, display few strong emotional outbursts, and may avoid or ignore a parent's responses toward them."

Bowlby (1979) believed that children whose parents are confident and available tended to experience less fear of new situations, knowing that their parents would be there to assist them if necessary. This, in turn, caused them to feel confident in their dealings with others and their environment. Schore (2001) has shown how this works with respect to brain development:

> The infant's early developing right hemisphere has deep connections into the limbic and autonomic nervous systems and is dominant for the human stress response, and in this manner the attachment relationship facilitates the expansion of the child's coping capacities. This model suggests that adaptive infant mental health can be fundamentally defined as the earliest expression of flexible strategies for coping with the novelty and stress that is inherent in human interactions. This efficient right brain function is a resilience factor for optimal development over the later stages of the life cycle. (p. 7)

What this means is that children whose family environment allowed them to be securely attached to their original caregivers have brains that develop the capacity to solve problems, form relationships, and develop resilience to better cope with life's challenges.

Conversely, Shi, Bureau, Easterbrooks, Zhao, and Lyons-Ruth (2012, p. 55) found the following about child maltreatment to be true:

> [It is] significantly associated with anti-social personality disorder (ASPD) features, but [it] did not account for the independent effect of early referral to parent-infant services on ASPD features. In longitudinal analyses,

maternal withdrawal in infancy predicted the extent of ASPD features 20 years later, independently of childhood abuse. In middle childhood, disorganized attachment behavior and maladaptive behavior at school added to prediction of later ASPD features. Antisocial features in young adulthood have precursors in the minute-to-minute process of parent–child interaction beginning in infancy.

In this way the authors demonstrated that early caregiver-child interactions that led to insecure attachment were predictors for later development of anti-social personality disorder.

Not all children with insecure attachment develop this condition. Nevertheless, they do have more difficulty showing trust of others, more disruption in relationships with others, and a more negative view of life in general.

It is easy to see how family disruption can cause interruption of secure attachment in children. Johnny tries to avoid being near a father who gets abusive when drunk. Jenny is afraid to go home after school, not knowing if her mother will be drunk or sober. Maya is afraid to leave home and suffers separation anxiety and school phobia because she doesn't want to leave her mother alone for fear her father will assault her in her absence. Murray, whose father is in prison for aggravated assault and whom he has not seen for almost two years, gets into trouble for fighting at school.

So what types of family dynamics can be expected to produce a securely versus an insecurely attached child? Cherry (2014) points out that children who are securely attached tend to have parents who play with them often, are highly responsive to their children's needs, and respond more quickly to a child. This tends to result in children who can seek comfort from parents when afraid, separate from parents without distress, and return to parents calmly, preferring their parents to strangers.

Conversely, Cherry (2014) says that insecure attachment is produced when parents respond inconsistently to children's needs and interfere more in their children's attempts to explore their world. This results in children who are more distressed and anxious, and who tend to not explore their worlds as much.

Where a parent or parents are depressed and therefore neglectful, or where a parent has never learned impulse control and takes their anger out on their children in the form of physical or emotional abuse, or where a parent has not been able to control their need for domination and commits sexual abuse—all of these interfere with the development of secure attachment, especially if the abuse and neglect occur in the first years of life, and can lead to avoidant-insecure attachment in a child. Insecure attachment has been found in many studies to be a predictor of depression in adulthood (Beck, 1987; Hankin & Abramson, 2001; Irons & Gilbert, 2005).

Marie has been diagnosed with borderline personality disorder. Her whole life has been characterized by the results of her emotional dysregulation. Her volatile emotions have caused her to get into one conflict after another—first with teachers in elementary and secondary school, and then with professors when she attempted to go to college but left after several explosive outbursts directed at other students and her professors. She struggles with issues related to rejection and abandonment. Looking at her family history, it is no wonder. Her mother was an alcoholic, and Marie herself has drug and alcohol issues. At times her mother was loving and concerned, and at other times she was rejecting and abusive. Marie never knew what to expect from her. Her father was largely absent, and her mother had affairs with numerous men during his absences. It should not be surprising that Marie sees threats in others and her environment where there are none, and repeatedly gets into conflicts that could easily have been prevented. Marie's attachment issues prevent her from being able to maintain relationships over the long term—something that causes her to feel lonely and to seek attention from others, often in mal-adapted ways. It is easy to see how her mother's inconsistent parenting, her mother's inability to maintain relationships, as evidenced by the numerous lovers she had during her husband's absences, and her mother's struggles with alcohol were transmitted to Marie. The inconsistency of Marie's mother's parenting and her father's repeated absences have likely changed her brain's ability to process information and regulate her emotions. Marie suffers from hyperarousal (when too much norepinephrine, a stress hormone, is released in response to a perceived threat and the prefrontal cortex is unable to properly regulate it), and a "reactive amygdala," which increases the likelihood of impulsive behaviour related to a perceived threat. Her core issue is anger—also related to an over-reactive amygdala. Greenberg (2018) describes it this way: "the amygdala-insula circuit also impacts the medial PFC, an area associated with assigning meaning to events and regulating emotions. Research shows overactivity of the amygdala-amygdala-insult circuit can suppress the medial PFC, thereby interfering with the ability to regulate negative emotions and assign more positive meaning to events."

Marie's story demonstrates how her early ability to form a secure attachment with her mother, the ongoing impact of inconsistent parenting, and being subjected to abusive behaviour resulted in brain damage, anxious attachment, and the resulting symptoms: volatile emotions, impulsivity, inability to form and maintain relationships, and conflicts with others, as well as self-injurious behaviour through attempts at self-medication using drugs and alcohol, thereby repeating her mother's maladaptive attempts to cope.

Marie is not beyond help. Because of the findings that the brain has some degree of plasticity (the "nervous system's ability to modify its organization and ultimately its function throughout an individual's lifetime" [Kolb, Gibb, & Robinson, n.d.]), with appropriate therapeutic input, often in the form of dialectical behaviour therapy, Marie can correct many of the symptoms now plaguing her and causing her to be unable to experience a more peaceful life. Psychotherapy is essential for survivors like Marie to uncover the basis for their trauma and insecure attachment and to begin to address the symptoms of a disordered and abusive childhood.

## INCONSISTENT PARENTING AND THE CHAOTIC FAMILY

Where a parent is ambivalent toward a child—perhaps the child resembles a divorced parent, or has a temperament the parent does not like—or where there is considerable chaos in the family, or a lack of safety caused by few or no routines, rules, or limits being set, ambivalent-insecure attachment can result. Highly inconsistent parenting, where the child cannot predict whether to approach or avoid a parent, can also lead to ambivalent-insecure attachment. Where there is serious mental illness, criminality, and/or severe substance abuse that causes a child's world to seem out of control, completely unsafe, and frightening, disorganized-insecure attachment can result.

All of these situations can create a system of core beliefs in a child about themselves, about caregivers, and about their environment and lives. Core beliefs are the lens through which we view the world and lead to our expectations of the present and future. They relate to self-esteem, to whether we can function independently or not, and to whether we can endure adversity and bounce back or not, and they set the stage for how we will view and handle our future relationships with intimate others and with authority figures. Will we have good, adaptive coping strategies? Will we develop a conscience and have compassion for others? Will we be able to function as members of a group? Do well in school? Function effectively at work? All of these are affected by our earliest relationships with caregivers, and our family life.

Children who grow up in families characterized by chaos, violence, inconsistent or rejecting parenting, substance abuse, and neglect are more likely to have rigid core beliefs, negative automatic thoughts about themselves, others, and the world, be more distrustful of others, and focus more on survival skills rather than on being able to thrive.

For example, Lynn's blended family has considerable power struggles and tensions within it. Two external former spouses add a dimension to the complex problems, as well as a mother-in-law who is at war with her son's new partner. Their family is largely in disarray and its members behave more like they are living in a boarding house than a family home. The children's torn allegiances with the external parents and extended family cause them to feel insecure and act out in various ways. The home is also chaotic. People do not eat together at a table, and most days the house looks like it has been hit by a hurricane. Lynn's mother is not close to her partner, who tends to neglect her and ignore her needs. The children are disgusted with him and love him at the same time, and act out by being precociously sexual and indulging in underage drinking. Lynn attempts to get her mother's attention by suggesting that she might be gay. The likelihood of this family surviving over the longer term is almost nil, especially once the children leave home. The couple relationship is unlikely to survive, and the children may seek to distance themselves at some point from both partners, who failed to provide a secure home environment.

A vital task for professionals working with families is helping families to see and understand their role in creating an environment that feels safe for all family members; that promotes an appropriate balance between togetherness and being apart; and that recognizes the need for flexibility in family roles, rules, and routines while maintaining expectations that are clear, and ensuring that limits are fair and appropriate boundaries are maintained.

## CHAPTER SUMMARY

This chapter has examined family functioning in the context of systems theory and the need to maintain homeostasis. It has outlined the challenges families face with respect to maintaining a balance between closeness and distance, how family members will triangulate to ease pressure on dyadic relationships, and how scapegoating occurs when a family is experiencing considerable anxiety, stress, and pain. The ways in which families either promote or prevent secure attachment in children and the consequent results of both have also been discussed.

## FURTHER READING

Coyle, S. (2014, May/June). Intergenerational trauma—legacies of loss. *Social Work Today, 14*(3), 18.

Fromm, G. M. (2012). *Lost in transmission: Studies of trauma across generations.* Abingdon, UK: Routledge.

Johnson, S. M. (2005). *Emotionally focused family therapy with trauma survivors: Strengthening attachment bonds.* New York, NY: The Guilford Press.

Napier, A. Y., & Whitaker, C. A. (2017, October 3). *The family crucible. The intense experience of family therapy.* New York, NY: Harper Perennial.

Rex, B. (2019). *(e)Scapegoat child: A guide on how to break out of the role as the scapegoat child in a narcissistic family.* Amazon Digital Services.

Thomas, S. (2016). *Healing from hidden abuse: A journey through the stages of recovery from psychological abuse.* Tempe, AZ: MAST.

## CLASSROOM RESOURCES

*The broken thread.* (2002). NFB. http://onf-nfb.gc.ca/en/our-collection/?idfilm=51221

*Family number one.* (2009). NFB. https://www.nfb.ca/film/hothouse_5_family_album_number_one/

*Growing up Canadian.* (2003). NFB. https://www.nfb.ca/film/growing_up_canadian_family/

*I was a child of Holocaust survivors.* (2010). NFB. http://onf-nfb.gc.ca/en/our-collection/?idfilm=56522

*Life with murder.* (2010). NFB. http://onf-nfb.gc.ca/en/our-collection/?idfilm=56712

## CLASSROOM ACTIVITIES

### Fishbowl

Choose a group of volunteers to construct a family including a mom with an alcohol problem, a dad who is disengaged, a son who tries to be perfect, and a daughter who is scapegoated. Each group member discusses the likely reasons each has taken on this role in the family, how it happened, and how, working as a therapist with this family, they might intervene to help the family. A second group observes the process, then shares their observations.

## Buzz Groups

Break the class into groups and ask each to choose a topic from those written on a whiteboard: scapegoating, distancing, attachment styles, triangulation, family structure and roles, intergenerational transmission and trauma, and inconsistent parenting and family chaos. Ask each group to identify what they have learned about the topic and how they are now seeing their own and others' families as a result. Have each group share their observations with the whole class.

## QUESTIONS FOR REFLECTION

1. Would you consider your own family members and those of your friends to be distanced from each other, overinvolved with each other, or balanced between closeness and distancing?
2. Is there a scapegoat in your family and in the families of those you know? What makes you believe this person is the family scapegoat?
3. Have you noticed any triangulation between yourself and other people or issues in your life?
4. In looking at your own life and that of your family, can you detect issues involving either secure or insecure early attachment? What makes you believe one or the other is present?

## REFERENCES

Ainsworth, M., Blehar, M., Waters, E., & Wall, S. (1978). *Patterns of attachment.* Hillsdale, NJ: Erlbaum.

Beck, A. T. (1987). Cognitive models of depression. *Journal of Cognitive Psychotherapy, 1,* 5–37.

Bowen Center. (2014). Eight concepts. Retrieved from https://thebowencenter.org/theory/eight-concepts/

Bowen, M. (1978). *Family therapy in clinical practice.* New York, NY: Jason Aronson.

Bowlby, J. (1979). *The making and breaking of affectional bonds.* London, UK: Tavistock.

Bowlby, J. (1988). *A secure base.* New York, NY: Basic Books.

Brotherson, S. (2005). Understanding attachment in young children. *Bright Beginnings #6.* North Dakota State University Extension Service. Retrieved from https://www.ucy.ac.cy/nursery/documents/attachement_3.pdf

Cassidy, J., & Berlin, L. J. (1994). The insecure/ambivalent pattern of attachment: Theory and research. *Child Development, 65*(4), 971–991.

Castelloe, M. S. (2012, May 28). How trauma is carried across generations. Retrieved from https://www.psychologytoday.com/ca/blog/the-me-in-we/201205/how-trauma-is-carried-across-generations

Cherry, K. (2014). Secure attachment. Retrieved from http://psychology.about.com/od/loveandattraction/ss/attachmentstyle_4.htm

Forward, S. (2002). *Toxic parents: Overcoming their hurtful legacy and reclaiming your life.* New York, NY: Bantam.

Greenberg, M. (2018, September 29). How PTSD and trauma affect your brain functioning. Retrieved from https://www.psychologytoday.com/us/blog/the-mindful-self-express/201809/how-ptsd-and-trauma-affect-your-brain-functioning

Guerin, P. J., Fogarty, T. F., Fay, L. F., & Kautto, J. G. (1996). *Working with relationship triangles: The one two three of psychotherapy.* New York, NY: The Guilford Press.

Hamilton-Giachritsis, C. E., & Browne, K. D. (2005, December). A retrospective study of risk to siblings in abusing families. *Journal of Family Psychology, 19*(4), 619–624.

Hankin, B. L., & Abramson, L. Y. (2001). Development of sex differences in depression: An elaborated cognitive vulnerability-transactional stress theory. *Psychological Bulletin, 12*, 773–796.

Hollingsworth, J., Glass, J., & Heisler, K. W. (2007). Empathy deficits in siblings of severely scapegoated children. *Journal of Emotional Abuse, 7*(4), 69–88. Retrieved from https://www.tandfonline.com/doi/abs/10.1300/J135v07n04_04

Irons, C., & Gilbert, P. (2005). Evolved mechanisms in adolescent anxiety and depression symptoms: The role of the attachment and social rank systems. *Journal of Adolescence, 28*, 325–341.

Janzen, C., Harris, O., Jordan, C., & Franklin, C. (2006). *Family treatment: Evidence-based practice with populations at risk.* Belmont, CA: Thomson Brooks/Cole.

Kolb, B., Gibb, R., & Robinson, T. (n.d.). Brain plasticity and behavior. Retrieved from https://www.psychologicalscience.org/journals/cd/12_1/kolb.cfm

Main, M., & Solomon, J. (1986). Discovery of an insecure-disorganized/disoriented attachment pattern: Procedures, findings and implications for the classification of behavior. In T. B. Brazelton & M. Yogman (Eds.), *Affective development in infancy* (pp. 95–124). Norwood, NJ: Ablex.

Mook, B. (1985). Phenomenology, system theory, and family therapy. *Journal of Phenomenological Psychology, 16*(1), 1–12.

Pillari, V. (1991). *Scapegoating in families: Intergenerational patterns of physical and emotional abuse.* Philadelphia, PA: Brunner/Mazel.

Scharp, K. M., & Dorrance Hall, E. (2018). Reconsidering family closeness: A review and call for research on family distancing. *Journal of Family Communication*, 1–14.

Schore, A. N. (2001). Effects of a secure attachment relationship on right brain development, affect regulation, and infant mental health. *Infant Mental Health Journal*, *22*(1/2), 7–66. Retrieved from http://allanschore.com/pdf/SchoreIMHJAttachment.pdf

Shi, Z., Bureau, J., Easterbrooks, M. A., Zhao, X., & Lyons-Ruth, K. (2012). Childhood maltreatment and prospectively observed quality of early care as predicators of antisocial personality disorder features. *Infant Mental Health Journal*, *33*(1), 55–60.

Urban Society for Aboriginal Youth, YMCA Calgary, & University of Calgary. (2012). Intervention to address intergenerational trauma: Overcoming, resisting and preventing structural violence. Retrieved from https://www.ucalgary.ca/wethurston/files/wethurston/Report_InterventionToAddressIntergenerationalTrauma.pdf

# CHAPTER 8

# Couple Relationships

*A great marriage is not when the "perfect couple" comes together. It is when an imperfect couple learns to enjoy their differences.*

—D. Meurer (2000)

## CHAPTER OVERVIEW

This chapter will cover some complex issues related to couple dynamics, including victim, rescuer, and persecutor styles of interaction, the importance of particular communication styles and their impact on a relationship, the stages of couple relationships, and the impact of early attachment on relationship and communication styles, including Lee's "love styles" or ideologies (Lee, 1977). It also includes the positive characteristics that hold relationships together and covers the importance of professionals helping couples to shift from negative to more positive forms of communication and interaction.

## THE KARPMAN TRIANGLE

In the 1970s, Dr. Steven Karpman developed what was then known as the "Karpman Triangle" to describe a relationship between two people. The triangle included three different roles that add up to a relationship pattern—the "rescuer," the "victim," and the "persecutor." Karpman (2007) theorized that most relationships begin with someone feeling in need of rescuing—perhaps from loneliness, a bad home situation, a troubled marriage or relationship, a difficult financial situation, emotional problems, and so forth. Enter the rescuer, usually in the form of a "nice person" who offers to help. Both play their roles, with the rescuer assisting the victim who is having difficulty coping. Trouble often sets in when the rescuer gets tired of taking most of the responsibility in the relationship and shifts to a persecutor role, expressed as "You're not pulling your emotional, financial, sexual, or task-related weight in the relationship." Underlying this are the rescuer's feelings of resentment, anger, hurt, and feeling used, which can appear in statements such as "You're so immature!" and "Why am I always having to do everything?" and "Why are you so thoughtless?"

Generally, when this occurs, the victim will move into a rescuer position in an attempt to calm things down. There is a raft of "I'm sorry, I didn't realize," and expressions of appreciation. Often the rescuer then feels guilty about having been a persecutor and may even become depressed themselves. Eventually, however, the couple will make up and return to their original roles. In this way, couple homeostasis is restored.

In most couple relationships, people are most comfortable playing particular roles based on their temperament, upbringing, and social conditioning. Those raised to be pleasers are more likely to be rescuers. Those who were indulged and did not fully grow up as others did things for them will feel most comfortable in the role of victim. As they shift positions, both will at times become resentful and take on the role of persecutor.

Taibbi's (2009) description of those most at risk of becoming rescuers and victims provides some interesting insights into the dynamics between couples. The rescuer is "often an only child, oldest, or grew up in a chaotic family" without "many buffers between [them] and [their] parents." Such people learned early in life that by "being good," they could avoid getting into trouble. Taibbi describes such a person as "very sensitive to others as a means of survival" and as someone who has "good radar and can pick up the nuances of emotions. [They are] hyper-alert, spend all [their] energy surveying the environment, and stay on [their] toes, ever ready to do what the parents want" (p. 26).

According to Taibbi (2009, p. 27), the victim is often the youngest child in a family, who was "overprotected as a child by parents or had older siblings who stepped in and took over all the time when [they were] stuck with a problem. What [they] missed in growing up were opportunities to develop the self confidence that comes from learning to manage problems on [their] own." In light of this theory, one can see how victims in general are going to try to marry rescuers, and vice versa, because this is what they have always known.

Taibbi (2009, p. 27) describes the persecutor as the "evil twin of the rescuer ... [who is] angry, critical, and blaming." The persecutor is someone who thinks "When I get scared, I get tough." It is a defence against losing control and ending up vulnerable.

The goal in working with the victim/rescuer/persecutor triangle is to help each person to become an adult—someone who is "responsible for what they think, do, say" (Taibbi, 2009, p. 27) and who recognizes that they are capable of both problem solving and of asking for help when necessary. An adult does not feel inordinately responsible for others but will help if they can, and does not expect others to be inordinately responsible for them. The goal in working with couples is to help both partners become adults in the relationship.

## CLOSENESS AND DISTANCING IN COUPLES

Gottman (2001) sees the problem of closeness and distancing in couples as often being embedded in how couples communicate and in the kinds of messages they send to each other. He sees several types of communication as being either problematic or helpful in couple relationships. Couples who "turn toward" each other "react in a positive way to another's bids for emotional connection" (p. 16). Couples who "turn against" each other appear more "belligerent and argumentative" and reject each other's communication bids. Couples who "turn away" from each other tend to ignore each other's communication bids by "acting preoccupied" (p. 17). He refers to the last two as "unrequited turning" and suggests that all three types of communication are learned in one's family of origin (p. 18).

Gottman (2001) also sees couple communication as a complex interaction of beliefs that lead to feelings that lead to behaviour. A great deal, in his view, has to do with a family's "philosophy of emotion" (p. 145). He sees this as generally falling under four categories: "coaching, dismissing, laissez-faire, and disapproving" (p. 145). Coaches tend to "accept the expression of all feelings ... [and] in emotional situations ... often help one another solve problems and cope with difficult feelings" (p. 145). Those who are dismissers, however, "tend to keep their feelings hidden, especially negative feelings" (p. 145). They tend not to understand or provide much guidance to each other or to family members in how to handle feelings. Those who subscribe to a laissez-faire philosophy see emotional expression as fine but are not helpful in dealing with feelings. They are more likely to do nothing and let them pass. Finally, disapprovers also believe feelings should remain hidden, but can become hostile toward others who display feelings, especially negative ones (p. 146). Gottman believes that understanding one's emotional style and breaking through communication barriers, especially in understanding how we use verbal and non-verbal cues such as tone of voice, facial expression, gestures, and so on, can assist greatly in improving couple relationships. He sees communicating "heart to heart" and developing "shared rituals of emotional connection" (p. 221) that incorporate meaning into the relationship as vital to maintaining strong couple ties. These daily rituals can be related to mealtimes, bedtime, and formal and informal activities.

In the previous chapter, the impact of early attachment issues was discussed. Nowhere are these issues more prominent than in couple relationships. How someone bonded with their early caregivers has significant implications for how they are likely to bond with an intimate partner.

## ATTACHMENT AND THE STAGES OF COUPLE RELATIONSHIPS

Mikulinger and Shaver (2007, pp. 285–286) have identified three stages in couple relationships: the flirtation and dating, consolidation, and maintenance stages. In the initial stage, the authors point out that both "hopes of care and support" and "fears of disapproval and rejection" can be activated. Both are heavily tied to early attachment in one's family of origin in that "more attachment anxious people anticipate feeling anxious with their new dating partner, and more avoidant people anticipate being more avoidant," while "secure individuals typically manage tension and uncertainty constructively, transforming potential threats into challenges." So, depending upon early attachment style, individuals are likely to be anxious, avoid confrontation and commitment, or relaxed and easygoing in getting to know someone. In the first two cases, interactions are likely to be fraught with neediness, distancing, and fearful game playing, while in the latter, interactions are more likely to be light and lively, possibly with a humorous component.

Because of the impact of early attachment in this early stage, individuals whose self-worth is not high, or who are inhibited and secretive, are likely to have more difficulty forming and maintaining healthy relationships with others. Their "self-presentation" and "self-disclosure" skills are likely to be lacking. Schlenker (1980) describes self-presentation as the manner in which someone projects who they are to someone else—what and how much do they wish to reveal? What kind of impression are they likely to create: one of being helpless or needy, or one of being capable and in charge? Individuals with a more avoidant attachment style may attempt to present themselves as not really needing someone else when in fact they do, in spite of also needing considerable independence and autonomy.

When it comes to self-disclosure, disclosing too much too soon can be taken as a sign of neediness and a desperate desire to be liked and understood, whereas failure to disclose can lead to a lack of trust in a relationship or to an assumption that one is not really interested. A person who has had stable early attachment is more likely to be balanced in their self-presentation and self-disclosure, focusing on the other person as much as on themselves, and disclosing more as a relationship progresses and trust is established. Anxious individuals are more likely to be focused on themselves and how they are doing in the interaction rather than responding appropriately to a partner (Grabill & Kerns, 2000).

To summarize, at this stage, anxious people are likely to disclose too much too soon in a desperate attempt to establish a relationship where they can feel secure and avoid rejection, rather than establishing a reciprocal relationship with another person (Mikulinger & Shaver, 2007, p. 287). Avoidant people are more likely to withhold information, not wanting too much connection that might impede their strong desire for independence. However, they may also want sex, so their goal may be to avoid commitment while attempting a one-night stand or a sexual relationship without commitment. They are also interested in ensuring that their creature comforts are met, so they may seek relationships with rescuers who take care of them without demanding much emotionally.

Securely attached individuals will want to explore the possibility of commitment that involves both intimacy and mutual joy. Their disclosures are more likely to be tied to a potential partner's receptivity (Keelan, Dion, & Dion, 1998), and they are also more likely to return a potential partner's bids for communication and intimacy.

But does attachment also have some impact on whom we are likely to select as possible partners? The answer is yes. Regardless of one's own attachment style, people want to find partners who seem secure and positive in their presentation. Avoidant people were the least likely to be attractive to others upon an initial meeting, and anxious people were also considered less attractive (Mikulinger & Shaver, 2007).

It is easy to see how those with insecure attachment issues are more likely to end up with others who are either anxious or avoidant in their attachment styles, because both styles are more familiar to them. An avoidant partner may choose an anxious partner who is eager to please and who may project an image of strength onto them, which is appreciated. This is a very likely relationship combination. Or two anxious partners may feel more secure in sharing their personal anxieties, as might two avoidant partners who are both comfortable with distancing in order to meet their need for independence.

Insecurely attached people in relationship with other insecurely attached people do tend to fare less well in relationships in general than those in which at least one partner is more securely attached (Buss, 1998).

The trouble may really begin during the consolidation stage of a relationship, where couples are more likely to spend considerable time together developing goals for the future. Mikulinger and Shaver (2007, p. 290) point out that this is the stage where "mutual support, nurturance, and intimacy as determinants of relationship quality increases as early infatuation and sexual passion recede in relative importance." One can see how this may be a problematic time for two anxious or avoidant individuals or for an anxious and avoidant couple.

Securely attached people have several advantages when it comes to this stage. Not only are they likely to trust that their partners will be supportive and caring over the long term, but they are also less likely to attribute other negative characteristics to their partners. In other words, they are more likely to give their partners the benefit of the doubt, whereas anxious or avoidant partners are not. Not doing so can set the stage for considerable conflict in a relationship. Believing that someone is deliberately annoying or deliberately sabotaging when they behave in ways that a partner does not like can seriously undermine both trust and optimism in a relationship and lead to considerable conflict characterized by bitter accusations, defensiveness, and recrimination.

Because avoidant people tend to have little trust in the likelihood of a relationship surviving, they can turn this into a self-fulfilling prophecy. Anxious people, who see themselves as largely unlovable, may have similar fears for the longevity of their relationships.

## LEE'S LOVE IDEOLOGIES

Lee (1977) identified a variety of "love ideologies," or styles, that can be easily attributed to problems in early attachment because they are based on core belief systems. The styles he identified are eros (passionate, erotic), ludus (game playing, uncommitted), storge (friendship), pragma (practical, calculating), agape (altruistic, giving), and mania (obsessional) (see also Sternberg & Weis, 2008, p. 150). Eros is characterized by "strong physical attraction, emotional intensity, a preferred physical appearance, and a sense of inevitability" (Sternberg & Weiss, 2008, p. 153). Ludus is distinguished by deception and game playing with a series of partners over time and a lack of self-disclosure. Today, someone with a ludus love style may be referred to as a "player." Storge is a style that is generally charac-terized by quiet companionship. Pragma tends to typify someone who is shopping for desirable characteristics in a mate, for example, on dating websites. The agape style often features extreme sacrifice—putting another's needs before one's own. This is the style most likely to transform over time. A person with a mania love style alternates between feelings of ecstasy or devastation. This style is extremely intense and the relationship may not end well.

It is easy to see from these descriptions how early attachment may play a role in one's choice of love styles. Those who are anxiously attached are more likely to exhibit eros, agape, and mania, characterized by eroticism, giving at cost to oneself, and intense absorption in another, whereas those who are avoidant often model ludus, typified by game playing and avoidance of commitment. Securely attached people are most likely to look for specific characteristics in a partner and settle into a long-term, companionable relationship over time.

All of these styles are based on behaviour and core beliefs acquired in families of origin and are also somewhat related to temperament. As discussed earlier, the ability to balance closeness and distance is a core issue in a relationship. So too the notion of fairness and the ability to solve problems based upon this notion are strong indicators of whether or not a relationship will survive, as are the presence of strong emotional regulation and communication skills. Long-term relation-ships require true intimacy and commitment—something that will be difficult for insecurely attached people to achieve. Those who are anxiously attached are likely to demand too much intimacy and commitment in an effort to shore up their poor self-esteem, while avoidant people are likely to see even normal demands for in-timacy and commitment as too taxing. These tendencies will impede the sense of safety and security necessary for a relationship to survive over the long term.

Mikulinger and Shaver (2007, p. 297) have correctly concluded that "the chal-lenging and demanding task of maintaining a satisfying and stable relationship beyond the initial stages of ardent passion and deep self-disclosure depends largely on partners' interpersonal skills, the quality of their daily interactions, and their ability to manage disagreements and conflicts." Each attachment style will have an impact on these relationship skills and abilities. Fitzpatrick, Fey, Segrin, and Schiff (1993) point out that those who are securely attached tend to not get involved in as many demand-withdrawal interactions. Those with avoidant attachment issues are more likely to not share their feelings with their partners, thereby undermining the chance of intimacy. Simpson and Rholes (1998) found that anxious individ-uals usually had high levels of "empathic accuracy" but also noted that this could have negative implications for a relationship—by reading others too well, they could cause them to feel too closely scrutinized. Guerrero (1996) concluded that conversations between partners where one or both had anxious attachment issues tended to be more intense because of the high degree of distress expressed during these interactions. Because anxious people are more likely to "hang in" when a partner is disinterested or even emotionally or physically abusive, the likelihood of their remaining in dysfunctional relationships is high. Others found that avoidant people made less physical contact with partners, showed less humour, made less eye contact, and laughed or smiled less than securely attached people (Tucker & Anders, 1998).

Gaines and Henderson (2002) have identified what they term "neglect responses" (shutting a partner out and/or refusing to discuss issues that arise between them) and active attempts to hurt a partner or threaten to walk out as being particularly "relationship-destructive" ways of interacting. Securely attached people seem more willing and able to discuss relationship issues, even those involving deception, whereas anxiously attached people tended to be much more indirect, avoiding important discussions but reacting intensely in other ways. Avoidant partners tend to distance themselves from a cheating spouse while not discussing the impact the deception had on them (Mikulinger & Shaver, 2007, p. 299).

It is obvious that individuals with anxious or avoidant attachment face many more challenges in attempting to maintain relationships than do securely attached people. However, this does not mean that they are unable to learn the skills needed to maintain relationships. Professionals working with couples where one or both partners have attachment issues can assist by pointing out destructive interactions and helping to shift them to more positive ones.

## FEATURES OF RESILIENT RELATIONSHIPS

Two relationship skills that are likely to lead to longevity are the ability to solve problems constructively and the ability to forgive and recognize that a partner's inadequacies in a situation are likely to be short-lived. Optimism, the belief that things will get better, is also helpful in maintaining long-term relationships. Those who are insecurely attached tend to demonstrate these qualities far less so than those who are securely attached.

Gottman (1994) has identified the qualities that can destroy long-term relationships. He has also identified their antidotes. Qualities that can destroy relationships are criticism, contempt, defensiveness, and stonewalling. The antidotes to each are "gentle start-ups," using *I* statements of positive need, building a culture of appreciation where positive qualities are acknowledged, taking responsibility and offering an apology for wrongdoing, and taking time out to do things that are soothing and distracting (The Gottman Institute, 2013). Markman, Stanley and Blumberg (1994) claim that commitment, intimacy, and forgiveness are the glue that hold a relationship together. The goal is to make a partner feel loved and appreciated, which in turn will often cause the other partner to reciprocate.

In any relationship, maintaining an appropriate level of togetherness as well as separateness to ease tension in the relationship is important, as are the qualities of forgiveness and the expression of positive regard. Helping couples to focus more on the positives of their relationship, assisting them to communicate with each other in non-accusatory ways when problems do arise, and aiding them in identifying any tendencies to be overly distant or dependent can help partners overcome many difficulties that they may encounter.

## CHAPTER SUMMARY

This chapter has looked at several important issues facing couples: triangulation, victim/rescuer/persecutor dynamics, the importance of returning communication bids and maintaining positive communication strategies, the impact of secure, anxious, and avoidant attachment styles, as well as Lee's "love ideologies." It has also outlined the positive characteristics likely to support long-term relationships and how professionals can assist couples by helping them to identify communications that are destructive versus ones that are more likely to support the relationship. Having an objective third party provide supportive feedback can be a valuable resource for couples. Professionals can do this by maintaining their alliances with both partners and demonstrating positive ways to communicate.

## FURTHER READING

Fruzzetti, A., & Linehan, M. (2006). *The high conflict couple: A dialectical behavior therapy guide to finding peace, intimacy and validation*. Oakland, CA: New Harbinger.

Gottman, J. S., & Gottman, J. (2015). *Ten principles for doing effective couples therapy*. New York, NY: W.W. Norton.

## CLASSROOM RESOURCE

*Scenes from a marriage*. (1973). Cinema 5. https://www.imdb.com/title/tt0070644/

## CLASSROOM ACTIVITY

### Three-Part In-Class Assignment and Sharing of Highlights

(From the Gottman Institute. [2019]. https://www.gottman.com/blog/
weekend-homework-assignment-turning-towards/)

Ask students to write down each of these questions and respond to them with respect to their relationships with a significant other:

1. During this week **I felt**: defensive / hurt / unappreciated / unattractive / sad / lonely / criticized / worried / misunderstood / like leaving.
2. **What triggered these feelings was**: feeling excluded / that my partner was not attracted to me / that I was not important to my partner / that I felt no affection toward my partner / that I felt rejected.
3. **These feelings about my relationship came from**: how I was treated in my own family / a previous relationship / past trauma / my own basic fears and insecurities / things and events that I have not yet resolved or put aside / unrealized hopes that I have / the way that others have treated me in the past.

Ask students what they have discovered, if anything, through this exercise.

## QUESTIONS FOR REFLECTION

1. How would you describe your own attachment style as demonstrated by your relationship interactions?
2. Which of Lee's "love ideologies" apply to you?
3. Given the communication skills that tend to support relationship building, what changes could you make in your own communication style?
4. Have your parents' ways of communicating with each other influenced how you communicate with your partner?

## REFERENCES

Buss, D. M. (1998). Sexual strategies theory: Historical origins and current status. *Journal of Sex Research*, *35*, 19–31.

Fitzpatrick, M. A., Fey, J., Segrin, C., & Schiff, J. L. (1993). Internal working models of relationships and marital communication. *Journal of Language and Social Psychology*, *12*, 103–131.

Gaines, S. O., Jr., & Henderson, M. C. (2002). Impact of attachment style on responses to accommodative dilemmas among same-sex couples. *Personal Relationships*, *9*, 89–93.

Gottman Institute. (2013). The four horsemen. The antidotes. Retrieved from https://www.gottman.com/blog/the-four-horsemen-the-antidotes/

Gottman, J. M. (1994). *What predicts divorce? The relationship between marital processes and marital outcomes*. Hillsdale, NJ: Erlbaum.

Gottman, J. M. (2001). *The relationship cure*. New York, NY: Three Rivers Press.

Grabill, C. M., & Kerns, K. A. (2000). Attachment style and intimacy in friendship. *Personal Relationships*, *7*, 363–378.

Guerrero, L. K. (1996). Attachment style differences in intimacy and involvement: A test of the four category model. *Communication Monographs*, *63*, 269–292.

Karpman, S. B. (2007). The new drama triangles. Retrieved from www.karpmandramatriangle.com/pdf/thenewdramatriangles.pdf

Keelan, J. R., Dion, K. K., & Dion, K. L. (1998). Attachment style and relationship satisfaction: Test of a self-disclosure explanation. *Canadian Journal of Behavioral Science*, *30*, 24–35.

Lee, J. A. (1977). A typology of styles of loving. *Personality and Social Psychology Bulletin*, *3*, 173–182.

Markman, H. J., Stanley, S., & Blumberg, S. L. (1994). *Fighting for your marriage: Positive steps for preventing divorce and preserving a lasting love*. San Francisco, CA: Jossey-Bass.

Meurer, D. (2000). *Days of our wives: A semi-helpful guide to marital bliss*. Ada, MI: Bethany House.

Mikulinger, M., & Shaver, P. R. (2007). *Attachment in adulthood: Structure, dynamics and change*. New York, NY: The Guilford Press.

Schlenker, B. R. (1980). *Impression management: The self-concept, social identity, and interpersonal relations*. Monterey, CA: Brooks/Cole.

Simpson, J. A., & Rholes, W. S. (Eds.). (1998). *Attachment theory and close relationships*. New York, NY: The Guildford Press.

Sternberg, R. J., & Weis, K. (2008). *The new psychology of love*. New Haven, CT: Yale University Press.

Taibbi, R. (2009). *Doing couple therapy*. New York, NY: The Guilford Press.

Tucker, J. S., & Anders, S. L. (1998). Adult attachment style and nonverbal closeness in dating couples. *Journal of Nonverbal Behavior*, *22*, 109–124.

## CHAPTER 9

# Families and Disability

*Families are developing health problems, there is marital stress, family breakdown, and the heartache of having to place someone in a long term care institution because of a lack of support to maintain them in the community.*

    —P. Spindel (2013)

## CHAPTER OVERVIEW

In this chapter, several issues and concepts concerning families and disability will be explored. These include the impact on both children and their families where there is a mental, physical, learning, behavioural, neurological, intellectual, and/or developmental disability. These conditions may range from mild to severe. The chapter outlines the stages that families pass through when they have a child or children with a disability, and discusses the challenges and opportunities these families face at every stage. The impact of factors external to the family—stigma, lack of financial and moral support, isolation, and discrimination—will also be examined.

## EARLY STAGES OF ADJUSTMENT

When parents first learn that their child has a disability, they experience shock. This shock is felt because the child and the life they had imagined is forever altered. Some parents adjust quickly and become their child's advocate and strongest supporter, while other parents may adjust more slowly and experience a prolonged grief. In 2000, the Roehr Institute completed a study entitled "Beyond the Limits: Mothers Caring for Children with Disabilities" (2000a). The mothers in this study were reported to have more health problems and as having to resort to counselling, friends, and medications to get by. But these mothers also claimed that it was not their disabled child who was the source of their stress; rather, it was the lack of support that they received. This lack of support can sometimes lead to the heart-breaking decision to place their son or daughter in residential care.

According to Hanvey (2002, p. 8), however, these mothers also reported feeling that they "had grown ... become stronger ... learned skills and tended to look at life in new ways ... [that they had] become better people, increased their awareness of a wide range of issues ... [and now] look at the world and other people differently ... have greater insights, learned acceptance, became more sensitive to others' differences, learned new talents and gained a sense of fulfillment." But all of this does not mean that their lives have been, or are, easy. They have had to make adjustments that other families do not have to make, and they face frustrations and setbacks that are hurtful and, in some cases, threaten the well-being of their children and families. Sometimes the stress of having to cope with little to no support leads to family breakdown, substance abuse, and mental health issues.

Each disabled child is unique, as is each family. What is true for one family may not be true for another. Some families struggle with grief and loss, others with guilt, and still others believe strongly that their disabled child is a gift in their lives. Professionals working with families need to be especially sensitive to both the child's and the family's feelings and needs, and be supportive of their goals and dreams for themselves and their child or children.

Most families have no idea of what resources may be available to them to help them care for a child with a disability. Little to no information is provided to new parents at a time when they need it most. For many, especially parents with adult children with disabilities, their first contact was with doctors many years ago, some of whom recommended that they place their child in institutions and carry on with their lives. In some cases, this is still occurring. Some parents did place their children in care and consequently left themselves and future children—the siblings of these "lost children"—with a terrible legacy, that of always wondering what happened to the "other child." Clearly this "advice" that many received did not serve them or their children well. This illustrates the importance of professionals listening carefully to what a family wants and helping them to find the resources to make their goals achievable.

# EXTERNAL CHALLENGES

Families that choose to raise their disabled child at home often face a myriad of problems—a service system that is often unhelpful, a school system that they have to fight to ensure the inclusion of and appropriate education for their children, a lack of support in the home, stereotyping and discrimination, a lack of inclusion in community life and activities, and pitying looks from others with no understanding at all of disability. In most cases, the needs of parents looking after children with disabilities at home are completely overlooked (Hanvey, 2002). In fact, many parents may face open hostility from government officials and service providers whose role it is to support them (Spindel, 2013).

Parents of children with disabilities want the same things for their children as any other parent—that they be secure and happy, and have friends and a full life. But for parents of children with disabilities, providing these can involve a much higher degree of responsibility and stress. In addition to ordinary parenting responsibilities, parents of children with disabilities often have extraordinary caregiving tasks as well as seeking to improve their children's lives by helping them to build friendships and be included in school and community activities: "Parents take on responsibility not only for the care related to their child's disability but also for creating friendships and building acceptance in the community. The responsibilities that other parents are able to share with the community, neighbours and society are often borne exclusively by parents who have a child with a disability. This is overwhelming for many" (Canadian Association for Community Living, 2001).

Hanvey (2002, p. 7) points out that "many children with disabilities and their parents are not fully included in all aspects of society and do not enjoy full citizenship. What does it mean to be fully included in society? It means children and families are able to participate with choice. It means that individual children are involved in activities and social structures in a way that is meaningful to their own unique experience. It means that they truly belong, have community, and are equal participants in that community." Inclusion has not become a reality for many families, who must adapt to inflexible service systems rather than having service systems fit their needs, and who must struggle to have their children included in community life and activities (Freiler, 2002).

Not only are these children and families often not included in society, they may also be poor. This can occur for a variety of reasons, but the main one is often that one parent must stay at home to care for the child while the other works—something that other families do not have to contend with. Poverty can also itself lead to disability in that living in unsafe circumstances can increase the risk of illness. According to the Roehr Institute (cited in Hanvey, 2002, pp. 8–9), "29% of children with disabilities live in households where the total income is in the lower-middle and lowest income quintiles, compared with 17% of children without disabilities." Not only that, but families of children with disabilities also have higher expenses for a variety of goods and services related to their children's special needs.

## IMPACT ON COUPLE RELATIONSHIPS

Poverty is also more likely because parents who have a child with a disability are more likely to split, leaving one partner, a single parent, attempting to cope on their own. When one or both parents have to act as caregivers, advocates, case managers, and nurses, the stress can become unbearable. It is difficult for couple relationships to function well under these circumstances. Hanvey (2002, pp. 12, 13) has summarized this situation:

> Parents, particularly mothers, spend an incredible amount of time caring for and supporting their children. On average, they spend 50 to 60 hours per week on personal care, advocacy, coordination of services and transportation directly related to their child's disability. This includes an average of 14 hours per week in advocacy and coordination related to their child's education. All of this is in addition to time they put into general domestic responsibilities and paid work. In order to do so, they have taken on a number of roles that greatly increase their responsibilities and impact on their physical, emotional and social status. In some cases these external roles actually impede or undermine effective parenting.

For example, June has a daughter with severe disabilities whom she originally cared for as a foster mother. Her husband, Tom, agreed to the arrangement, but often behaves in a passive-aggressive manner: he acts as if he is incompetent when it comes to caring for their child. June has taken on all the responsibility of caring for her daughter, but as she is now in her sixties, she is feeling the strain. June and Tom's relationship has become completely distanced over the years, to the point where June's husband is almost irrelevant to her. Her focus is almost entirely on her daughter.

June and Tom are a perfect example of a couple that is emotionally divorced but still living together. Their son has developed serious mental health problems and is suicidal at times. Where attention is not paid to the couple relationship and instead is given only to a child with a disability, it can cause separation, divorce, and severe distancing. In this instance, it is possibly contributing to the mental health problems of the other sibling.

As difficult as it may be, parents of children with disabilities need to find ways to support one another and remain close to better support themselves and their families. Failure to do this can spell serious problems for the family as a whole.

## STIGMA

An additional source of stress for these families is the stigma that society attaches to disability. The Mental Health Commission of Canada (2013) has defined stigma as "negative, unfavourable attitudes and the behaviour they produce. It is a form of prejudice that spreads fear and misinformation, labels individuals and perpetuates stereotypes." In addition to all their daily struggles, parents of children with disabilities also have to face the negative judgment of others. In August 2013, a grandmother in the Region of Durham whose autistic grandson sometimes played outside in the yard received a letter, allegedly from a neighbour, saying that the teen was "a hindrance to everyone." The writer went on to say, "Do the right thing and move or euthanize him!!! Either way, we are ALL better off!!!" The letter closed with "Sincerely, one pissed off mother!" (Daubs, 2013). This letter was not considered a hate crime because it was not widely distributed. It does, however, demonstrate the often hateful ways in which people with disabilities are still treated in society, and it adds enormously to the stress and isolation that families with a disabled family member feel.

It is still a common societal belief that children with disabilities do not belong in schools with other children, should not be able to take part in community recreational activities, and should not be a "burden" on society. Some even favour the return of large institutions where people with disabilities could be shut away, out of sight and out of mind of the general public. A great deal of work still needs to be done to change social attitudes and thereby shift government policy concerning the provision of services and supports to these families. To date this has not occurred, and they continue to struggle with all the challenges facing them.

Parents of children with mental, behavioural, emotional, and psychological disabilities often face the highest level of stigma and may also be blamed for their children's problems. While this may well be true where children are acting out because of serious difficulties in a couple's relationship or because of poor parenting styles, the cause of children's challenges may also be genetic, the result of an allergic condition, neurological, the result of injury, physical illness, and so forth.

## BEHAVIOURAL CHALLENGES

Where a child acts out violently, tension in the home is greatly increased, as parents may fear for their own or other children's safety. The absence of adequate clinical and educational supports for many children experiencing these difficulties greatly exacerbates parents' stress levels and places them at the same risk for family breakdown as parents of children with physical and developmental disabilities. Where there is a dual diagnosis—a child with mental health and developmental disabilities and/or autism—stress levels can skyrocket. The Center for Education and Human Services (2010) found that "parents of children with emotional disturbances were 81% more likely to get divorced, compared to [a] reference group ... and mothers of children identified with more than one disability were 81% more likely to become [or continue to be] unemployed than mothers of children identified with one disability."

## STRESSORS AT EACH DEVELOPMENTAL STAGE

Stressors can be different at each stage of a child's development. As infants, many children with disabilities may have accompanying health issues that can disrupt sleep. They may also have repeated doctor visits and/or hospitalizations. Exhausted, sleep-deprived parents must then confront the medical establishment, which can, at times, be unsympathetic to their plight. If they do not have family or friends who can periodically take over, the likelihood of exhaustion is even greater. Consequently, infancy can be a particularly challenging time for parents and siblings alike.

As children become toddlers, the search for specialized daycare often occurs. With subsidized daycare being largely unavailable, parents are financially stretched to pay for care for their children with special needs—if they can even find a service that is able to take their children. They may have to teach daycare workers how to respond to their children, and regularly monitor conditions to ensure that their child is receiving adequate care and attention. Where health problems exist, they may be regularly called away from work to take the child to doctors or to the hospital. This can place the parents' jobs at risk if they do not have sympathetic employers.

As children reach school age, parents may find themselves in conflict with an education system that is not geared to meet children's individual needs. Programs, support, and in-class assistance may be lacking. Teachers and teacher's aides may not be adequately trained to support their children in the classroom, or their children may face segregated classrooms or activities. Often parents must become strong advocates to ensure that their children are not left behind. Children with disabilities are also more likely to be subject to bullying. This can have an extremely detrimental effect on any child's life, but especially on the mental health of children who are already struggling with psychological, emotional, behavioural, learning, developmental, and/or physical disabilities. Parents may find school systems unresponsive or ineffective in dealing with this kind of bullying and therefore attempt to address the problem on their own.

As children become teenagers and face the many challenges that confront all teens, their school problems may increase. Now that the children are physically larger, parents may be less able to handle them if they become aggressive. If they have behavioural challenges, educators and fellow classmates may also see them as more threatening. This can lead to suspensions or suggestions that home schooling would be a better option. In some cases, it can lead to criminal charges.

Once children with disabilities become adults, they are often not able to leave home and live on their own, have relationships with others, and work at a paying job. Many people with disabilities cannot find work or housing, and are infantilized when it comes to having relationships, especially sexual ones. This may mean that a parent's job is never over. They may have their children living with them all of their lives and may also face the stress of trying to find accommodation for them when they are older. Extremely long waiting lists for residential accommodation may force people with disabilities to be institutionalized in long-term care facilities—a heartbreaking decision for aging parents.

## IMPACT ON SIBLINGS

What impact does having a brother or sister with a disability have on siblings? A new study has found that parents of children with disabilities, already stretched to the limit in meeting all the demands associated with caring for one child, may not be physically, emotionally, or mentally able to bond securely with their other children. This puts siblings at risk of anxiety and depressive disorders (Rivas, 2013). Gray (2013) refers to a 2013 study by Goudie, Havercamp, Jamieson, and Sahr, who found that "siblings of children with a disability experienced more problems with interpersonal relationships, psychological issues, functioning at school, and getting involved with sports and hobbies than did kids without such siblings."

There can be reasons other than insecure parent-child bonding for these disorders in siblings. Having parents who are feeling depressed or stressed has an impact on all children in the household. Beresford, Rabiee, and Sloper (2007, p. 2) have pointed out the following:

> Lifting, sleep problems, and the chronic care and supervision needs of the children were some of the factors that threatened parents' physical and emotional well-being. Accepting and adjusting to the child's diagnosis was an on-going emotional task, with changes in the child's condition and times of transition bringing such issues back to the surface. Watching the child suffer from ill-health or pain was emotionally distressing. Accessing and dealing with services was identified by many parents as stressful and distressing. Having to use a service that was inadequate or inappropriate was a source of anxiety and even despair.

One can only imagine how all of these parental stressors impact on siblings. In some instances, older children may feel the need to take over and bear some of the parental responsibilities. These "hero" children may in turn suffer anxiety and depression themselves.

## HOW CAN PROFESSIONALS HELP?

What can professionals do to help these families? First, they can listen carefully, not just to what a family is saying, but to what they are feeling. What are the dreams of each family member, and how can a professional help them to achieve them? For example, would the parents like a break to spend time with their other children? Can respite services be arranged? Does the family want their disabled family member to be more accepted and included in the community? Can the professional talk to leisure and recreational coordinators about including more people with disabilities in their programs? Is the family short of money? Would problem solving with the family about how their financial situation may be addressed be helpful? Do the parents need support and encouragement from others? Are there friends and family members who may be willing to assist? Are there local students needing volunteer hours who could help out by doing an occasional overnight with a sleepless child to give parents a break? Can the local high school be approached to see if a youth-to-youth program could be launched to twin disabled and non-disabled teens so that they can become more involved in social activities and make friends at school? If a family is continuing to process a sense of grief and loss, can a professional help them with this by listening, encouraging them through each stage of loss—overcoming denial, anger, bargaining for a different outcome, depression—and helping them to reframe their experiences in a more positive and meaningful way?

Listening to and validating family members while helping them to examine other ways of thinking and other possibilities can be very helpful. Where families are too afraid, too tired, or too overwhelmed to ask for help, providing support and encouragement can make a huge difference. What may be most important is pointing out to families all the things that they are doing right and what qualities they have that are helpful and admirable. Also important is helping everyone to function as a team, and ensuring that there are happy, playful times, as well as helping them to support each other when times are tough.

Sometimes providing additional information on new approaches and research can also be helpful. Providing advocacy assistance when families run into difficulties with the service system, or helping them to write letters to political representatives, local ombudsmen, and government officials may be what is needed.

Perhaps the key thing a professional can do is to listen carefully and validate family members' experiences. Help the family to identify their strengths and build on their resilience, encourage them to have fun together—playing games, doing a craft, watching a movie—to bring enjoyment into their lives, and point out ways that they are already doing this. All of these things can be helpful. Being on the family's side is one of the fundamental ways professionals can help to overcome the isolation families with disabled family members often feel, as is helping them to connect to others who will also be supportive.

One mother had this to say:

I have always felt alone in attempting to advocate for my daughter who has significant disabilities. I had to fight for integrated daycare, had to fight the school system so that she would be included in a regular classroom, had to fight for recreation and leisure opportunities, and now that she is 19, it is as if she has dropped off the end of the earth. There is nothing for her. She sits at home and watches TV day after day, both of us getting more depressed. Waiting lists for day programs or employment programs are years long. No college wants to take people with developmental disabilities and the ones that do have very few spaces and they are already filled. Everywhere I go, the answer is no. Elected officials don't even answer the letters I write to them. Is it any wonder I feel like I'm going insane?

And a father had this to say:

> I work at two jobs just to pay for the extra support my son needs. This means that I work 16 hours a day. I am not there to provide emotional support to my wife and son, and it is hurting our family. The only time we have is on the weekend, and by then I am so exhausted that I have to push myself to spend quality time with them. This whole situation is heartbreaking. I sometimes wonder if I will make it to 40 before I have a heart attack. And then what will they do?

In both of these situations, the mother and father feel unsupported by friends, family, and community. Assisting them to access funding and resources so that their children are better able to be included in their communities, and linking them with family, friends, and other parents who can provide assistance would help them to feel less alone and provide the social support that might be the difference between exhaustion and a more balanced family life.

## CHAPTER SUMMARY

This chapter has covered the often heartbreaking situation of families of children with disabilities. It includes a look at the challenges facing people with disabilities and their families at each stage of a child's development. It has examined in detail the day-to-day frustrations and stresses that families undergo, and has also examined their resourcefulness. Additionally, it has discussed the impact of stigma and stereotyping, as well as what professionals can do to help families to address these challenges.

## FURTHER READING

Eichenstein, R. (2015). *Not what I expected: Help and hope for parents of atypical children.* New York, NY: TarcherPerigee.

Wang, M., & Singer, G. H. S. (2016). *Supporting families of children with developmental disabilities: Evidence-based and emerging practices.* Oxford, UK: Oxford University Press.

## CLASSROOM RESOURCES

*Becky belongs.* (1986). CBC. https://www.youtube.com/watch?v=E_ZTY-GqdfY

*The ties that bind.* (2006). NFB. http://onf-nfb.gc.ca/en/our-collection/?idfilm=54521

## CLASSROOM ACTIVITY

Engage in a full-group discussion after watching one of the films listed under "Classroom Resources." Ask students the following questions: What did you learn? Why does society create barriers for people with disabilities and their families? How can non-disabled people help remove these barriers?

## QUESTIONS FOR REFLECTION

1.  Do you know anyone who has a child with a disability in the family? If so, have you ever thought of how you might be able to help out?
2.  What are your own feelings about people with disabilities? Where do you think your values, views, and feelings about disability came from?
3.  Have you gone to school with those who have disabilities? What was your experience of them?
4.  If you were working with a family with a disabled member, what are some of the ways you might try to help?

## REFERENCES

Beresford, B., Rabiee, P., & Sloper, P. (2007). Outcomes for parents with disabled children. *Research Works*. Social Policy Research Unit, University of York. Retrieved from www.york.ac.uk/inst/spru/pubs/rworks/aug2007-03.pdf

Canadian Association for Community Living. (2001). Don't exclude our children. Toronto, ON: Author.

Center for Education and Human Services. (2010). Effects of child disability on families. Retrieved from http://www.sri.com/sites/default/files/brochures/201104_enewsletter.pdf

Daubs, K. (2013, August 20). Letter attacking boy with autism not a hate crime police say. *Toronto Star*. Retrieved from www.thestar.com/news/gta/2013/08/20/letter_attacking_autistic_boy_not_a_hate_crime_police_say.html

Freiler, C. (2002). *Understanding social inclusion*. Toronto, ON: The Laidlaw Foundation.

Goudie, A., Havercamp, S., Jamieson, B., & Sahr, T. (2013, July 29). Assessing functional impairment in siblings living with children with disability. *Pediatrics*. Retrieved from http://pediatrics.aappublications.org/content/early/2013/07/23/peds.2013-0644.full.pdf+html

Gray, B. B. (2013). Siblings of disabled kids may show emotional effects. *Health Day*. Retrieved from http://consumer.healthday.com/kids-health-information-23/

child-development-news-124/siblings-of-disabled-kids-show-emotional-effects-678727.html

Hanvey, L. (2002). Children with disabilities and their families in Canada: A discussion paper. National Children's Alliance. Retrieved from http://citeseerx.ist.psu.edu/viewdoc/download?doi=10.1.1.457.3999&rep=rep1&type=pdf

Mental Health Commission of Canada. (2013). What is the issue? Retrieved from www.mentalhealthcommission.ca/English/issues/stigma?routetoken=38639626ca252e26858f97fb1a443bb7&terminitial=31

Rivas, A. (2013, July 30). Siblings of disabled children more likely to develop functional problems from household stress. *Medical Daily*. Retrieved from www.medicaldaily.com/siblings-disabled-children-more-likely-develop-functional-problems-household-stress-248186

Roehr Institute. (2000a). *Beyond the limits: Mothers caring for children with disabilities*. North York, ON: Author.

Roehr Institute. (2000b). *Count us in: A demographic overview of childhood and disability in Canada*. North York, ON: Author.

Roehr Institute. (2000c). *Finding a way in: Parents on social assistance caring for children with disabilities*. North York, ON: Author.

Spindel, P. (2013). *Abuse by ministry: Power dynamics, lack of resources, and the troubled relationship between the Ministry of Community & Social Services and families of people with developmental disabilities*. Toronto, ON: Spindel & Associates.

## CHAPTER 10

# Family Violence

*If we are going to stop violence in our society, in our schools and on our streets, we first need to stop the violence in our homes.*

   —Erin Gray, actress

## CHAPTER OVERVIEW

Family violence continues to be prevalent in Canada and the United States. In this chapter, the extent of this problem, its root causes, and the individual and family dynamics that contribute to it are discussed. It will examine how professionals can help individuals and families where violence is occurring, and explore the legal duties of professionals to not only report child abuse but to warn any individuals against whom a direct threat of violence has been made.

## PREVALENCE OF VIOLENCE IN FAMILIES

The Government of Canada (2016) reports that "one quarter of all violent crime resulted from family violence and that almost 67% of family violence victims are women or girls. 79% of police reported intimate partner violence is against women. Women were victims of intimate partner homicide at a rate four times greater than men." Because of the fear and stigma associated with it, family violence is also underreported.

Thirty percent of violence against children and youth is perpetrated by family members, and "girls are 4–5 times more likely than boys to be victims of child sexual abuse by a family member." Girls aged "14–17 were almost twice as likely to be victims of family-related violence" as their male counterparts (Government of Canada, 2016). Statistics Canada reports "in 2017, there were 59,236 child and youth victims (aged 17 years and younger) of police-reported violence in Canada. Females represented over half (56%) of victims in this age group" (Statistics Canada, 2018, p. 4). Statistics Canada further states the following:

> In 2017, nearly six in ten (58%) child and youth victims of police-reported family violence were victimized by a parent. This was most common among victims aged 5 years and younger (73%) and least common among those aged 15 to 17 years (44%). Among child and youth victims of family violence, the majority (53%) of females were victimized by a parent, and this was even more common among their male counterparts (66%). The next most common relationship was another type of family member, such as a grandparent, uncle, aunt, cousin or in-law (25% of females and 18% of males), followed by a sibling (18% of females and 15% of males). (Statistics Canada, 2018, p. 4)

Older adults are also victims of family violence.

> In 2015, more than 9,900 seniors (65 years and older) were victims of police-reported violent crime in Canada. Of these victims, one-third (33%) were victimized by a grown child, spouse, sibling or extended family member (a rate of 60 per 100,000 population) ... Six in ten (60%) senior victims of family violence were female, with a rate 26% higher than that of male seniors (66 versus 52) ... Common (level 1) assault was the most frequently reported form of family violence against seniors in 2015. This type of offence was experienced by more than half (55%) of seniors victimized by a family member, followed by uttering threats (19%), major assault (levels 2 and 3) (15%) and criminal harassment (4%). (Conroy, n.d.)

Between 2010 and 2015, 418 people died at the hands of family members, with 80 percent of the adult victims being women. "More than 50 per cent of victims were vulnerable and either identified as Indigenous, immigrant, refugee or a young person. Those victims could've also hailed from a rural, remote or northern community." Risk factors included "recent separation, history of domestic violence, verbal threats, issues around addiction and depression, stalking behaviour"

(Ghonaim, 2018). Among the victims, "37 children were killed in those domestic homicides, 70 per cent of which were biological children of the victim and/or accused" (Ghonaim, 2018). The report by the Canadian Domestic Homicide Prevention Initiative identified several other features of domestic homicides in Canada, and these included the following: "28 per cent of the adult victims were between the ages of 25 to 34; 443 of the accused were identified, 21 per cent of which committed suicide and seven per cent attempted suicide following the homicide; 38 per cent of the victims died as a result of stabbing, sometimes followed by either a shooting, strangulation or beating; second-degree murder was the most common initial charge laid (50 per cent) followed by first degree murder charges (37 per cent) (Ghonaim, 2018)."

There are also significant geographic disparities in family violence across the country, with Saskatchewan and Manitoba having the highest rates, and Ontario, British Columbia, and Prince Edward Island having the lowest. Family violence against children and youth was highest in the territories (Statistics Canada, 2018).

It is quite clear from these statistics that family violence is an epidemic in Canada, and that many families are not the safe, stable oases they are intended to be. Some would argue that men are just as much at risk of violence as women, and this is true. However, most violence against men is perpetrated by strangers, whereas violence against women tends to be perpetrated by current or former spouses or lovers. And the violence tends to be serious, with about half of all women murdered in Canada being killed by a current or former intimate partner, compared to only 7 percent of men (Statistics Canada, 2011, p. 11).

There are geographic disparities in intimate femicide. "Consistent with the pattern of women and girls killed overall, the largest group of intimate femicides occurred in Ontario (45%) followed by Alberta (16%) and Quebec (10%). Intimate femicide victims in both Ontario and Alberta are overrepresented slightly relative to the proportion of Canadian women living in those jurisdictions (39% and 11% respectively). Intimate femicide victims in Quebec were underrepresented compared to the proportion of women living in that province (23%)" (Canadian Femicide Observatory for Justice and Accountability, 2018, p. 34).

The number of people willing to report incidents of violence to police declined by 6 percent from 2004 to 2009—from 28 to 22 percent. The Canadian Women's Foundation (2013) states that only 22 percent of domestic violence incidents are actually reported. Lack of reporting is a significant problem because it tends to distort the reality of how many people, especially women, are actually assaulted. An Angus Reid poll conducted for the Foundation found that "67% of all Canadians say they personally know at least one woman who has been sexually or physically assaulted." What does this translate to in actual numbers? The Canadian Women's Foundation (2013) says that "in a 2009 Canadian national survey, women reported 460,000 incidents of sexual assault in just one year. Only about 10% of all sexual assaults are reported to police." According to the Foundation, many women do not report because they fear being blamed for the assault or simply not being believed. They may have to deal with insensitive treatment by police, poor collection of evidence, and untried cases that never make it to court. Few cases result in a conviction (Johnson, 2012).

Indigenous women have even higher levels of risk of domestic violence and homicide. With 582 Indigenous women either missing or murdered since 2010, Amnesty International and the United Nations have unsuccessfully asked the Government of Canada to address this issue (Amnesty International, 2011; Canadian Women's Foundation, 2013). The Native Women's Association of Canada has said that "if this figure were applied proportionately to the rest of the female population, there would be over 18,000 missing Canadian women and girls" (Canadian Women's Foundation, 2013). "According to the 2014 General Social Survey (GSS) on Victimization, the rate of self-reported sexual assault of Indigenous people (58 per 1,000) was almost triple that of non-Indigenous people (20 per 1,000). The rate of sexual assault self-reported by Indigenous women (113 per 1,000) was more than triple that of non-Indigenous women (35 per 1,000)" (Government of Canada, Department of Justice, 2017).

## FEMICIDE

The Canadian Women's Foundation (2013) reports that, "on average, every six days a woman in Canada is killed by her intimate partner. In 2011, from the 89 police reported spousal homicides, 76 of the victims (over 85%) were women." In 2018 "a woman or girl was killed every 2.5 days on average in Canada" (Thompson, 2019). Most were killed by people they knew. The risk factors included "72% history of domestic violence; 67% actual or pending separation; 50% perpetrator depressed; 46% obsessive behavior by perpetrator; 45% perpetrator made prior threat/attempts to commit suicide; 44% victim had intuitive sense of fear; 41% perpetrator displayed sexual jealousy" (Ontario [Canada] Domestic Violence Death Review Committee, 2017).

Children and youth were also victims of murder by family. From 2000 to 2009, 326 children or youth were murdered by a family member, with parents committing 84 percent of these homicides, and infants being most at risk. Infants were most likely to be shaken or beaten to death, while weapons were generally used against older children. "Parents and step-parents accounted for the majority (95%) of those accused of family-related murder-suicides of children and youth, with other family members such as aunts and uncles accounting for the remaining 5%" (Statistics Canada, 2013).

## TYPES OF VIOLENCE

However you look at it, family violence remains a major problem. It can take many forms: sexual, physical, emotional, and financial. Sexual violence can involve everything from unwanted fondling, to rape, to attacks on sexual organs, to forcing someone to perform sexual acts that they do not wish to perform. It can also include wrongful accusations of infidelity, undermining the individual's sexuality through continuous criticism, undermining the victim's body image, and treating the person in a derogatory manner sexually (United Nations, 1993).

Physical violence can involve pushing and shoving, hitting, grabbing, pinching, arm twisting, kicking, punching, and the use of weapons. It can also involve withholding resources to maintain health (i.e., medications), sleep deprivation, drugging with alcohol or other substances, cutting off access to food and fluids, medical care, and anything else that is a necessity of life (Government of Alberta, n.d.). The Government of Alberta (n.d., p. 4) has added medication abuse as another form of violence. It includes using medication for purposes other than what it was intended; "manipulating of medications to cause pain or reduce ability; over or under medicating against a doctor's direction … not filling a prescription … stealing a person's medication for financial or convenience reasons or for other reasons or resale."

Emotional or psychological violence includes threats and intimidation of the person, children, loved ones, and pets; blackmail; mind games; and harassment. Spiritual abuse might include using religion to manipulate or control someone, and criminal harassment or stalking may involve following, watching, or invading someone's privacy (Government of Alberta, n.d.). Financial abuse often involves the withholding of money, forcing one partner to rely on the other even when they contribute financially to the family.

## CAUSES OF VIOLENCE

What causes this kind of violence in families? Goldsmith (2006) cites several reasons: one partner needing to control another because of low self-esteem, problems with emotional regulation, strong emotions such as jealousy, feelings of inferiority because a partner may be better educated or earn more, and beliefs in some cultures that controlling, dominating, and abusing women is acceptable. Abusers may learn to be violent in their own families or from others in their communities. Boys may have witnessed violence against their mothers while growing up. Girls may become victims as adults for similar reasons. Substance abuse may also play a role in lowering inhibitions against violence.

Researchers at Princeton found that there may be some genetic, biochemical, and brain-related reasons for domestic violence in that some abusive men may have histories of head injury. This can undermine their problem-solving ability and cause impulsivity and/or lack of emotional regulation (Perry, 1997).

Others believe that children learn about domestic violence in their families of origin, where it is rewarded or supported as acceptable. It may also be supported by a society that does nothing about it and appears to want to ignore it (Emery & Laumann-Billings, 1998). This has been confirmed by early research that shows that sons with violent fathers were more likely to be violent (Hotaling & Sugarman, 1986). It has also been found that as adults, children who have witnessed violence and abuse are more likely to become involved in a violent and abusive relationship themselves (Royal College of Psychiatrists, 2019). Not all children repeat this pattern. Some try not to repeat the mistakes of their parents. However children from violent, abusive homes are considered to have more struggles with anxiety, depression, and maintaining good relationships with others (Royal College of Psychiatrists, 2019).

Still other researchers believe that psychopathology is the cause of domestic violence. Dutton (1997) found that "dysfunctional personality structures" are sometimes shaped by early childhood experiences of seeing domestic violence. These personality structures are contributing factors, in that witnessing violence in the family can undermine the development of trust and emotional regulation and lead to symptoms of anxious and avoidant attachment in the form of hostility, dependency, and the inability to form healthy relationships. Maikovich and Jaffee (2008) also found that psychopathology is increased in children where there is domestic violence, specifically harsh physical punishment.

Baker, Jaffe, and Moore (2001) have also outlined the specific effects on children of witnessing domestic violence, which include anxiety and fear, aggression, withdrawal, lack of interest or feelings, regression to previous behaviours typical of younger children, weakened family bonds, premature independence, taking on inappropriate responsibilities, adolescent struggles such as running away, leaving home too young or dropping out of school, and/or abusing substances.

Cahn and Lloyd (1996) suggest that the problem lies in the communication styles of couples—the characteristics, family dynamics, and context in which violence occurs.

For example, Ron has repeatedly beaten and abused his wife, Jill, for many years. Jill's spirit has been broken and she stays in the relationship because she is afraid she cannot make it on her own. Ron has a drinking problem and suffers from depression related to problems in his own upbringing. His father also beat his mother. Jill's mother was abused by her father, who also had a drinking problem. The last beating Jill endured was particularly serious, and she ended up in the hospital. The hospital called the police, and Ron has since been charged with aggravated assault. Jill is frantically afraid now that she is on her own. She has become depressed and has considered suicide. She is not co-operating with the police in ensuring that Ron is found guilty of assaulting her, and she visits him in jail. Attempts by women's rights advocates to help her have failed. She is determined to get Ron back. This has been a particularly frustrating problem for the professionals who work with her because they are concerned, given the severity of the last beating, that Ron will eventually kill her.

The Canadian Panel on Violence Against Women (1993) suggests that one of the main causes of family violence is the underlying problem of a society that condones it. Where there is a power imbalance that supports patriarchy or male domination of women and children by reinforcing male control of finances, politics, and social institutions, there also exists an acceptance and reinforcement of domestic violence. The Panel saw the causes of domestic violence as being rooted in the inequality between men and women.

As this brief review indicates, the causes of family violence are many and complex.

## WHAT CAN BE DONE?

So what can be done about family violence? Some of the answers may lie in primary, secondary, and tertiary prevention strategies, according to Wolfe and Jaffe (1999). Primary prevention seeks to change the attitudes in society that can lead to family violence by challenging the values, communication skills, and distorted thinking that accompany it, and replacing these with a focus on building respect for others, empathy, the development of trust, and healthy relationship skills that promote non-violence and personal growth. These efforts can be directed to the population in general. Secondary prevention efforts are usually targeted toward specific individuals and families that have either identified themselves or others as engaging in family violence. Similar strategies would be used to assist them. Tertiary prevention efforts often involve inter-agency co-operation in providing direct services and support to families where violence occurs.

Wolfe (1989) found that intervening early with children from violent families can improve their functioning in the areas of empathy and self-control. Teaching children early how to communicate well, share, and control their feelings can help them to use these skills effectively later in life.

There are also strategies that individual professionals can use to help to defuse family violence. However, it should be mentioned that consideration for the safety of family members and themselves must come first. It is not feasible to have family meetings and counselling sessions when family members are afraid to speak out because of the consequences they may face when they go home.

## THE DUTY TO REPORT

It must also be mentioned that professionals are under a legal obligation to report child abuse, as well as specific threats made by one individual against another.

In Ontario, Section 125 of the Child, Youth, and Family Services Act (2017), which became effective April 30, 2018, requires professionals to promptly report any suspicions that a child is in need of protection to a Children's Aid Society (CAS). Children in need of protection need only to appear to be suffering the effects of abuse and neglect. The Ministry of Children and Youth Services makes it clear that "it is not necessary for you to be certain a child is or may be in need of protection to make a report to a CAS.... 'Reasonable grounds' refers to the information that an average person, using normal and honest judgment, would need in order to decide to report" (Ontario Ministry of Children and Youth, 2010). This duty is on each individual professional and is, therefore, not an agency responsibility. Any professional who believes they have reasonable grounds to report must report, whether or not their agency is in agreement. This report cannot be made by someone else. The legal duty lies with each professional. Suspicion of child abuse and neglect requiring a report overrides any confidentiality requirement and any other provincial statute (law) (Government of Ontario, 2011, s. 72[1]). There are legal sanctions in Ontario against any professional who fails to make a report in the course of their professional duties.

A fine of up to $5,000 may be applied upon conviction if they obtained information requiring a report as part of their official duties.

The argument that a professional's relationship with a family could be compromised if they report is invalid, given that the needs of a vulnerable child must come first under the law. This duty is "ongoing": even if a report has been made, should a professional continue to suspect child abuse or neglect, they must continue to report to the Children's Aid Society.

The Ontario Child, Youth, and Family Services Act, Section 125(1) specifically sets out this duty as follows:

Despite the provisions of any other Act, if a person, including a person who performs professional or official duties with respect to children, has reasonable grounds to suspect one of the following, the person shall forthwith report the suspicion and the information on which it is based to a society:

1.  The child has suffered physical harm, inflicted by the person having charge of the child or caused by or resulting from that person's,
    i.   failure to adequately care for, provide for, supervise or protect the child, or
    ii.  pattern of neglect in caring for, providing for, supervising or protecting the child.
2.  There is a risk that the child is likely to suffer physical harm inflicted by the person having charge of the child or caused by or resulting from that person's,
    i.   failure to adequately care for, provide for, supervise or protect the child, or
    ii.  pattern of neglect in caring for, providing for, supervising or protecting the child.
3.  The child has been sexually molested or sexually exploited, by the person having charge of the child or by another person where the person having charge of the child knows or should know of the possibility of sexual molestation or sexual exploitation and fails to protect the child.
4.  There is a risk that the child is likely to be sexually molested or sexually exploited as described in paragraph 3.
5.  The child requires medical treatment to cure, prevent or alleviate physical harm or suffering and the child's parent or the person having

charge of the child does not provide, or refuses or is unavailable or unable to consent to, the treatment.

6. The child has suffered emotional harm, demonstrated by serious:
   i. anxiety
   ii. depression
   iii. withdrawal
   iv. self-destructive or aggressive behaviour, or
   v. delayed development,

   and there are reasonable grounds to believe that the emotional harm suffered by the child results from the actions, failure to act or pattern of neglect on the part of the child's parent or the person having charge of the child.

7. The child has suffered emotional harm of the kind described in sub-paragraph i, ii, iii, iv or v of paragraph 6 and the child's parent or the person having charge of the child does not provide, or refuses or is unavailable or unable to consent to, services or treatment to remedy or alleviate the harm.

8. There is a risk that the child is likely to suffer emotional harm of the kind described in subparagraph i, ii, iii, iv or v of paragraph 6 resulting from the actions, failure to act or pattern of neglect on the part of the child's parent or the person having charge of the child.

9. There is a risk that the child is likely to suffer emotional harm of the kind described in subparagraph i, ii, iii, iv or v of paragraph 6 and that the child's parent or the person having charge of the child does not provide, or refuses or is unavailable or unable to consent to, services or treatment to prevent the harm.

10. The child suffers from a mental, emotional or developmental condition that, if not remedied, could seriously impair the child's development and the child's parent or the person having charge of the child does not provide, or refuses or is unavailable or unable to consent to, treatment to remedy or alleviate the condition.

11. The child has been abandoned, the child's parent has died or is unavailable to exercise [their] custodial rights over the child and has not made adequate provision for the child's care and custody, or the child is in a residential placement and the parent refuses or is unable or unwilling to resume the child's care and custody.

12.  The child is less than 12 years old and has killed or seriously injured another person or caused serious damage to another person's property, services or treatment are necessary to prevent a recurrence and the child's parent or the person having charge of the child does not provide, or refuses or is unavailable or unable to consent to, those services or treatment.

13.  The child is less than 12 years old and has on more than one occasion injured another person or caused loss or damage to another person's property, with the encouragement of the person having charge of the child or because of that person's failure or inability to supervise the child adequately.

A precedent-setting court case in the United States dubbed the "Tarasoff Decision" also creates a duty to warn for professionals where a specific threat is made against an individual. It is based on both ethical and legal principles. In the Tarasoff case, a psychologist who worked at the counselling centre at the University of California at Berkeley was told by a graduate student he was counselling that he wished to kill his girlfriend, Taliana Tarasoff. The psychologist took this threat seriously and reported his concerns to campus police, as well as ordering his client committed for a psychiatric evaluation. Unfortunately, even though campus police did interview the student, they released him on the promise that he would stay away from Ms. Tarasoff. Neither the campus police nor the psychologist warned her, and two months later, the student fatally stabbed her on the steps of her parents' home. Her parents sued the psychologist, the campus police, and the board of regents of the university. The claim was dismissed twice in lower courts, but the Supreme Court of California concluded that the psychologist did have a duty to warm Ms. Tarasoff and/or her parents of the threat posed by his client. The Court further found that concerns related to confidentiality are overridden by the need to prevent foreseeable danger to another person. To quote the judge, "The protective privilege ends when the public peril begins" (Sheppard, 2003; Supreme Court of California, 1976).

Since this case, a number of Canadian cases have referred to this decision. Various authors of legal publications have suggested that even though there is not a large amount of Canadian case law regarding this duty, it is nevertheless likely that in a similar circumstance, a Canadian court would probably rely on the general legal principles underlying the California court decision because of the need to protect individuals from "imminent danger" and a professional's legal obligation to warn a person who may be at risk (Picard & Robertson, 2007).

## SAFETY PROTOCOL

The Government of Alberta (n.d.) has created a valuable protocol for professionals working with violent families. It includes the following actions that professionals are urged to take when working with a child and/or an adult who may be at risk of serious harm:

- Ask: When alone with a client, pose a question in a non-judgmental way as part of normal conversation, such as "what happens when you argue?" This might also involve asking a woman about any bruises or lacerations. Children will sometimes give indications that they are being abused, and may disclose this directly to a professional. It is important not to ask leading questions if a child discloses, and to remain calm and reassure the child that they were right to tell you. A disclosure of abuse from a child places a duty on a professional to make a report to the local Children's Aid Society.
- Listen without interruptions, judgment, or overreaction.
- Seek clarification if necessary once the adult has stopped talking, but do not ask for details. "Are you saying that they sometimes hurt you physically when you argue?"
- Take safety precautions: Reassure the person that it is not their fault, and that they deserve to be safe.
- Provide reassurance and let the adult or child know that you will try to help them. Do not make promises that you are not certain that you can deliver.
- Deal with any immediate safety concerns. Try to ensure that your client(s) and you will be safe once you exit the dwelling or office where the conversation took place. If there is an immediate threat, call 911. If you think an adult is in danger, say so, and strongly encourage them to call police. If you think a child is in immediate danger, call 911 and the Children's Aid Society.
- If you are speaking to a woman or an older person who is being abused or neglected, provide whatever information you can. Advise the person that abuse will not stop on its own and that the person will likely need to be stopped. Let the person know that abuse is a crime and that the risk they face may be higher than they are anticipating. In the case of stalking or harassment, the risk may be very high. Explain the effect of domestic

abuse on children in the household, specifically the effect on brain development, even if the abuse does not happen in front of them. Advise the person of what help is available, preferably in writing so that they can call if necessary. You will need to discuss with them how to keep the written information out of the hands of an abuser, possibly by hiding it outdoors or with another person.

- Never recommend joint counselling where there is danger of violence. Instead, encourage separate counselling, even if the couple wants joint counselling. Make sure you have a list of information that can be helpful to someone in a domestic violence situation that includes where to go or whom to call in an emergency. Suggest photographing any injuries. Again, this will need to be done carefully and in a way that the abuser cannot obtain the pictures.
- Help work out a safety plan. This is to reduce the risk of possible further harm.
- A safety plan has eight parts: The person needs to tell someone they trust. Care will need to be taken with specific collectivist cultures since the person the individual tells may feel obligated to discuss matters with the abuser. The person will need to let the other person know what signals mean they are in trouble and what the person should do in response.
- Work out where the person can go in an emergency, and how they can ensure they have access to their car keys, a car, and gas or some other means of transportation in an emergency.
- Help the person to memorize any emergency numbers and/or decide where they can keep these safely to access in an emergency.
- Help the person learn how to erase a number from call display and to advise people to never leave messages.
- Provide information about emergency protection orders.
- Help the person to pack a small emergency bag and leave it in a place where they can access it quickly and where the abusive person is not likely to find it. The bag should include cash, a debit card, health card, driver's licence, car keys, any important documents—passport, immigration papers, financial info, etc.—prescription medication, copies of any no-contact orders, plus clothing and other personal items for a few days.
- Help the person to document the abuse (including times and dates) if they are being stalked or harassed, and to call police. Advise them to alert co-workers, friends, and teachers at a child's school if the person is being stalked. Providing a picture of the stalker to these individuals can be helpful.

- Help the person to tell children what they should do in an emergency, and advise them of how they will know it is an emergency—where they should go and what they should do.
- Always end by reassuring the person or child that they were right to tell you and tell them what you will be doing next.
- Report child abuse. And if someone has made a direct threat against another person, warn both the person and the police.
- Document what you saw or heard as quickly as possible after someone discloses that they are being abused. Focus on facts, not opinion, and write as clearly and concisely as possible. Document having made the report to the Children's Aid Society as well, and/or having warned an individual, and the police, where a direct threat has been made. Document this as quickly as possible.
- Never discuss possible abuse with the individual implicated in taking part in the abuse. This would put their victim at extreme risk.

## THE PROFESSIONAL RESPONSIBILITY TO STAY SAFE

Finally, as a professional, it is very important to ensure your own safety. You will need to develop a safety plan for yourself in consultation with a supervisor if you regularly work with violent families, especially in their homes, or in a location where you would be working alone. You will also need to establish an emergency call system with code words to let another worker or supervisor know that you are in danger. If working in a family home, make sure others know where you are and when you are expected back, and have them call and check if you are not back on time. Park somewhere that is well lit and allows for a quick exit if necessary. Check for exits in an apartment building or home where you can leave quickly.

Never discuss possible abuse while an abusive person is nearby. If you witness an assault, leave and call police immediately. Do not confront an aggressive person. If confronted, speak calmly, reassuring the person that your first priority is to protect everyone's safety.

If you are being threatened, call police, advise your supervisor, and talk to any security staff to work out a safety plan for yourself (Government of Alberta, n.d.).

---

## CHAPTER SUMMARY

This chapter has covered family violence, its type and prevalence, its causes, and how professionals should respond, including reporting requirements and assisting in the development of a safety plan. Specific information on professionals' duty to report child abuse was outlined. Legal requirements related to the Tarasoff decision in the United States concerning professionals' obligations to report direct threats against any person were also included.

## FURTHER READING

Statistics Canada. (2018, December 5). Family violence in Canada: A statistical profile, 2017. https://www150.statcan.gc.ca/n1/en/pub/85-002-x/2018001/article/54978-eng.pdf?st=-1CrEZ8g

## CLASSROOM RESOURCES

*Finding dawn.* (2006). NFB. https://www.nfb.ca/film/finding_dawn/
*A safe distance.* (1986). NFB. https://www.nfb.ca/film/safe_distance/
*To a safer place.* (1987). NFB. https://www.nfb.ca/film/to_a_safer_place/

## CLASSROOM ACTIVITY

After showing a film on family violence, break the group into dyads and have them discuss what about the film touched them most and why. Report findings to the whole class as appropriate.

## QUESTIONS FOR REFLECTION

1. Has someone you know been victimized in their family? If so, what impact did it have?
2. Have you dealt with family violence in a placement or work situation, and if so, what would you do differently after reading this chapter?
3. Was anything in this chapter surprising to you? If so, what and why?

## REFERENCES

Amnesty International. (2011, March 8). Canada: Missing and murdered Aboriginal women and girls: Families deserve answers—and justice. Retrieved from https://www.amnesty.ca/news/news-item/canada-missing-and-murdered-aboriginal-women-and-girls-families-deserve-answers-%E2%80%93-and

Angus Reid. (2012). Omnibus Survey for the Canadian Women's Foundation. Retrieved from www.canadianwomen.org/facts-about-violence#2

Baker, L., Jaffe, P., & Moore, K. (2001). Understanding the effects of domestic violence: A handbook for early childhood educators. Centre for Children and Families in the Justice System. Retrieved from http://www.lfcc.on.ca/wp-content/uploads/2017/02/PDF-Copy-1.pdf

Cahn, D. D., & Lloyd, S. A. (Eds.). (1996). *Family violence from a communication perspective*. Thousand Oaks, CA: Sage.

Canadian Femicide Observatory for Justice and Accountability. (2018). #CallItFemicide. Retrieved from https://femicideincanada.ca/callitfemicide.pdf

Canadian Panel on Violence Against Women. (1993). *Changing the landscape: Ending violence-achieving equality. Final report*. Ottawa, ON: Minister of Supply and Services.

Canadian Press. (2008, November 24). Canada must probe cases of slain, missing Aboriginal women: UN. CBC News. Retrieved from www.cbc.ca/news/canada/story/2008/11/24/missing-women.html

Canadian Women's Foundation. (2013). The facts about gender-based violence. Retrieved from www.canadianwomen.org/facts-about-violence#3

Conroy, S. (n.d.). Section 5: Police reported family violence against seniors. Highlights. Retrieved from https://www150.statcan.gc.ca/n1/pub/85-002-x/2017001/article/14698/05-eng.htm

Dutton, D. (1997). Male abusiveness in intimate relationships. *Clinical Psychology Review, 15*, 367–581.

Emery, R. E., & Laumann-Billings, L. (1998). An overview of the nature, causes, and consequences of abusive family relationships: Toward differentiating maltreatment and violence. *American Psychologist, 53*, 121–135.

Ghonaim, H. (2018, December 7). 418 cases of domestic homicide in Canada and what they have in common. Retrieved from https://www.cbc.ca/news/canada/london/canada-wide-report-women-at-risk-domestic-violence-1.4936047

Goldsmith, T. (2006). What causes domestic violence? *Psych Central*. Retrieved from http://psychcentral.com/lib/what-causes-domestic-violence/000344

Government of Alberta. (n.d.). What the health care community can do about family violence. Retrieved from http://humanservices.alberta.ca/documents/NCN1578-what-the-health-care-community-can-do-booklet.pdf

Government of Canada. (2016). Family violence: How big is the problem in Canada? Retrieved from https://www.canada.ca/en/public-health/services/health-promotion/stop-family-violence/problem-canada.html

Government of Canada, Department of Justice. (2017, July). Victimization of Indigenous women and girls. Retrieved from https://www.justice.gc.ca/eng/rp-pr/jr/jf-pf/2017/july05.html

Government of Ontario. (2011). Child and Family Services Act (CFSA). Retrieved from www.e-laws.gov.on.ca/html/statutes/english/elaws_statutes_90c11_e.htm

Hotaling, G. T., & Sugarman, D. B. (1986). An analysis of risk markers in husband to wife violence: The current state of knowledge. *Violence and Victims, 1*, 101–124.

Johnson, H. (2012). Limits of a criminal justice response: Trends in police and court processing of sexual assault. In E. Sheehy (Ed.), *Sexual assault in Canada: Law, legal practice, and women's activism* (pp. 613–634). Ottawa, ON: University of Ottawa Press.

Maikovich, J. K., & Jaffee, S. R. (2008, September/October). Effects of family violence on psychopathology symptoms in children previously exposed to maltreatment. *Child Development, 79*(5), 1498–1512.

Ontario (Canada) Domestic Violence Death Review Committee. (2017). 2017 report findings. Retrieved from http://cdhpi.ca/sites/cdhpi.ca/files/DVDRC-2018-Infographic.pdf

Ontario Ministry of Children and Youth. (2010). Reporting child abuse and neglect: It's your duty. Retrieved from http://www.children.gov.on.ca/htdocs/English/childrensaid/reportingabuse/abuseandneglect.aspx

Perreault, S., & Brennan, S. (2009). Criminal victimization in Canada. *Statistics Canada*. Retrieved from www.statcan.gc.ca/pub/85-002-x/2010002/article/11340-eng.htm#a3

Perry, B. D. (1997). Incubated in terror: Neurodevelopmental factors in the "cycle of violence." In J. D. Osofsky (Ed.), *Children, youth, and violence: The search for solutions* (pp. 124–148). New York, NY: Guilford Press.

Picard, E. L., & Robertson, G. B. (2007). *Legal liabilities of doctors and hospitals in Canada*. Toronto, ON: Carswell.

Royal College of Psychiatrists. (2019). Domestic violence and abuse: The impact on children and adolescents. Retrieved from https://www.rcpsych.ac.uk/mental-health/parents-and-young-people/information-for-parents-and-carers/domestic-violence-and-abuse-effects-on-children

Sheppard, G. (2003). Duty to warn. Retrieved from https://www.ccpa-accp.ca/wp-content/uploads/2015/05/NOE.Duty-to-Warn.pdf

Statistics Canada. (2009). Highlights—Family violence in Canada: A statistical profile. Retrieved from www.statcan.gc.ca/pub/85-224-x/85-224-x2010000-eng.pdf

Statistics Canada. (2011). Homicide in Canada. Retrieved from www.statcan.gc.ca/pub/85-002-x/2012001/article/11738-eng.pdf

Statistics Canada. (2013). Section 2: Family related murder suicides. Retrieved from https://www150.statcan.gc.ca/n1/pub/85-002-x/2013001/article/11805/11805-2-eng.htm

Statistics Canada. (2018). Family violence in Canada: A statistical profile, 2017. Retrieved from https://www150.statcan.gc.ca/n1/en/pub/85-002-x/2018001/article/54978-eng.pdf?st=-1CrEZ8g

Supreme Court of California. (1976). *Tarasoff vs Regents University of California*. Retrieved from https://law.justia.com/cases/california/supreme-court/3d/17/425.html

Thompson, N. (2019, January 30). Every 2.5 days, a woman or girl is killed in Canada, new report shows. Canadian Press reported on Global News. Retrieved from https://globalnews.ca/news/4904975/a-woman-or-girl-is-killed-every-2-5-days-in-canada-report/

United Nations. (1993). *United Nations Declaration on the Elimination of Violence against Women*. Retrieved from www.un.org/documents/ga/res/48/a48r104.htm

Wolfe, D. A. (1989). *Child abuse: Implications for child development and psychopathology* (2nd ed.). Thousand Oaks, CA: Sage.

Wolfe, D. A., & Jaffe, P. G. (1999). Emerging strategies in the prevention of domestic violence. *Journal of Domestic Violence and Children*, *9*(3). Retrieved from https://pdfs.semanticscholar.org/61ce/0df79b88b189cb45f7b8786a2dca413593e6.pdf

## CHAPTER 11

# Addiction and the Family

*No one is immune from addiction; it afflicts people of all ages, races, classes, and professions.*

    —Patrick J. Kennedy

## CHAPTER OVERVIEW

Almost everyone knows a family member who struggles with addiction. This chapter focuses on the widespread problem of addiction and its impact on individuals and family members. It also examines extended family reactions and the transmission of negative effects to the next generation, as well as the underlying causes of addiction and what roles and dynamics result when one or both parents abuse substances or engage in other addictive behaviours. The chapter concludes by outlining some helpful interventions.

## DEFINITION AND SYMPTOMS OF ADDICTION

The American Society of Addiction Medicine (ASAM) (2014) defines addiction as follows:

> Addiction is a primary, chronic disease of brain reward, motivation, memory and related circuitry. Dysfunction in these circuits leads to characteristic

biological, psychological, social and spiritual manifestations. This is reflected in an individual pathologically pursuing reward and/or relief by substance use and other behaviors. Addiction is characterized by inability to consistently abstain, impairment in behavioral control, craving, diminished recognition of significant problems with one's behaviors and interpersonal relationships, and a dysfunctional emotional response. Like other chronic diseases, addiction often involves cycles of relapse and remission. Without treatment or engagement in recovery activities, addiction is progressive and can result in disability or premature death.

This was considered a controversial definition, in that it essentially said all addictions are the same. *Addiction Treatment Magazine* ("New Definition of Addiction," 2011) made the following comment:

Over 80 experts from the ASAM spent four years developing the new definition, which is that addiction is a chronic brain disease. It develops from physical abnormalities in the reward circuitry of the brain, particularly in atypical differences in the way areas of the brain communicate regarding memory, emotional response and pleasure. If you look at the brain of an addict on a CAT scan, abnormalities show up in the same way tumors show up in the lungs of people with lung cancer. A drug addict spends most of his waking hours thinking about drugs, using them, and seeking them out because his brain has an abnormal circuitry, and his behaviors associated with addiction in turn make his abnormalities worse, according to the ASAM.

The World Health Organization (WHO) (2014) prefers the term *substance misuse* to *substance abuse* because it is less judgmental; however, it does define substance abuse with reference to the *Diagnostic and Statistical Manual of Mental Disorders* (4th edition): "In DSM-IV, 'psychoactive substance abuse' is defined as a 'maladaptive pattern of use indicated by ... continued use despite knowledge of having a persistent or recurrent social, occupational, psychological or physical problem that is caused or exacerbated by the use [or by] recurrent use in situations in which it is physically hazardous.'" WHO defines substance misuse as the "use of a substance for a purpose not consistent with legal or medical guidelines, as in the non-medical use of prescription medications" (WHO, 2014).

## ADDICTION STATISTICS

Fortunately, substance abuse and misuse appear to be declining among youth and older Canadians. Health Canada (2011) reports the following:

> Among youth, aged 15–24 years, past-year use of at least one of 5 illicit drugs (cocaine or crack, speed, hallucinogens [excluding salvia], ecstasy, and heroin) decreased from 11.3% in 2004 to 4.8%.... The rate of past-year psychoactive pharmaceutical use decreased among Canadians aged 15 years and older from 26.0% in 2010 to 22.9%. Of those who indicated they had used an opioid pain reliever, a stimulant or a sedative or tranquilizer in the past year, 3.2% reported they abused such a drug. Abuse is use for the experience, the feeling caused, to get high or for other non-prescribed reasons.

## ALCOHOL ADDICTION

Health Canada also reports that alcohol use is holding steady in adults and declining among young people: "Among Canadians 15 years and older, the prevalence of past-year alcohol use was 78.0%, not statistically different from previous years.... Less than three quarters of youth (70.8%) reported consuming alcohol in the past year. This is a decrease from 2004 when 82.9% of youth reported past-year use of alcohol" (Health Canada, 2011). The Centre for Addiction and Mental Health (CAMH) (2013) says that about 20 percent of individuals with mental health issues may also have co-occurring addiction.

One group that is experiencing increasingly dangerous effects of alcohol addiction is women. "The rate of women who died from causes linked directly to alcohol has increased by 26 per cent between 2001 and 2015. The rate for men only increased by about five per cent during that same period" (Canadian Institute for Health Information, 2018a). The Institute's findings are a red flag that increasingly dangerous use of alcohol may be occurring across the board. It found that girls aged 10 to 19 were hospitalized more frequently than boys the same age, and that the average number of people in Canada who were hospitalized for conditions related directly to alcohol grew from 2016 to 2017. There was an increase in the proportion of avoidable deaths from conditions that could be 100 percent attributed to alcohol, from 2.7 percent in 2001 to 3.8 percent in 2015 (Canadian Institute for Health Information, 2018a).

## ABUSE OF NON-PRESCRIPTION DRUGS

In the United States, the National Survey on Drug Use and Health (NSDUH) says that pain relievers are the most common type of illicit drugs used and are also the most commonly involved in overdoses (Drug Enforcement Agency, 2018). However, the decline in drug use in the United States parallels that of Canada.

In spite of the apparent decline in the use of illegal substances or misuse of prescription medications, substance abuse and misuse continue to have an impact on families in both Canada and the United States. Other types of addictions—to food, sex, the Internet, gaming, and so forth—also have negative financial, interpersonal, and emotional impacts on families. When a family member is essentially missing in action because of their focus on their addiction rather than on the needs of the family, negative consequences result.

## THE FENTANYL EPIDEMIC IN CANADA

More than 10,000 Canadians died of opioid related events between January 2016 and September 2018 (Government of Canada, 2019b). The greatest number of these were in Ontario and British Columbia. Many of these deaths were accidental. A major problem is that "a variety of street drugs are tainted with toxic substances, such as fentanyl, without the knowledge of the people consuming them" (Government of Canada, 2019b), and it is believed that fentanyl accounted for 73 percent of accidental opioid-related deaths. Fentanyl is highly potent and used as a pain reliever. What makes it so dangerous is that "it is 20 to 40 times more potent than heroin and 100 times more potent than morphine, which makes the risk of accidental overdose very high; a very small amount (about the size of a few grains of salt) of pure fentanyl is enough to kill the average adult; it is odourless and tasteless, so you may not even know you are taking it; it can be mixed with other drugs such as heroin and cocaine, and is also being found in counterfeit pills that are made to look like prescription opioids" (Government of Canada, 2019a).

Opioid addiction has been devastating for families, especially when it involves the loss of a loved one through accidental death.

Joe was 19 years old when he first graduated from weed to opioids. He was not worried and considered himself to be "experienced." His family knew that Joe smoked weed and were not all that concerned until his mother came home from work one day and found him unconscious in his room.

Desperate, she called 911, but to no avail. Joe was pronounced dead on arrival—another victim of drugs laced with fentanyl. Since Joe's death, his mother has been extremely depressed, blaming herself for not having acted. His father is angry and often spends long periods away from the family as he tries to deal with his own grief. Joe's 14-year-old sister has started acting out at school, getting into fights with other girls. The aftermath of Joe's death is blowing his family apart.

Doctors now know that legal opiate medications (codeine, oxycodone, morphine, and fentanyl) were over-prescribed, and because they are highly addictive, they have created an opioid addiction epidemic in Canada. Fentanyl is a particularly dangerous part of this epidemic. Opioids should only be prescribed for short periods of time, but many were given for lengthy periods, resulting in addictions that are very difficult to overcome (Canadian Institute for Health Information, 2019b). Sadly, many families like Joe's have now fallen victim to this epidemic and have lost family members to the opioid crisis.

## CAUSES OF ADDICTION

Considerable research has been done on the underlying causes of addictive behaviours. Volkow (2013) believes that there are genetic, developmental, social, and environmental factors in the development of addiction. It is now thought that genetics may account for 50 percent of someone's vulnerability, with "culture, neighborhoods, schools, families, and peer groups likely affecting the rest, or interacting with genetic factors to affect the rest." Research now seems to indicate that stress and drug exposure "can cause lasting changes to genes and their function … which can result in long term changes to brain circuits" (Volkow, 2013). Genetic factors can also prevent addiction.

It is suggested that adolescents are particularly vulnerable to addiction. Volkow (2013) states, "Because their brains are still undergoing rapid development in areas that contribute to decision-making, judgment, and risk-taking, adolescents tend toward immediate gratification over long-term goals. This can lead to risk-taking, including experimenting with drugs. When coupled with their increased sensitivity to social or peer influences and decreased sensitivity to negative consequences of behaviour, it is easy to see why adolescents are particularly vulnerable to drug abuse."

## IMPACT ON FAMILIES

Several authors have outlined the impact that substance abuse and misuse can have on families (Center for Substance Abuse Treatment, 2004; Lameman, 2014; Reilly, 1992). These authors have outlined distancing as one of the major impacts, as dependency on a particular substance places the need for it before family relationships. This sends an uncaring message to spouses and children who suffer emotional trauma as a result, and it interferes with bonding and attachment. It also leads to a failure to accept responsibility by the individual who is abusing the substance, meaning that remaining family members must bear additional burdens and must adapt to both the behaviour and lack of responsibility shown by the substance abuser. This and the problem of distancing can lead to family arguments that can become explosive and end in violence. This can lead to affairs and, ultimately, separation and divorce. Furthermore, it distorts family roles as individuals take on responsibilities that do not rightly belong to them, and these dysfunctional roles can lead to the intergenerational transmission of these dynamics. As those who abuse substances age, they may also have inappropriately dependent relationships with their children, who are also often faced with risks to both their parents' and their own health.

Lameman (2014) has listed a number of other impacts on individuals and families that occur when there is substance abuse. These include jealousy, marital conflict, conflict with children, financial problems, emotional trauma, violence, cheating, separation and divorce, intergenerational transmission of patterns of substance abuse, and health risks.

For example, Jim has a serious drinking problem. His wife of many years, June, sticks with him, in spite of having threatened to leave many times. Jim manages to manipulate her into staying, usually by getting close to other women. This makes her jealous and causes her to seek favour with Jim again. Jim and June's finances are tight, but they still take expensive vacations. Jim continues to drink and smoke, and engages in expensive hobbies, as does June. Tension has greatly increased in their family lately with the death of Jim's mother, who was also an alcoholic. Jim has become depressed and is in trouble at work because of his attempt to "self-medicate" his depression by increasing his drinking. Jim and June teeter constantly on the brink of financial ruin and divorce, but have done so for years. Jim has lately entered therapy, but it is debatable whether or not he will continue.

Jim and June's situation illustrates the kind of marital conflict, financial problems, infidelity, and other issues that can surface in a family where a member struggles with alcoholism. Quite often the alcoholic is completely unaware of the negative impact their drinking has on others, especially if they have managed to hold a job or function relatively normally. Counselling can sometimes help a person to develop this insight, but it can also be frightening to an already insecure person and cause them to leave therapy.

Normative development cannot occur in families where substance abuse is common, and this interferes with normal attachment processes and the development of trust. Sometimes extended family who feel anxiety, embarrassment, fear, or guilt about substance-abusing relatives may cut ties, leaving family members isolated. Work relationships can also be affected since substance abusers are likely to be unreliable, thereby placing additional burdens on co-workers. This can cause conflict at work or even job loss.

In some cases a child may act as a surrogate spouse to a substance-abusing parent, and may subsequently become controlling and overprotective with their own children, refusing to allow them sufficient autonomy and impeding their progress toward adulthood.

Reilly (1992) has outlined how interactional patterns in families can be affected by substance abuse. Negativism, complaints, and criticism may be common. The family may be beaten down, and family members may only get attention by creating crises. This may cause the person abusing substances to do so more often, in an effort to manage repressed anger. Because of a lack of parental consistency, children may not understand limits or develop appropriate boundaries. Denial of the problem in the family may be common. The substance abuser or misusers may also be self-medicating against intolerable thoughts or personal pain rather than addressing them directly, and this can create further dysfunctional dynamics in a family. Unrealistic parental expectations may cause children to become over- or underachievers as they either fight to meet parental expectations or attempt to avoid them altogether.

Addiction has varying impacts, depending upon the type of family. Where only two people are involved, the effects can include the non-addicted partner having to take on the provider role, denying the problem, or protecting the addicted partner. There may be "chronic anger, stress, anxiety, hopelessness, inappropriate sexual behavior, neglected health, shame, stigma, and isolation" (Center for Substance Abuse Treatment, 2004). Should either partner obtain help, especially for co-dependency, it will have an impact on both partners. Co-dependency is defined as "being overly concerned with the problems of another to the detriment of attending to one's own wants and needs" (Center for Substance Abuse Treatment, 2004). It is generally characterized by controlling behaviour, believing the other person is incapable of caring adequately for themselves, low self-esteem and denial of their own feelings, excessive compliance and compromising of their own values to avoid rejection, hyper-vigilance, a high degree of sensitivity to trouble or disappointment, and loyalty to someone who may not be deserving of it.

Children of an alcoholic parent may feel guilt about possibly causing the drinking, or shame as a result of it (Brooks & Rice, 1997). Further impact on children may include learning problems, risk factors for addiction, relationship problems, and mental health problems including depression, anxiety, and low self-esteem (Johnson & Leff, 1999).

However, some research shows that the impact may not be all negative. Some children develop resilience (Werner, 1986) and highly adaptive coping strategies because of early exposure to stress and a chaotic environment. They may be mature beyond their years, autonomous, and able to shoulder more responsibility than most (Wolin & Wolin, 1993). These qualities can be double-edged swords for children who may not have had the opportunity to experience childhood because of having to play an adult role in the family at too young an age. Adult children of parents with addiction issues may take on more than their fair share of responsibility and often end up in caregiving roles in their relationships.

Roles tend to be skewed in families struggling with addiction. Downs and Wampler (2009) have outlined the hero, lost child, mascot, and scapegoat roles, which many children take on in such families. The hero tends to be mature, trustworthy, helpful, and organized; the lost child is quiet, shy, lonely, and solemn; the mascot is entertaining, excitable, cheerful, and playful; and the scapegoat is disobedient, deceitful, hostile, and irritating. All of these roles are attempts to either fix or draw attention away from the anxiety and pain experienced in families confronting addiction.

## BEST PRACTICES IN ADDICTION TREATMENT

What are the best treatments for individuals and families struggling with addiction? Treatments that promote "prolonged abstinence" offer the best chance of helping individuals who are addicted recover and regain at least some of their former functioning and control over their lives (Downs & Wampler, 2009). Changing addictive behaviours requires a treatment program that challenges "deeply embedded behaviours," with the understanding that relapse simply means that treatment may need to be "reinstated or adjusted" or changed in some way.

In the end, however, the responsibility rests with the individual to obtain and stick with treatment.

The National Institute on Drug Abuse (2009) informs us that addiction treatment likely needs to be long term, involve medication as well as counselling (especially behavioural therapies), meet the multiple needs of an individual and not just focus on the addiction, be flexible and change according to needs and conditions, involve possible treatment of any mental illness that accompanies it, and involve medically assisted detoxification as the first stage of treatment. Treatment need not be voluntary to be effective, and individuals, especially those who use injected drugs, should be carefully monitored for other infectious diseases. This is also true for individuals who live on the street and abuse alcohol or other drugs.

Relapse prevention as part of a "continuum of care that includes a customized treatment regimen—addressing all aspects of an individual's life, including medical and mental health services and follow-up options (e.g., community- or family-based recovery support systems)—can be crucial to a person's success in achieving and maintaining a drug-free lifestyle" (National Institute on Drug Abuse, 2009).

Anyone going through a detox process will likely require medication to assist with withdrawal symptoms and to help re-establish "normal brain function and prevent relapse and diminish cravings" (National Institute on Drug Abuse, 2009). Medications may also act either as substitutes for an addictive substance (for example, methadone) or as a blocking agent to alter the feelings of reward someone receives from drinking or using drugs.

Behavioural treatments are largely geared toward helping individuals and families recognize the attitudes and behaviours that support and enable addiction and replace them with healthier lifestyle and communication choices. Behavioural treatments are available from community-based agencies, and these may include cognitive behavioural counselling, multidimensional family therapy, and/or motivational interviewing and incentives. Cognitive behavioural counselling helps individuals to recognize, steer clear of, and find new ways to cope or adapt rather than using drugs. Multidimensional family therapy is designed to help families function more effectively by examining the adaptivity of current roles and ways of relating. Motivational interviewing capitalizes on individuals' desires to change their lives by identifying and eliminating the discrepancies between where someone is in their life and where they would like to be.

These treatments can also be offered through residential programs, especially if a person's addiction is quite severe. Residential programs will often attempt to influence the "attitudes, perceptions, and behaviors associated with drug use" (National Institute on Drug Abuse, 2009).

Whatever treatment method is used, family involvement will likely be critical. The tendency of families to attempt to maintain homeostasis, even if it involves non-adaptive ways of functioning, can be very strong and must be overcome if the family member struggling with addiction is to recover. This will involve therapy that assists the entire family to determine how rigid roles and functions, and negative communications, thoughts, and behaviour, contribute to and fuel addictive behaviours.

## CHAPTER SUMMARY

This chapter has included definitions of addiction and substance abuse and misuse, and examined the underlying causes of addiction and the impact it has on individual and family functioning. It has also provided an overview of treatments for individuals and families struggling with addictions.

## FURTHER READING

Canadian Mental Health Association. (2019). Understanding and finding help for substance abuse. https://ontario.cmha.ca/documents/understanding-and-finding-help-for-substance-abuse/

Mager, D. (2016, May 2). Addiction as a family affliction. https://www.psychologytoday.com/ca/blog/some-assembly-required/201605/addiction-family-affliction

MyHealth.Alberta.ca. (2017, March 7). Addiction in the family. https://myhealth.alberta.ca/Alberta/Pages/addiction-in-the-family.aspx

## CLASSROOM RESOURCES

*Cottonland*. (2006). NFB. https://www.nfb.ca/film/cottonland/
*Here at home: The wound inside*. (2012). NFB. https://www.nfb.ca/film/at_home_wound_inside/

## CLASSROOM ACTIVITY

### Task Groups

Form groups and assign each group one of the following tasks. Each group can focus on a different geographic area.

1.  Find out where the drug and alcohol addiction services are in your area and put together a list of them, including descriptions, to share with the class.
2.  Describe the descent into addiction of family or friends and compile a list of potential warning signs.
3.  Research the ways that families can attempt to address addiction issues, citing the barriers and opportunities they may encounter.

## QUESTIONS FOR REFLECTION

1.  Have you ever abused substances? If so, what do you consider to be the underlying causes?
2.  Has anyone in your family ever abused a substance or struggled with any other addiction? If so, what impact did this have on the family?
3.  Have you, or anyone you know, played one of the childhood roles that are common in substance-abusing families? What evidence do you have of this?
4.  Which of the treatment options for addictions interests you the most?

## REFERENCES

American Society of Addiction Medicine. (2014). Definition of addiction. Retrieved from www.asam.org/for-the-public/definition-of-addiction

Brooks, C. S., & Rice, K. F. (1997). *Families in recovery: Coming full circle*. Baltimore, MA: Paul H. Brookes.

Canadian Institute for Health Information. (2018a, May 31). Alcohol harm on the rise for Canadian women. Retrieved from https://www.cihi.ca/en/alcohol-harm-on-the-rise-for-canadian-women?utm_source=crm&utm_medium=email&utm_campaign=yhsccq&utm_content=mediareleaseEN

Canadian Institute for Health Information. (2018b, June). Amount of opioids prescribed dropping in Canada: Prescriptions on the rise. Retrieved from https://www.cihi.ca/en/amount-of-opioids-prescribed-dropping-in-canada-prescriptions-on-the-rise

Center for Substance Abuse Treatment. (2004). Substance abuse treatment and family therapy. Retrieved from www.ncbi.nlm.nih.gov/books/NBK64265/

Centre for Addiction and Mental Health. (2013). Mental illness and addiction statistics. Retrieved from www.camh.ca/en/hospital/about_camh/newsroom/for_reporters/Pages/addictionmentalhealthstatistics.aspx

Downs, A. B., & Wampler, R. S. (2009). Development of a brief version of the children's roles inventory. Retrieved from https://www.tandfonline.com/doi/abs/10.1080/01926180902754687?journalCode=uaft20

Drug Enforcement Agency. (2018). National drug threat assessment summary. Retrieved from https://www.dea.gov/sites/default/files/2018-11/DIR-032-18%20 2018%20NDTA%20final%20low%20resolution.pdf

Government of Canada. (2019a). Fentanyl. Retrieved from https://www.canada.ca/en/ health-canada/services/substance-use/controlled-illegal-drugs/fentanyl.html#a2

Government of Canada. (2019b, April). National report: Apparent opioid related deaths in Canada. Retrieved from https://infobase.phac-aspc.gc.ca/datalab/national-surveillance-opioid-mortality.html

Health Canada. (2011). Canadian Alcohol and Drug Use Monitoring Survey (CADUMS). Retrieved from www.hc-sc.gc.ca/hc-ps/drugs-drogues/stat/index-eng.php

Johnson, J. L., & Leff, M. (1999). Children of substance abusers: Overview of research findings. *Pediatrics, 103*, 1085–1099.

Lameman, B. A. (2014). Effects of substance abuse on families. *Chicago Tribune*. Retrieved from www.chicagotribune.com/sns-health-addiction-families,0,2311189. story

National Institute on Drug Abuse. (2009). Drug facts: Treatment approaches for drug addiction. Retrieved from www.drugabuse.gov/publications/drugfacts/ treatment-approaches-drug-addiction

New definition of addiction causing controversy among doctors. (2011, August 19). *Addiction Treatment Magazine*. Retrieved from www.addictiontreatmentmagazine. com/addiction/new-definition-addiction-controversy/

Reilly, D. M. (1992). Drug-abusing families: Intrafamilial dynamics and brief triphasic treatment. In E. Kaufman & P. Kaufmann (Eds.), *Family therapy of drug and alcohol abuse* (2nd ed., pp. 105–119). Boston, MA: Allyn and Bacon.

Volkow, N. (2013). The essence of addiction. National Institute on Drug Abuse. Retrieved from https://science.education.nih.gov/supplements/webversions/ BrainAddiction/guide/essence.html

Werner, E. E. (1986). Resilient offspring of alcoholics: A longitudinal study from birth to age 18. *Journal of Studies on Alcohol, 47*, 34–40.

Wolin, S. J., & Wolin, S. (1993). *Bound and determined: Growing up resilient in a troubled family*. New York, NY: Yilfard Press.

World Health Organization. (2014). Abuse (drug, alcohol, chemical, substance, or psychoactive substance). Retrieved from www.who.int/substance_abuse/ terminology/abuse/en/

## CHAPTER 12

# Family Assessment

*My manager was under pressure to reduce the number of cases so I was told to close cases and move them on to a CAF (common assessment framework).*

—Comment by a UK social worker (Community Care, 2014)

## CHAPTER OVERVIEW

In chapter 2, strengths-based assessment was presented as one of the most helpful forms available (Spindel, 2013). This assessment strategy allows family members to determine their own strengths and redefine problems as needs. It avoids the negative dynamic of a professional observer making assumptions about a family's functioning based only on their observations or answers to a routine set of questions, thereby allowing the family to be the experts on their own lives.

Most other forms of family assessment, whether formal or informal, help professionals to evaluate family functioning by using specific criteria, philosophies of practice, or models. While none of these types of assessments are endorsed here, because of their tendency to create a "we-they" approach to working with families, it is useful for readers to know of them and the forms that they take. In this chapter, various types of family assessment will be briefly described.

## WHY ASSESS?

Before choosing which type of assessment to use with a family, a professional should first ask "Why assess?" What benefit is likely to accrue to a family because of the assessment? If the answer is that there is more benefit for the professional, or agency, or funder than to a family, then an ethical question arises. Should the family be warned that the assessment will offer little to no benefit for them, given that the benefit is largely for others?

Many family assessments are driven by legal, policy, or program requirements established by funding bodies, such as government, or in legislation, with respect to child protection. This may mean that there is a legal or political agenda behind the assessment that may or may not make it more difficult for families to obtain assistance or funding, or that may result in the apprehension of a child. Does the family understand that they may be refused assistance or informed that they do not meet criteria for assistance because of the outcome of a family assessment? Is the family aware that an assessment may result in a child being taken into care? In any of these scenarios, is a professional under a moral obligation to inform the families? Ethically, the answer is yes, irrespective of whether or not there is a legal obligation to do so.

Any assessment that attempts to fit individuals or families into specific frameworks is likely to fail, as there are many more factors that inform family functioning than are easily assessed. No assessment can possibly capture the fullness of a family's experiences, history, culture, beliefs, feelings, and behaviours. Therefore, to some extent, almost all assessments are doomed to fail because they will be incomplete. Should professionals attempt to assist families based upon incomplete information? Should professionals be making assumptions about families, or logging observations based on incomplete information in agency files? The correct ethical answer is no, unless the family is able to complete the documentation by contributing to their own file. Professionals who use an empowerment approach will often write their notes along with the family. This is helpful for many reasons. It aids communication between the professional and family, creates trust, establishes an egalitarian framework for the work that will be done together, and ensures a more complete picture of the family.

## FAMILY-DRIVEN ASSESSMENT

The obvious way out of the usual assessment dilemma is to ensure that any "assessment" is family-driven—that the family determines what information they wish to provide, how they would like it used, and what priorities they would like to address first. The only caveat to this is if a family is under investigation for possible child abuse or other forms of family violence. If that is the case, legal requirements demand that parenting or other forms of assessment be done to determine the level of risk family members face.

Ideally, professionals will use a family-driven assessment to help them determine how the family sees itself, what it considers its main strengths and challenges to be, and what, specifically, family members would like to accomplish in working with a professional. This does not preclude the need for difficult conversations if a professional is concerned about particular family dynamics, but the key will be to discuss these with the family openly, with diplomacy and tact.

Other types of assessments, and their flaws, are discussed below.

## ASSESSMENTS USED IN EARLY INTERVENTION

The early intervention literature discusses several assessments being used in this sector. Bronfenbrenner (1992) bases assessment on an ecological theory of child development, wherein there is reciprocity between the developing child and multiple environments. Assessment using this model focuses on the interactions between a child and their environment—how the child influences the environment and how the environment influences the child. Since the family is the closest and most frequent influence on a developing child, the reciprocity of interactions between the child and their family are of primary importance.

Guralnick (2004) posits that there are three kinds of family interactions that can be assessed: "the quality of the parent-child transactions, family-orchestrated child experiences, and health and safety provided by the family" (p. 120). Each of these is tied directly to childhood development. The parent-child transactions interaction appears to be directly linked to "children's cognitive and social competence" (Guralnick, 2004, p. 121) and the parent's ability to be supportive and responsive in a variety of contexts. Guralnick acknowledges that maintaining a very high degree of parental responsiveness can be quite a challenge on a 24/7 basis.

The second interaction—family-orchestrated child experience—includes "providing developmentally appropriate toys and materials, and organizing social experiences that are stimulating and that extend the advantageous parent-child transactions previously noted" (Guralnick, 2004, p. 121). This has implications for what type of child care the parent selects, what social networks the parent introduces the child to, as well as the family's own social network. This area also affects the cognitive and social development of the child.

The third type of family interaction—providing a safe and secure environment—also has significant implications for child development and involves "protecting their child from experiencing or even witnessing violence … obtaining proper immunizations, accessing health care as needed, and providing adequate nutrition" (Guralnick, 2004, p. 122).

Guralnick is largely concerned with whether or not family patterns are within normative ranges. If they are, children's development will proceed within normal parameters. If they are not, and negative factors, such as a depressed mother, are present, child development will not proceed within normal parameters. This might seem fairly obvious. However, it has been found that examining the specifics of the three types of interaction is helpful in understanding which family dynamics may lead to particular child development outcomes.

## ADAPTATION-ORIENTED ASSESSMENTS

Adaptation theories form another of the underpinnings of family assessment. How well do parents and children adapt to changing life circumstances? And what are the mechanisms that foster and/or prevent appropriate adaptation? Ryff and Seltzer (1996) have examined the specifics of how families adapt to raising children but also what impact grown children have on their parents in midlife—an area that has, until recently, been largely unexplored. The longest relationship period between parents and children does not occur in the first 20 years, but over the next 30 years, as parents and children grow older and must cope with intergenerational issues. For example, parents may wish to retire, travel, and enjoy their lives at a time when their children want help with babysitting.

## STRESS AND COPING ASSESSMENTS

Other theories examine stress and coping strategies. McCubbin and Patterson (1983a) have looked at the characteristics of particular stressors, the perception of the stressor by the family, and the resources that are used to cope with it. They examine how well families are able to see stressful events as a process, and at what point "stress pileup" occurs in a family, forcing it to reorganize or adapt in order to survive. They question whether or not "high levels of disorganization in some cases might be essential to the maintenance of family relationships and may push families into creative solutions in problem solving" (Mederer & Hill, 1983, p. 46).

Pearlin, Mullan, Semple, and Skaff (1990) have done considerable work ex-amining families under stress, such as those where a family member is ill or has a significant disability, and have also mapped the areas where caregiving has be-come stressful. They identify what they term primary and secondary stressors, with primary stressors referring to "hardships and problems anchored directly in caregiving" and secondary stressors referring to "the strains experienced in roles and activities outside of caregiving, and intrapsychic strains, involving the dimin-ishment of self-concepts" (p. 583). They suggest that professionals can assist fam-ilies by increasing and broadening coping strategies and increasing levels of social support to ease family stress.

## CHILD PROTECTION ASSESSMENT

The Ontario Child Protection Tools Manual of the Ministry of Children and Youth Services (2016) provides considerable information related to determining risk factors in families as well as strengths that are protective factors. There is a comprehensive safety assessment tool included, as well as other detailed assess-ment material too extensive to cover here. Professionals or students wishing to work in child welfare should acquaint themselves with this good example of a government-mandated child and family assessment tool.

## THEORETICALLY BASED ASSESSMENTS

Assessments are also based upon theoretical constructs. Major theoreticians in the family therapy field include Bowen (1978); McGoldrick, Gerson, and Petry (2008); Minuchin (1974); and Satir (1983).

Bowen (1978) considered families to be an "emotional unit," which established the notion of "systems thinking" with respect to family assessment. Theoretically, whatever affected one family member affected them all, and this could be seen in the level of anxiety present in individuals and the family as a whole. Family relation-ship patterns were assessed to determine how families dealt with stressors, includ-ing triangulation, conflict, distancing, and over- or under-functioning in the area of reciprocity in couple relationships. He developed the differentiation of self scale to detail the degree to which family members were fused and the degree to which they were able to develop an identity separate from the group, postulating that those who were more "fused" had higher levels of anxiety (Gilbert, 2006). Self-differentiation can often be seen in the extent to which people have boundaries or not.

Bowen (1978) assessed the degree to which families "triangulated" as a coping strategy to ease anxiety, and explored the "cutoff" process, where family members stopped any form of communication with each other:

> The family projection process describes the primary way parents transmit their emotional problems to a child. The projection process can impair the functioning of one or more children and increase their vulnerability to clinical symptoms. Children inherit many types of problems (as well as strengths) through the relationships with their parents, but the problems they inherit that most affect their lives are relationship sensitivities such as heightened needs for attention and approval, difficulty dealing with expectations, the tendency to blame oneself or others, feeling responsible for the happiness of others or that others are responsible for one's own happiness, and acting impulsively to relieve the anxiety of the moment rather than tolerating anxiety and acting thoughtfully. (Bowen Center, n.d.)

Family projection, especially as it manifests in children is an especially vital part of family assessment. Bowen also considered sibling position to be an important part of the assessment process, hypothesizing that birth order had a great deal to do with how children functioned in families.

Minuchin (1974) developed what was considered to be a structural approach to work with families, believing that individuals' problems are the result of relationships in the present or past or both. Taking this into account, Minuchin believed that families developed patterns of interacting that were effective for them, and that these patterns became interdependent and complementary as well as necessary for the family to function. These patterns tended to be played out through both explicit and implicit rules. Explicit rules might involve routines (e.g., mealtimes, bedtimes), whereas implicit rules had to be observed to be determined (e.g., which family member makes the decisions or does the nurturing).

More recently, Minuchin, Reiter, and Borda (2013) appear to argue the opposite of what empowerment theorists suggest—that the family is the expert on its own life. The authors purport that families who show up for assistance come with the wrong assumptions; that the family's "certainty is the enemy of change" (p. 4); that it is the therapist's role to join with the family, but also to challenge it and help it to explore alternatives; that assessment is done using "the content of family communications to determine the process of family dynamics"; that humour and "metaphoric language" should be used to help the family; and that therapists should be introducing new knowledge to families (p. 6).

Virginia Satir's (1983) landmark book defined the role of those working with families as that of easing their pain. She believed that family pain is often acted out by one family member, but is present in all family members. Where others refer to the family member who carries the family's pain as the scapegoat, Satir considered them to be the "identified patient." According to Satir, a dysfunctional marital relationship resulting in flawed parenting takes the highest toll on the "identified patient," and careful consideration of this individual's symptoms is required to begin to understand the marital difficulties at their base. The resultant low self-esteem and dependency cripple an individual's ability to function independently and develop individuality, and the anxiety created by this also causes anxiety in offspring. The selection of mates, states Satir, is not accidental, in that each partner is seeking a sense of completion in the other: the qualities that they themselves lack as well as those that cause them some degree of fear and distrust, not unlike what they experienced in their family of origin. Like Bowen (1978), Satir believed that family members strive through repetitive and predictable interactions to maintain homeostasis in the family, and that observation of these interactions can provide clues to their underlying issues.

## GENOGRAMS

McGoldrick et al. (2008, p. 1) introduced the concept of genograms as a way of "tracking family history and relationships." The North American Primary Care Research Group, which included, among others, Murray Bowen, established standardized symbols and a format that could be used to create family genograms. Genograms "record information about family members and their relationships over at least three generations. They display family information graphically in a way that provides a quick gestalt of complex family problems; as such they are a rich source of hypotheses about how clinical problems evolve in the context of the family over time" (McGoldrick et al., 2008, p. 2). McGoldrick et al. set out clinical guidelines for the interpretation of genograms as an assessment method.

## CHILD CUSTODY ASSESSMENTS

The Ontario College of Social Workers and Social Services Workers (OCSWSSW) defines custody/access assessment as "a comprehensive clinical exploration of the needs of a child within the context of [their] family and environment and resulting in recommendations relevant to custody and/or access, regarding how those needs can best be met" (OCSWSSW, 2009, p. 5). Courts may order these types of assessments, but not always. Some are requested by both parties in a custody/access dispute, and as such may be subject to private contracts between individual parents, their legal counsel, and whoever completes the assessment.

According to OCSWSSW (2009), these assessments can recommend how parents may carry out their responsibilities toward their child or children and may also define their parental rights. Many will also contain a recommendation for a specific care plan for a child. Professionals completing these types of assessment will be affected by their own personal and professional values, and, for this reason, these kinds of assessments may be open to the criticism that they contain bias.

## CHAPTER SUMMARY

This chapter has examined family assessment from a variety of perspectives, including various theorists as well as particular models. It has also included a brief reference to child welfare and custody/access assessments. Also included is the caveat that all assessments are biased in some manner by the views of the individual doing the assessment. Since assessments are as plentiful as the theorists, jurisdictions, and organizations that use them, readers are advised to acquaint themselves with the assessments most commonly used in their areas of work.

## FURTHER READING

Devine, L. (2015, January 12). Considering social work assessment of families. *Journal of Social Welfare and Family Law, 37*(1). https://www.tandfonline.com/doi/full/10.1080/09649069.2015.998005

## CLASSROOM RESOURCE

*Lymelife*. (2008). Bartlett Films. https://www.imdb.com/title/tt0363780/?ref_=ttls_li_tt

## CLASSROOM ACTIVITIES

### Debate

Resolved that assessment is necessary to assist families and that professionals should use their professional judgment in applying assessments. (Or, resolved that assessments are not ethical ways to practice unless families themselves set the assessment agenda.) Each "team" takes a position and makes its points after researching the topic.

## Film Analysis

Using the film *Lymelife* as a basis, divide the class into groups to discuss how they would assess the family. Group One uses a strengths assessment. Group Two an ecological assessment. Group Three uses a child welfare assessment. The class will have had a homework assignment asking them to summarize each of the forms of assessment listed and to have watched the film.

## QUESTIONS FOR REFLECTION

1. Why do you feel assessment will be important in your work with families?
2. Of the assessments mentioned, which interests you most, and why?
3. Which type of assessment do you consider to be the least interesting? For what reasons?
4. Examine your own family using whichever assessment tool appeals to you most. What have you discovered?

## REFERENCES

Bowen Center. (n.d.). Eight concepts: Family projection process. Retrieved from https://thebowencenter.org/theory/eight-concepts/

Bowen, M. (1978). *Family therapy in clinical practice*. New York, NY and London, UK: Jason Aronson.

Bronfenbrenner, U. (1992). Ecological systems theory. In R. Vasta (Ed.), *Annals of child development. Six theories of child development: Revised formulations and current issues* (pp. 187–249). London, UK: Jessica Kingsley.

Community Care. (2014). 100 quotes from social workers that the government shouldn't ignore. Retrieved from www.communitycare.co.uk/2013/11/25/100-quotes-social-workers-government-shouldnt-ignore/#.UxNy14VQMns

Gilbert, R. M. (2006). *The eight concepts of Bowen Theory*. Front Royal, VA: Leading Systems Press.

Guralnick, M. J. (2004). Family investments in response to the developmental challenges of young children with disabilities. In A. Kalil & T. Deleire (Eds.), *Family investments in children's potential: Resources and parenting behaviors that promote success* (pp. 119–137). Mahwah, NJ: Lawrence Erlbaum.

Landau, B., Wolfson, L. H., & Landau, N. (2009). *Family mediation, arbitration, and collaborative practice handbook* (5th ed.). Markham, ON: LexisNexis.

Lappin, J. (1988). Family therapy: A structural approach. In R. Dorfman (Ed.), *Paradigms of clinical social work*. New York, NY: Brunner/Mazel.

L'Heureux-Dube, C. (1993). Supreme Court of Canada decision *Young v. Young*, [1993] S.C.R. 3 at 87, 49 R.F.L. (3d) 117 at 213. *Coleman Family Law Centre.* Retrieved from www.complexfamilylaw.com/Articles-by-Gene-C-Colman/Custody-Access-Assessments.shtml#Is%20an%20assessment%20always

McCubbin, H. I., & Patterson, J. M. (1983a). The family stress process: The Double ABCX Model of adjustment and adaptation. In H. I. McCubbin, M. B. Sussman, & J. M. Patterson (Eds.), *Social stress and the family: Advances and developments in family stress theory and research* (pp. 7–37). New York, NY: Haworth Press.

McCubbin, H. I., & Patterson, J. M. (1983b). Family transitions: Adaptation to stress. In H. I. McCubbin & C. R. Figley (Eds.), *Stress and the family: Vol. 1. Coping with normative transitions* (pp. 5–25). New York, NY: Bruner/Mazel.

McGoldrick, M., Gerson, R., & Petry, S. (2008). *Genograms: Assessment and intervention.* New York, NY: W.W. Norton.

Mederer, H., & Hill, R. (1983). Critical transitions over the family life span: Theory and research. In H. I. McCubbin, M. B. Sussman, & J. M. Patterson (Eds.), *Social stress and the family: Advances and developments in family stress theory and research* (pp. 39–60). New York, NY: Haworth Press.

Ministry of Children and Youth Services. (2016). Ontario Child Protection Tools Manual. Retrieved from http://www.children.gov.on.ca/htdocs/English/documents/childrensaid/Child-Protection-Tools-Manual-2016.pdf

Minuchin, S. (*1974*). *Families and family therapy.* Cambridge, MA: Harvard University Press.

Minuchin, S., Reiter, M. D., & Borda, C. (2013). *The craft of family therapy: Challenging certainties.* New York, NY: Routledge.

Ontario College of Social Workers and Social Services Workers. (2009). Practice guidelines for custody and access assessments. Toronto, ON: Author.

Pearlin, L., Mullan, J., Semple, S., & Skaff, M. (1990). Caregiving and the stress process: An overview of concepts and their measures. *The Gerontologist, 30*, 583–594.

Ryff, C. D., & Seltzer, M. M. (Eds.). (1996). *The parental experience at midlife.* Chicago, IL: University of Chicago Press.

Satir, V. (1983). *Conjoint family therapy.* Palo Alto, CA: Science and Behavior Books.

Spindel, P. (2013). *Case management from an empowerment perspective.* Toronto, ON: Spindel & Associates.

## CHAPTER 13

# Positive Strategies for Working with Families

*Call it a clan, call it a network, call it a tribe, call it a family. Whatever you call it, whoever you are, you need one.*

—Jane Howard

## CHAPTER OVERVIEW

Irrespective of which assessment tool is used, there are some ways of working with families that appear to be more helpful than others. Nichols (2010) has outlined over 14 different models of work with families. Some of these will be described in this chapter.

## FAMILY-CENTRED POSITIVE PSYCHOLOGY

Family-centred positive psychology is defined as "a framework for working with children and families that promotes strengths and capacity building within individuals and systems, rather than one focusing on the resolution of problems or re-mediation of deficiencies" (Sheridan, Warnes, Cowan, Schemm, & Clarke, 2004, p. 7). It has links to ecological theory in that it recognizes the presence of the microsystem (home, child-care providers, and school), the mesosystem (connections between the child and parent, the parent and school, and the school and the family), the exosystem (the larger system, such as the community that surrounds the family), and the macrosystem (including "cultural values, customs and laws") (Sheridan & Burt, 2009, p. 553), and seeks to build strengths and connections at all levels. Fundamental to this approach is the Search Institute of Minneapolis's 40 assets that, when emphasized in the family, are likely to result in young people who cope well, have self-confidence, are able to solve problems, relate positively to others, achieve at school, are engaged in their communities, and avoid high-risk behaviours such as drug and alcohol abuse, unprotected sex, and violence (Search Institute of Minneapolis, 1990). These 40 assets "identify a set of skills, experiences, relationships, and behaviors that enable young people to develop into successful and contributing adults" (Search Institute of Minneapolis, 1990). They are research-based and are being widely used to promote positive child development from early childhood through adolescence. The more of these assets young people have, the more likely they will be successful in life.

Several features of family-centred positive psychology make it a successful approach with families. These include the identification of strengths upon which families can build to promote a sense of control over their lives, redefining problems as needs, and addressing these needs by setting goals that are measurable and achievable and that help family members to strengthen their personal and family capacities and abilities. The focus is on helping families to learn and grow together rather than on addressing identified problems. It emphasizes building family capacity to allow the family to develop the resources necessary to confront current and future challenges.

Another feature of this approach is that the family identifies its own strengths and needs instead of a professional doing so through an assessment process. The underlying assumption is that families are the experts in their own lives and know best what they want to address.

This is also a model that promotes the strengthening of social support systems by using various linkages to help families mobilize helpful resources. Is budgeting an issue? Uncle Phil is good at that and can be used as a resource. Are Mom and Dad having trouble getting along? Perhaps Grandma and Grandpa can help, given that they have been married for almost 40 years. And Aunt Aneesha works in the college system, so maybe she can help the young people to prepare for their higher education.

Professionals working collaboratively with families, rather than "treating" them, is central to this model. Professionals are encouraged to view families as already having strengths and capacities that can be used to promote further growth and resilience (Sheridan & Burt, 2009).

## SUBSTANCE ABUSE TREATMENT IN FAMILIES

Interpersonal relationships in families are an important factor in whether or not someone relapses. Therefore, treatment of the entire family where substance abuse is present is a vital part of preventing relapse (McCrady, Epstein, Cook, Jensen, & Hildebrandt, 2009). The family adjustment model (Jackson, 1954) assumes that family members attempt to cope in a variety of ways with the stress of living with a person who abuses substances, and suggests that this attempt to cope is a normal adjustment to substance abusers' behaviours (Miller, Forcehimes, & Zweben, 2011). What other models stigmatize as "enabling" behaviour is seen by Jackson as "understandable attempts to adjust to and cope with the chaos of addiction" (Miller et al., 2011, p. 203). Within this framework, the goal is to positively reinforce recovery by helping families to determine which of their coping strategies favour recovery and which do not (Meyers, Miller, Smith, & Tonigan, 2002).

Other methods for helping families of individuals with addictions is the Al-Anon approach of "loving detachment." Family members are urged to stop attempting to influence another's addiction and to seek appropriate personal support elsewhere, thereby focusing more on self-care. This may be good advice for any family member dealing with someone who has any kind of addiction, including to sex, food, gambling, or the Internet. Such a strategy is likely to "reduce emotional distress and improve their coping skills; however, it appears to have little to no effect on addictive behavior" (Miller et al., 2011, p. 205).

Since many families do not voluntarily seek assistance but may be referred by schools, the courts, child welfare agencies, or hospitals, professionals working with them must often first overcome families' suspicion. Because of possible negative experiences with various "helping or legal systems" or previously encountered racism or classism, the establishment of rapport and careful attention to the professional's own impact on the family become vital (Boyd-Franklin & Bry, 2000). This challenges professionals to develop a high degree of self-awareness and cultural competence.

## STAGES OF CHANGE

Prochaska and DiClemente (1982) have suggested that many families are ambivalent about change and that they may go through stages of readiness in this regard. There are actually five stages of change that many families go through: contemplation, preparation, action, maintenance, and relapse. To further complicate the process, it is possible that different family members may be at different stages of change. There are several ways that professionals can address this issue, among them the use of a variety of engagement strategies. Where someone is resistant to taking part in a whole-family process, a professional may, with the consent of others in the family, reach out to a particular individual. This process may be particularly helpful when one or more family members are fed up because previous attempts to improve family functioning have failed due to a family member's mental health or substance abuse issues (Boyd-Franklin, Cleeck, Wofsky, & Munday, 2013). Asking a peripheral family member their opinion about why there is a problem in the family, and encouraging them to provide advice to a professional in this regard, can be an effective engagement strategy that may bring that member in closer over time.

A non-judgmental approach is also helpful in reducing fear of stigma because the parents are not working or a child is in trouble at school and the parents fear being blamed. Approaching multi-problem families in a calm, non-judgmental manner, focusing first on family strengths and later asking them to redefine their problems as needs, can be a good way to engage formerly resistant families. The goal is to decrease blaming behaviour and the reactions it engenders, while building hope by reframing situations and people in a more positive light. The professional can help the family to improve its problem-solving skills as well as model and teach more effective communication strategies (Boyd-Franklin et al., 2013).

## RESILIENCY-BASED APPROACHES

Many families are struggling with extreme adversity. They may be military families, or families caring for an aged or severely disabled individual. Resiliency-based approaches are best suited to these circumstances. This model has identified three domains of family functioning—belief systems, organizational patterns, and communication processes (see Walsh, 2006). Belief systems incorporate a "meaning-making" process regarding whatever adversity the family is facing. This may involve professionals assisting families to see a family crisis as a challenge that is occurring for a reason, and helping them to consider it as manageable, though perhaps not solvable. Providing encouragement and helping families to "master the possible" while accepting the inevitable, as well as embedding their experience in their own spiritual values, seeing the challenge as an opportunity for transformation, and finding new possibilities that will result in change and growth can be especially helpful.

In the domain of organizational patterns, assisting families to reorganize in a way that may better meet the challenge and find whatever stability they can, while offering one another nurturance and mutual support, and collaborating in a way that respects individual needs and differences, is useful. This may, at times, mean mobilizing extended family members and community support networks (Walsh, 2006).

With respect to the domain of communication processes, professionals can help families send each other "clear and consistent messages," share their feelings, and show "mutual empathy" (Walsh, 2006, p. 107). The professional can help the family members find any humour they can in a situation and own their feelings while avoiding blame. What can be especially important is assisting families to solve problems together by agreeing on goals, with each family member taking responsibility to reach them (Walsh, 2006). Complaints refocused as aims are more likely to be successfully resolved.

Families experiencing trauma and loss are going through a painful process, but with supportive and caring assistance from professionals, they can make the transition and grow stronger and more resilient in the process.

## FAMILY WORK IN MENTAL HEALTH

In 1945, Henry Richardson wrote a book about mental health recovery entitled *Patients Have Families*. It was the first time that psychiatry turned its focus toward families. Initially, this was not a positive development, in that families tended to be stigmatized and blamed for the mental illness of family members. However, more recent efforts seek to help family members who are caring for someone with mental illness to manage their stress levels using cognitive behavioural therapy. The goal is to support more effective problem-solving capability on the part of both the individual with mental illness and the family to help them address their life goals (Falloon, Boyd, & McGill, 1984). There is also a focus on stress reduction related to symptoms of mental illness, which is achieved through family education related to mental health diagnoses (Anderson, Reiss, & Hogarty, 1986).

## SOCIOLOGICAL CONTRIBUTIONS

The field of sociology has made contributions to work with families through the notion of social constructionism, which suggests that people together construct reality through shared meanings in which communication plays a key role (Leeds-Hurwitz, 2009). Brief solution-focused therapy is based upon this concept, helping families to envision what they would like the future to be and then coming up with ways that this might be achieved. Building this future often involves using family members' strengths, previous successes, and existing resources (Guterman, 2006).

Specific approaches used are miracle, exception, coping, scaling questions, and compliments (Institute for Solution Focused Therapy, 2013).

Miracle questions involve asking what small steps the family might take to begin improving things right away. Exception questions ask families to describe situations where problems could have developed, but did not, and why they did not. Coping questions ask families to focus on how they have managed in the past or are managing in the present. Scaling questions tune in to a family's level of hope, sense of progress, optimism, and feelings of confidence.

Symbolic interaction theory, a theory developed by George Herbert Mead, was designed to examine face-to-face interactions in families and how these were interpreted by family members. It is based on an understanding that family members use language and symbols in interacting with each other and the world. Subjective meaning derived through interaction with others is how individuals make sense of their world, and how they behave as a result. In families, meaning is constantly created and recreated through family interactions (Carter & Fuller, 2015).

Conflict theory, developed by Karl Marx, is concerned with power relations and social inequalities, and how those with power and status are able to control resources in a society and in a family. Conflict theorists believe that family structures contribute to maintaining social inequality through reinforcement of the status quo. Conflict theorists would also argue that male dominance in a family contributes to the inequality of women in society, and that it teaches girls to acquiesce to boys from an early age. It also examines the impact of social inequality on families, and how poverty and racism contribute to family distress (Hammond & Cheney, n.d.).

Structural functional theory, developed by Herbert Spencer and Robert Merton, defines a family as a complex system that either creates stability and a sense of solidarity or detracts from both. Families are considered to behave in ways that promote the positive social functioning of their members or contribute to their inability to function appropriately in the larger society. This theory has been widely criticized for being a conservative approach, intended to maintain the status quo. It was challenged and, in some ways, discredited by later conflict theorists (Elwell, 2013).

## DIRECTIVE APPROACHES

A much more directive type of family intervention is strategic family therapy, also called problem-solving therapy, developed by Jay Haley. This approach incorporates aspects of Minuchin's structural family therapy, wherein the professional uses direct influence on each family member to bring about change in addressing their concerns. In this model, the professional decides what will occur during family meetings, and gives direction as well as interpreting communication metaphors—the various meanings in chosen communications (Haley, 1987).

What most empowerment-oriented interventions have in common is a focus on strengths, encouraging families to set their own agendas and identify their own successes and future directions. It is assumed that the family knows best what will help them.

What more directive interventions have in common is that problems are identified, and the professional determines, based upon their assessment, what the family needs to work on and then gives direction and suggestions to family members on how to better their situation.

There is no clear consensus on which modes of intervention are best. With so many possibilities available, each professional should choose which model best suits their own philosophy of practice since the comfort level of the professional is critical in helping the family to feel at ease.

## CHAPTER SUMMARY

This chapter has provided an overview of the different ways that professionals can choose to work with families, based on their particular perspective and preferences. While no one approach is recommended, it is suggested that strengths-based approaches may prevent a "professional knows best" perspective and allow families to choose their own change agendas.

## FURTHER READING

Becvar, R. J., & Becvar, D. S. (2017). *Systems theory and family therapy: A primer* (3rd ed.). Lanham, MD: Hamilton Books.

Gehart, D., & Tuttle, A. (2002). *Theory based treatment planning for marriage and family therapists: Integrating theory and practice.* Pacific Grove, CA: Brooks Cole.

## CLASSROOM RESOURCES

*An evening with Salvadore Minuchin.* (2017). Milton H. Erickson Foundation. https://www.youtube.com/watch?v=MG-UvrVEkzw

*Salvador Minuchin on family therapy.* (2012). PsychotherapyNet. https://www.youtube.com/watch?v=2evU02UocpQ

## CLASSROOM ACTIVITY

### Debate

Resolve that structural-functional (or conflict, or symbolic interactionism) theory is the best approach to understanding families. Each "team" takes a position and makes its points after researching each approach.

## QUESTIONS FOR REFLECTION

1. Would an empowerment or a directive approach suit you best, and why?
2. Why do you think there are so many different models for working with families?
3. If you were to use a resiliency-based model to work with families, what kinds of interactions might you have with family members?
4. Can you foresee any problems in using a problem-solving model, and if so, what do you think those problems might be?

## REFERENCES

Anderson, C. M., Reiss, D. J., & Hogarty, G. E. (1986). *Schizophrenia and the family.* New York, NY: The Guilford Press.

Boyd-Franklin, N., & Bry, B. H. (2000). *Reaching out in family therapy: Home-based, school, and community interventions.* New York, NY: The Guilford Press.

Boyd-Franklin, N., Cleeck, E. N., Wofsky, M., & Munday, B. (2013). *Therapy in the real world: Effective treatments for challenging problems.* New York, NY: The Guilford Press.

Carter, M. J., & Fuller, C. (2015). Symbolic interactionism. California State University. Retrieved from http://www.sagepub.net/isa/resources/pdf/symbolic%20 interactionism.pdf

Elwell, F. W. (2013, June). Sociocultural systems: Principles of structure and change. Edmonton, AB: AU Press

Falloon, I. R. H., Boyd J. L., & McGill C. W. (1984). *Family care of schizophrenia.* New York, NY: The Guilford Press.

Greenberg, G. R., Ganshorn, K., & Danilkewic, A. (2001). Solution-focused therapy: A counseling model for busy family physicians. *Canadian Family Physician, 47,* 2289–2295.

Guterman, J. T. (2006). *Mastering the art of solution-focused counseling.* Alexandria, VA: American Counseling Association.

Haley, J. (1987). *Problem-solving therapy.* San Francisco, CA: Jossey-Bass.

Hammond, R., & Cheney, P. (n.d.). Family theories. Utah Valley University. Retrieved from https://www.canyons.edu/Offices/DistanceLearning/OER/Documents/Open%20Textbooks%20At%20COC/Sociology/SOCI%20103/Family%20Theories.pdf

Institute for Solution Focused Therapy. (2013). What is solution focused therapy? Retrieved from www.solutionfocused.net/solutionfocusedtherapy.html

Jackson, J. K. (1954). The adjustment of the family to the crisis of alcoholism. *Quarterly Journal of Studies on Alcohol, 15*, 562–586.

Leeds-Hurwitz, W. (2009). *Social construction of reality*. In S. Littlejohn & K. Foss (Eds.), *Encyclopedia of communication theory*. Thousand Oaks, CA: Sage.

McCrady, B. S., Epstein, E. E., Cook, S., Jensen, N., & Hildebrandt, T. (2009). A randomized trial of individual and couple behavioral alcohol treatment for women. *Journal of Consulting and Clinical Psychology, 77*(2), 243–256.

Meyers, R. J., Miller, W. R., Smith, J. E., & Tonigan, J. S. (2002). A randomized trial of two methods of engaging treatment refusing drug users through concerned significant others. *Journal of Consulting and Clinical Psychology, 70*, 1182–1185.

Miller, W. R., Forcehimes, A. A., & Zweben, A. (2011). *Treating addiction: A guide for professionals*. New York, NY: The Guilford Press.

Nichols, M. P. (2010). *The essentials of family therapy* (5th ed.). Don Mills, ON: Pearson.

Prochaska, J. O., & DiClemente, C. C. (1982). Transtheoretical therapy: Toward a more integrative model of change. *Psychotherapy: Theory, Research and Practice, 19*, 276–288.

Richardson, H. B. (1945). *Patients have families*. New York, NY: Commonwealth Fund.

Search Institute of Minneapolis. (1990). Developmental assets. Retrieved from www.search-institute.org/research/developmental-assets

Sheridan, S. M., & Burt, J. D. (2009). Family-centered positive psychology. In S. J. Lopez & C. R. Snyder (Eds.), *Oxford handbook of positive psychology* (2nd ed.). New York, NY: Oxford University Press.

Sheridan, S. M., Warnes, E., Cowan, R. J., Schemm, A., & Clarke, B. L. (2004). Family-centered positive psychology: Building on strengths to promote student success. *Psychology in the Schools, 41*, 7–17.

Walsh, F. (2006). *Strengthening family resilience* (2nd ed.). New York, NY: The Guilford Press.

# CHAPTER 14

# Working with Parents with Complex Needs

*Disability is a matter of perception. If you can do just one thing well, you're needed by someone.*

—Martina Navratilova

## CHAPTER OVERVIEW

Sometimes professionals work with parents who have complex needs because of an intellectual, mental health, neurological, or physical disability. Having a disability does not preclude someone being a parent, but someone with a disability may require accommodation, and in some cases intensive assistance, to facilitate parenthood, especially if they have difficulty processing information, solving problems, and engaging appropriately with others. This special clinical assistance should be considered the same as what they receive to help them with activities of daily living (The Arc, 2014).

There are, however, situations where the rights of a child do conflict with a parent's right to have a child. Just as with individuals who do not have disabilities, where a parent places a child in jeopardy, child welfare authorities must intervene. This chapter outlines the many aspects of parenting when someone has a disability.

## THE IMPACT OF STIGMA AND DISCRIMINATION

Parenthood and disability is a sensitive topic because of the long and painful history associated with it. Historically, discriminatory attitudes led to authorities in some jurisdictions denying parenthood to people with disabilities. In some cases, this involved involuntary sterilization. In other cases, the children of parents with disabilities were immediately removed from their care. There was a presumption underlying these actions: having a disability equalled being an unfit parent. People tended to see deficits rather than abilities. This sometimes caused people with disabilities to avoid authorities altogether, fearing that their children would be taken away from them.

Parents who internalized society's negative views of their ability to parent may have developed traits based upon these views that actually undermined their ability to parent. These traits include learned dependency, wherein they rely on others to make decisions and to take the initiative. They may also be overly compliant, lack self-sufficiency, fail to question and instead fear authority figures, have limited social and problem-solving skills, and have low expectations of being treated equally while feeling stigmatized and unwanted. Some have learned compensatory behaviours to conceal any shortcomings in order to avoid harsh consequences for failing to live up to others' expectations. In some cases, parents themselves have suffered significant abuse and neglect, thereby increasing the danger of intergenerational transmission or overcompensation with their own children. They may also live in poverty and sometimes fall prey to unscrupulous "helpers" (Green & Cruz, n.d.b). Add to this the fact that day support to parents with disabilities continues to be lacking, as are other types of support, and being able to parent becomes especially difficult. Specialized parenting programs, for example, are almost non-existent.

What many do not see are human beings who love their offspring and, like all parents, want to do what is right for them. They have good intentions but need help to bring these to fruition and raise healthy children who adapt well to the world.

## THE CHALLENGES FOR PROFESSIONALS

Professionals working with parents with developmental disabilities may need to overcome their clients' fears and distrust because of previous negative encounters with the "helping professions." Only then can they establish a rapport and an understanding of parents' individual needs and required supports in raising children. They will have to be on the lookout for any minimization of difficulties in an effort to avoid having children taken away. By being supportive and offering choices in how to parent, rather than criticism, professionals will be able to earn trust over time. Humour also helps (Green & Cruz, n.d.b). Of particular importance will be determining whether or not the family's basic needs for food, shelter, housing, transportation, and social support are met. Parents may need assistance in filling out any applications for financial or social assistance from municipalities or government-funded agencies. Also important is to help parents focus on and learn one task at a time, sometimes breaking it down into smaller steps, and demonstrating it by using concrete examples, pictorial manuals, guided instruction, and positive reinforcement. Expectations may have to be kept at reasonable levels and additional support built in initially, until the parent is able to take on more responsibilities. As Green and Cruz (n.d.b) point out, it can be helpful for professionals to reflect on their own attitudes toward parents with disabilities, to ensure that their treatment of the parents is respectful, and to ask how they might feel in a similar situation.

## PARENTING ASSESSMENT

Cruz and Green (n.d.a) recommend using an ecological assessment to examine strengths and stresses in determining how families where parents and/or children have disabilities interact with their environment. It is especially important to ascertain how much of an informal support network the family has, including extended family, neighbours, and religious and other community support. Where assistance is lacking, professionals need to help the family access more formal supports through social assistance programs and various community social services. Items that should be considered as part of an ecological assessment are daily living skills, such as feeding and bathing; any type of behaviour that may be self-injurious; safety, health, and medical needs; relational needs, including cultural factors; financial and other resources; and coping strategies.

Given appropriate support, it is likely that parents with developmental disabilities will learn good parenting skills and be able to function effectively as parents. A study done by Feldman et al. (1992, p. 205) found that "parent training may be a viable option to the removal of the child from the home when parenting skill deficits place the child's well-being in jeopardy."

## PARENTING WITH A MENTAL ILLNESS

With one in five Canadians having some form of mental illness, it is likely that there are a high number of people who struggle with mental illness who are also parents (Government of Canada, 2006). Gopfert, Webster, and Seeman (2006) have suggested that 50 percent of individuals with mental illness have children. Bassani, Padoin, Philipp, and Veldhuizen (2009) have found that the number of children living with parents with affective disorders like depression may in fact be much higher than reported. Therefore, many children live in families where parents are struggling with mental illness. Parents with mental illness wrestle with a host of issues that make parenting a challenge. Individuals with depression may also suffer from insomnia—a chronic lack of sleep. They may have problems with focus and concentration and be moody and irritable. This has an impact on their children in many ways, including making the parent less available and unable to actively interact with them. This can cause children to lag behind in language and social skills (Tartakovsky, 2011). The stigma of mental illness may cause children to feel shame and not discuss any family problems with school or other counsellors.

Particular attention should be paid to children who have a parent or parents with mental illness. They may feel stigmatized, lonely, and vulnerable. They may experience hypervigilance and extreme anxiety because of the unpredictable nature of their environment while growing up. It is important to share information about parental mental illness with children to avoid them blaming themselves when incidents occur in their lives related to a parent's mental health crisis. Some may have taken on caregiving responsibilities with younger siblings and require help to allow them to be children instead of young adults (Mehta, 2017).

## THE IMPORTANCE OF INFORMATION

Tartakovsky (2011) suggests several ways that professionals can help parents with mental illness. Because of the risk of children also developing mental illness, and because of the lack of good information, it is up to professionals to provide this to the whole family in a caring and supportive way.

Many children of all ages lack information concerning mental illness, and this can result in younger children fearing that their parent will die, especially if they are hospitalized. Older children may be concerned that they themselves could develop the same type of mental illness (Mordoch, 2010). In some cases, children hear fragments of conversations, especially when there is a crisis and other family members become involved. This leaves them with partial information that may add to their fears. It is especially important to be honest with children and to provide them with good, clear information about mental illness, since attempting to shield them or offering them vague answers seems to increase their fears.

# RISKS FOR CHILDREN OF PARENTS WITH PSYCHOTIC DISORDERS

Wang and Goldschmidt (1996) found children to be at special risk where parents have what are termed psychotic disorders that may involve hallucinations and distorted thinking. These authors found that children in 25 percent of these families ended up in foster care and institutions, and about 40 percent had never received any professional help. They found that 33 percent of parents with mental illness wanted support but never received it, and many did not know where to go to get help. Mordoch (2010, p. 1) says, "A culture of non-intervention in the organization of health and welfare services may inhibit prevention and early intervention efforts for this population. Thus children are left with few resources to assist them." Essentially, these children are abandoned by the system as well as, in some cases, by their parents.

# POSITIVE PROFESSIONAL INTERVENTIONS

There is a particular need for professional intervention in these situations, to connect these families with assistance in day-to-day parenting and to teach them how to maintain connections with extended family, friends, and neighbours in a positive way, all while assisting family members and individuals themselves to understand their condition (Nicholson, Sweeney, & Geller, 1998). Many parents with mental illness also fear having their children removed, and therefore lack trust in professionals, relying instead on familial support networks that can become exhausted unless additional assistance is provided.

Since improving parental functioning and helping parents to attend to their own needs helps children, urging parents to seek treatment and develop a crisis plan in collaboration with mental health professionals to manage their symptoms and keep themselves and their children safe will be helpful to the family. Reducing isolation and increasing social support by connecting with family and friends can help to normalize the situation for both parents and children and also give children a sense that there are others they can rely on. Having others who can take over if a parent is becoming symptomatic can be especially helpful, as is making sure that children have normal activities in their lives at school and in the community, and with parents when they are feeling well. Parents and children can use their strengths and passions to find activities that bring them both pleasure.

Marsh (2011) believes that it is especially important to reassure the children in these families that they are not to blame for their parents' illness. They also need to know that there is hope because the impact of having a parent with mental illness can be significant for them. She points out that there is a major grieving aspect, and the whole family "may mourn for the relative they have known and loved before the onset of the illness, for the anguish of their family, and for their own losses." Stability may often be out of reach in a family where a family member has mental illness, as families attempt to cope with the daily challenges that come with the illness as well as the social stigma associated with it.

## IMPACT OF PARENTAL MENTAL ILLNESS ON CHILDREN

Where there are very young children and a parent has a mental illness, their more limited coping skills and dependency on others make them much more vulnerable than older family members. Marsh (2011) informs us that there is a "significant relationship between age at the onset of a relative's mental illness and its impact … the younger the family member the greater the potential impact." A high degree of perfectionism, due to having to take on responsibilities too early, is only one outcome. If they have to spend much of their own time and emotional energy caring for a parent with mental illness, some children can grow into adults who have problems with identity formation and low self-esteem. They may look to others for approval and feel that they have to maintain control in every aspect of their lives to compensate for the chaos that is or was their home situation. Even where hospitalization does not occur, because of behaviour related to distorted thinking, hallucinations, or delusions, children can be negatively affected. Marsh points out that children may also experience "survivor syndrome" because their parent is suffering while they have been spared. This can negatively affect how well they do in school and their relationships with others, especially as they attempt to balance their two worlds: home and school.

As children who have parents with mental illness and/or addiction problems grow into adulthood, many are left with residual feelings of being isolated from others, alienated, and alone. They trust no one and have difficulty handling intimacy. They may take on partners who themselves need care, and many find it difficult to commit over the long term in relationships or work situations.

For example, John's father is narcissistic, and his mother is an alcoholic. His father's narcissistic demands on his mother caused her to invest much of her time and energy on him. While she cooked, cleaned, and served the children good meals, neither she nor their father were ever emotionally available for John and his two siblings. All three carry the scars of their parents' emotional neglect. John now takes on far too much responsibility in his life. He is married to a woman who is "high maintenance" and who regularly makes unreasonable demands of him that he feels he needs to fulfill. He is overly protective of his own children, perhaps psychically shielding them from his own pain or the pain caused him by his parents. He is a workaholic and often depressed. He comes home, makes dinner, then sits on the couch and watches movies until he falls asleep. The next day is exactly the same. He has a friend who is good to him, but he is unsure of how to accept being treated well, often disappears without a word, and tends not to return the caring his friend offers. He copes by drinking and suffers from anxiety to the point where his hands sweat and shake. He also suffers from gastrointestinal ailments, which may be part of a post-traumatic response to the chaos and pain of his childhood. John has no insight into why he is suffering; he only knows that he is. He does not understand the negative legacy given to him by his parents, and defends them, as he does his wife and dependent children. His sister also copes by drinking and is emotionally unavailable to her husband and children. She goes to pubs by herself, where she sometimes picks up men or women. She has distanced herself from her parents and wants little or nothing to do with them. She does hold a job, and has managed to maintain a reasonable lifestyle, but she is also depressed and experiences extreme neediness that she attempts to suppress. John's brother can best be described as a "lost child." He has a highly dependent relationship with his wife, lacks initiative, and has largely disappeared from the family scene. All three children from this narcissistic family have grown up with the terrible legacy left them by their parents, and continue to suffer into adulthood.

It is not uncommon for children who have parents with mental illness to take on caregiving roles with others in adulthood, and some are drawn to "helping professions" for this reason (Marsh, 2011).

## THE IMPACT OF PARENTAL NARCISSISM

Children with exceedingly narcissistic parents are often forced to fend for themselves, as their needs come last. Donaldson-Pressman and Pressman (quoted in

McBride, 2011) state that "the typical adult from a narcissistic family is filled with unacknowledged anger, feels like a hollow person, feels inadequate and defective, suffers from periodic anxiety and depression and has no clue about how [they] got that way." McBride suggests that children who grow up in narcissistic families live according to unspoken rules that prevent emotional connection to their parents: "They are basically invisible—not heard, seen or nurtured. Tragically, conversely, this set of rules allows the parents to have no boundaries with the children and to use and abuse them as they see fit." Common dynamics include possible abusive and neglectful behaviour; form over substance, with image being everything; judgmental and critical parenting that gives children the message that they are not good enough; not meeting children's needs because of a lack of parental empathy; seeing children as there for the convenience of their parents; indirect communication and messages that are sent through one family member to another; insufficient boundaries; neglecting the needs of the children on the part of the non-narcissistic parent to serve the needs of the other; pitting children against each other; denied and repressed feelings; and disguising any or all of these dynamics (McBride, 2011). The damage to children growing up in a narcissistic home is considerable.

## SINGLE PARENTS WITH MENTAL ILLNESS

Children assuming a parental role can be a common consequence of having a parent with a mental illness, especially if they are living in a single-parent family. The following case study illustrates this.

Robert's mother was often depressed, and sat in front of the TV almost every day in her housecoat. Robert took care of himself and his younger brothers and sisters, making sure they were fed, got ready for school, had their lunches, did their homework, and went to bed on time. The only problem is that Robert was only 12 years old, with two younger siblings, ages 6 and 9. Robert did not have time to play like other children, and was fearful of bringing friends home because of the state his mother was in. Robert did not have time to be a child and was missing important developmental milestones because of his need to meet others' needs as opposed to his own.

Children like Robert who grow up too soon may be left with scars that last a lifetime. They may become workaholics, always feeling too responsible, feeling that they have to take care of others at their own expense and never really being able to rest or relax. This can take its toll in emotional and physical illness, both in childhood and adulthood.

## PARENTS WITH BORDERLINE PERSONALITY DISORDER DIAGNOSIS

In the case of parents, especially mothers, diagnosed with a borderline personality disorder, the situation of children is likely to be just as difficult and possibly worse. Stepp, Whalen, Pilonis, Hipwell, and Levine (2011, p. 1) describe borderline personality disorder (BPD) as "characterized by a pattern of intense and stormy relationships, uncontrollable anger, poor impulse control, affective instability, identity and cognitive disturbances, and recurrent suicidal behavior.... Individuals with BPD are likely to face a host of negative outcomes, including poor treatment response, and poor social, occupational, and academic outcomes.... The day-to-day life of those with this disorder is fraught with high levels of misery, which often endures even after symptoms of impulsivity and suicide behaviors remit." This makes parenting with any degree of warmth and consistency almost impossible.

What makes all of this especially worrisome is the high degree of intergenerational transmission that occurs in children who have a parent with this diagnosis (White, Gunderson, Zanarini, & Hudson, 2003). In fact, there appears to be a 4- to 20-fold increase in BPD in first-degree relatives of someone with this condition (Barnow, Spitzer, Grabe, Kessler, & Freyberger, 2006). Not only that, but there is now evidence that this intergenerational transmission may also be genetic. Distel et al. (2007) have found that the tendency for children to inherit their parents' symptoms may be as high as 42 percent. These symptoms may include a high degree of reactivity and impulsivity.

For example, Marie had a mother with a diagnosis of borderline personality disorder, meaning that her mother had unstable relationships often characterized by high degrees of conflict. Her moods fluctuated significantly, as she at times loved and at other times hated various individuals in her sphere, including her own child. Marie's mother could be caring, but usually the caring had strings attached and an expectation that Marie would, in turn, take care of her. Her mother's demands for caring were sometimes beyond what Marie, at only nine years of age, could provide. When this happened, Marie's mother would become enraged and accuse her of not loving her. Marie lived in a constant state of fear that she would be rejected by her mother and placed in foster care.

Lamont (2006) states that a mother's own sense of instability can be a very destabilizing factor in a child's life: "Since it is through the unique relationship with the mother that the infant develops a sense of self, this distorted, unpredictable, and fluctuating self-image of the mother is likely to have negative effects on the child's own self-image."

Stepp et al. (2011, p. 76) consider children raised by mothers with a borderline personality disorder to be in a "high risk group ... given the wide array of poor psychosocial outcomes that have been found in these children." Because of these mothers' own fears of rejection and abandonment, these authors inform us that children may be subjected to "hostile control and passive aloofness in their interactions with their children," (p. 76) something that is possibly unique to mothers with this condition.

Lamont (2006) has also pointed out that many children who have mothers with this psychiatric diagnosis are victims of verbal and/or physical abuse because of the volatile nature of their mothers' personalities and their tendency to become intensely angry frequently. Furthermore, parents with this diagnosis may engage in risk-taking behaviours, including substance abuse, driving recklessly, and engaging in unsafe sex with different partners. They may also suffer from eating and other disorders. In some cases, they may have multiple sex partners and expose their children to these individuals, thereby raising the spectre of possible sexual abuse of their children.

Because of the highly disruptive, and in some cases, dangerous environments created for children when a parent or parents have a diagnosis of borderline personality disorder, intervention is often necessary, as well as child welfare involvement.

## PROFESSIONAL INTERVENTIONS

Stepp et al. (2011) suggest that attachment therapy, psychoeducational approaches that teach parenting, and therapeutic intervention for the parent, possibly using mindfulness approaches to self and in parenting, may be helpful in reducing the likelihood of harm to children. This is thought to increase self-awareness and objectivity in the parenting role, allowing the parent to differentiate their own emotions from those of children exhibiting strong emotions. This type of self-awareness may also help parents to understand when they have reached their own limits and it is time to seek support from others.

Significant assistance in the form of respite, parenting education, the building of social support systems, individual treatment, family therapy, and reparenting help are needed to assist parents who have developmental disabilities and mental health conditions.

Where parents have physical and neurological conditions, they may need direct assistance in the physical demands involved in parenting as well as help in teaching their children about their condition. The impact of stigma is also considerable for many of these families. Professionals can help greatly by engaging in public education related to parenting with a disability, and by encouraging community agencies and organizations to be supportive of these parents and children. If we accept that it takes a community to raise a child, then this becomes more critical when a child has a parent living with a disability.

Marsh (2011) has found that some children can have a highly resilient response to a chaotic family life caused by mental illness. They seem to "rebound from adversity" and "prevail over the circumstances of [their] lives." A large number of children report that they have acquired strength and higher levels of empathy and compassion toward others as a result of living with a parent who has mental illness. Some described having "healthier attitudes and priorities and greater appreciation of life," even as they mourn the loss of a stable family life. However, Mordoch (2010, pp. 1–2) has challenged this view, saying this research "mainly relied on imposed views of resiliency filtered through adult eyes and focused on behavioural competence which minimized children's subjective experiences." What this means is that researchers looked too closely for signs of resilience in children's behaviour without considering fully the quality of their daily lives.

By coming to recognize that their own needs matter as well as the needs of others, adult children who grew up in families where there was mental illness can make significant gains and improve the quality of their lives. Cognitive behavioural therapy can assist them to re-evaluate some of their belief systems. Facing and dealing with their own feelings of fear, disappointment, and rage because of their own unmet needs, and then seeking to meet these needs in a variety of ways, can help them to teach their own children that their needs are important and thereby aid them in circumventing the intergenerational transmission that often occurs in these families.

## CHAPTER SUMMARY

This chapter has outlined the challenges faced by children growing up in households where one or both parents have a disability, and examined the feelings, needs, and fears experienced by parents who have disabilities. It has included some ways that professionals can be helpful to these families and assist them in reducing the risk of intergenerational transmission of symptoms to future generations.

## FURTHER READING

Allen, D. M. (2018). *Coping with critical, demanding, and dysfunctional parents: Powerful strategies to help adult children maintain boundaries and stay sane.* Oakland, CA: New Harbinger.

Norah Fry Research Centre. (2009). *Supporting parents with learning disabilities and difficulties: Stories of positive practice.* Bristol, UK: Norah Fry Research Centre.

University of Hertfordshire. (2019). Parents with intellectual disabilities. http://www. intellectualdisability.info/family/articles/parents-with-intellectual-disabilities

## CLASSROOM RESOURCES

*Attachment and parents with intellectual disabilities.* (2018). Stockholm University. https:// www.youtube.com/watch?v=-zkP8PyvECw

*Parenting with a learning disability.* (2016). Attitude. https://www.youtube.com/ watch?v=FczB82C3T6g

## CLASSROOM ACTIVITY

Show the video *Parenting with a Learning Disability* and, in a whole-class discussion, ask students what they took from the video. Then ask for ways they might work with this father and daughter that would be positive and capitalize on strengths.

## QUESTIONS FOR REFLECTION

1. What is your view on whether or not someone with a developmental disability should be allowed to raise a child?
2. How might you try to assist someone with a developmental disability in raising a child? What resources might you rely on?

3. How would you feel about working with a family where both parents are narcissistic and lack insight?
4. What challenges do you think you might encounter as a worker attempting to help a parent with a borderline personality diagnosis?

## REFERENCES

The Arc. (2014). Parents with intellectual and/or developmental disabilities. Retrieved from www.thearc.org/page.aspx?pid=2375

Barnow, S., Spitzer, C., Grabe, H. J., Kessler, C., & Freyberger, H. J. (2006). Individual characteristics, familial experience, and psychopathology in children of mothers with borderline personality disorder. *Journal of the American Academy of Child and Adolescent Psychiatry*, *45*(8), 965–972.

Bassani, D., Padoin, D., Philipp, C., & Veldhuizen, S. (2009). Estimating the number of children exposed to parental psychiatric disorders through a national health survey. *Child and Adolescent Psychiatry and Mental Health*, *19*(1), 3–6.

Distel, M. A., Trull, T. J., Derom, C. A., Thiery, E. W., Grimmer, M. A., Martin, N. G., … Boomsma, D. I. (2007). Heritability of borderline personality disorder features is similar across three countries. *Psychological Medicine*, *38*(9), 1219–1229.

Donaldson-Pressman, S., & Pressman, R. M. (1997). *The narcissistic family: Diagnosis and treatment*. San Francisco, CA: Jossey-Bass.

Feldman, M. A., Case, L., Garrick, M., MacIntyre-Grande, W., Carnwell, J., & Sparks, B. (1992). Teaching child care skills to mothers with developmental disabilities. *Journal of Applied Behavioral Analysis*, *25*(1), 205–215.

Gopfert, M., Webster, J., & Seeman, M. V. (2006). *Parental psychiatric disorder: Distressed parents and their families*. New York, NY: Cambridge University Press.

Government of Canada. (2006). The human face of mental health and mental illness in Canada. Retrieved from http://publications.gc.ca/site/eng/296507/publication.html

Green, N., & Cruz, V. (n.d.a). Assessing strengths and stresses with families with children with special needs: An ecological perspective. Metropolitan State College of Denver Social Work Program.

Green, N., & Cruz, V. (n.d.b). Challenges facing parents with developmental disabilities. Metropolitan State College of Denver Social Work Program.

Lamont, A. E. (2006). How a mother with borderline personality disorder affects her children. Teacher's College, Columbia University. *Graduate Student Journal of Psychology*, *8*. Retrieved from http://bpdfamily.com/bpdresources/nk_a108.htm

Marsh, D. T. (2011). Children of parents with mental illness. BC Council for Families. https://youngparentoutreach.com/children-of-parents-with-mental-illness/

McBride, K. (2011). The legacy of distorted love: The narcissistic family tree. *Psychology Today*. Retrieved from https://www.psychologytoday.com/ca/blog/the-legacy-distorted-love/201105/the-narcissistic-family-tree

Mehta, V. (2017, September 5). Growing up with a mentally ill parent: 6 core experiences. Retrieved from https://www.psychologytoday.com/us/blog/head-games/201709/growing-mentally-ill-parent-6-core-experiences

Mordoch, E. (2010). How children understand parental mental illness. *Journal of the Canadian Academy of Child and Adolescent Psychiatry, 19*(1), 19–25. Retrieved from www.ncbi.nlm.nih.gov/pmc/articles/PMC2809442/

Nicholson, J., Sweeney, E. M., & Geller, J. L. (1998). Mothers with mental illness: I. The competing demands of parenting and living with mental illness. *Psychiatric Services, 49*, 635–642.

Stepp, S. D., Whalen, D. J., Pikonis, P. A., Hipwell, A. E., & Levine, M. D. (2011). Children of mothers with borderline personality disorder: Identifying parenting behaviors as potential targets for intervention. *Personality Disorder, 3*(1), 76–91. Retrieved from www.ncbi.nlm.nih.gov/pmc/articles/PMC3268672/

Tartakovsky, M. (2011). Tips for parenting with a mental illness. *Psych Central*. Retrieved from http://psychcentral.com/lib/tips-for-parenting-with-a-mental-illness/0005765

Wang, A., & Goldschmidt, V. (1996). Interviews with psychiatric inpatients about professional intervention with regard to their children. *Acta Psychiatrica Scandinavica, 93*, 57–61.

White, C. N., Gunderson, J. G., Zanarini, M. C., & Hudson, J. I. (2003). Family studies of borderline personality disorder: A review. *Harvard Review of Psychiatry, 11*, 8–19.

# CHAPTER 15

# Working with Military Families

*Military families are a direct reflection of the mutually reinforcing nature
of the relationship between the "military" and "family"—as one changes, so
does the other.*

  —V. Snyder (2013)

## CHAPTER OVERVIEW

Working with military families involves understanding military culture, the special demands faced by these families, and the military perspective that may influence the way that families seek help and what help they consider reasonable (Van Hook, 2014). Many in the military eschew seeking help for fear of being considered weak or facing career reprisals (Pryce, Pryce, & Shakelford, 2012). Recent military engagements in the Middle East have put considerable pressure on military families in both Canada and the United States as well as in other countries. Both men and women serve in the military, but men serve in far greater numbers than women. Since over half of active duty soldiers are married and just under half have children, in some cases very young children (Pryce et al., 2012), the impact on family life of duty overseas can be significant.

Military families tend to have higher education and income levels than the general population, and these can be protective factors (Pryce et al., 2012). Those who serve come from a variety of ethnic, cultural, and racial backgrounds, and some may be gay or lesbian, and these factors must be carefully considered by professionals working with military families.

Palmer (2008) has discussed different phases of stress for military families in the "relocation, deployment, and reunification" stages. Military families may be relocated several times. While this can be disruptive, it need not necessarily be harmful in that children may learn adaptation skills that can serve them well in life (Van Hook, 2014).

## PHASES OF STRESS IN MILITARY FAMILIES

When a nation is at war, deployment is extremely stressful for military families because of the danger posed and because of the reorganization demanded of the family in the absence of a key family member. The deployment phase can be quite unnerving for spouses and children as there is often confusion about what each particular deployment will entail and its impact on both parents, as well as fear for the deployed parent's safety. Children often express fear, helplessness, anger, sadness, nervousness, and worry during this period. Spouses suffer similar feelings and may also have to deal with depression and anxiety, along with their inherent sleep disruptions, and acute stress. All of these factors are exacerbated during lengthy deployments (Van Hook, 2014).

When a loved one is missing in action, families face what Van Hook (2014) terms "ambiguous loss," where there is no closure. Adjustment and adaptation become much more difficult when spouses and children are unsure of what they are adjusting and adapting to. Boss (2006) has dealt extensively with ambiguous loss and encourages professionals to acknowledge the ambiguity along with the family. Families will need help to find meaning in it, or to find the positives (such as the heroism and self-sacrifice of the loved one who is missing). Professionals can assist the family in developing healing rituals and their own spirituality to cope with the ambiguity sometimes presented by life.

The reunification phase may pose additional issues. As Van Hook (2014) points out, all parties (i.e., family members) will have changed during the deployment. Spouses will have learned to cope on their own, while children may have reached different developmental stages. The deployed family member will certainly have changed in a variety of ways because of their exposure to the war situation. All of these factors can complicate a homecoming.

Numerous stressors present themselves at this stage that deeply affect family life. This is especially true when the deployed family member has been injured or traumatized during active duty. Everyone in a family feels the impact of trauma through secondary traumatization. If someone has been injured, there will also be additional caregiving responsibilities for a spouse and possibly older children.

Armstrong, Best, and Domenici (2006) discuss various issues that can occur for military personnel deployed to a war-torn country. For instance, "one typical way to cope with the daily stresses of a war operation is to use drugs or alcohol. Drinking after a difficult day is a common way to unwind, relax, and enjoy some downtime with fellow service members" (p. 25). Alcohol, as Armstrong et al. point out, can be an avoidance strategy that helps someone cope with particularly distressing experiences and may become habitual if it is used to avoid disturbing feelings, to help with insomnia, and to allow someone to engage with others and fit in.

The difficulty with avoidance strategies is that they can deteriorate into "phobias, panic attacks, and post-traumatic stress" (Armstrong et al., 2006, p. 26), as well as continued alcohol use to cope with the symptoms of all of these. Some signs of alcohol abuse or dependence include having to drink more to gain the same effects and being unable to meet family responsibilities, resulting in conflict with other family members, drunk driving, and endangering others (Armstrong et al., 2006).

One of the most disturbing aspects of reintegration for those who have served in a war zone is the impact of post-traumatic stress on the individual and their family. Moore and Penk (2011, p. 24) state that PTSD can be a lifelong condition that is underreported because of the stigma associated with it within military culture, which "prides itself on a stoic response to extreme duress … [and where] emotional responses such as hyperarousal and nightmares may be considered a significant frailty." Because there are limits to confidentiality when someone sees a mental health professional, especially where family members may be in danger, some choose not to disclose their disturbing feelings. Nevertheless, family members become acutely aware of them.

## THE IMPACT OF RAPE ON FEMALE MILITARY PERSONNEL

Where a returning female family member has been raped, especially by a fellow service member, the situation can become especially complicated upon her return home to her spouse. Women exhibit numerous distressing rape-related symptoms because of rape trauma syndrome, and they are likely to experience three phases of adjustment.

During the acute phase that immediately follows a sexual assault, a survivor may experience ongoing anxiety and fear; feel constantly edgy and startle easily; be unable to focus; experience nightmares and extremely disturbed sleep or insomnia; experience anger, tension, and restlessness; suffer from gastrointestinal symptoms that interfere with eating; experience shaking; and possible self-blame (Moore & Penk, 2011). Because women react differently, and because of the nature of rape itself, each woman will react differently to the trauma. Some may seem calm on the outside and mask their feelings, while others may have obvious symptoms of trauma as well as physical injuries to the vagina, mouth, throat, or breasts (Moore & Penk, 2011). If the rape occurred close to the time of the woman's return to her family, her symptoms may be obvious to her spouse and children, and this can cause a range of reactions, from sympathy and protection to rejection. There are many pressures on the survivor during this period, including having to undergo medical examinations and worry about sexually transmitted diseases, as well as decisions about whether or not to press charges and how or whether to inform family members of what happened. Many survivors will choose not to disclose the reasons for these symptoms in fear of further humiliation or out of a sense of shame, and may also decide not to press charges for fear that they will not be believed or will face additional trauma during a police questioning and court process (University of Alberta Sexual Assault Centre, n.d.).

During the "outward adjustment phase," the victim may experience severe anxiety, a sense of hopelessness, abreaction (flashbacks), and suicidal thoughts. This can be a time where survivors begin a healing process to work through the trauma, or it may be a time where they attempt to repress or deny their feelings, and refuse to discuss the rape. Some may begin to make significant changes to their lives. They may become separated from spouses and old friends, attempt to move away, quit the military and go back to school, or travel to avoid having to relive what occurred.

During the "long-term reorganization" phase, repression and denial may no longer work, and the survivor is forced to begin a healing journey after something in their life triggers symptoms of the assault. If treatment is successful and the survivor is able to work with a therapist, this is a time when they may be able to integrate the assault into their lives and regain their sense of "safety, control, and trust" (University of Alberta Sexual Assault Centre, n.d.).

Protective factors for women during this phase and throughout recovery include support from family and friends, how they previously saw themselves, and the quality of treatment that they receive, as well as whether or not the perpetrator has been prosecuted and/or is now out of their lives.

## MENTAL HEALTH CHALLENGES OF RETURNING PERSONNEL

Men and women returning from a military deployment to a war zone may experience significant mental health and addiction issues that can have a severe impact on their families. Returning military personnel may have experienced a range of traumatic events that affect their mental health, including rape or having participated in particularly gruesome atrocities that could affect their military careers if they admitted to them. In some cases their actions during wartime deployments could lead to criminal charges and arrest. Living with this knowledge imposes additional stressors on them and their families. These individuals may return from war zones with a mixture of strong feelings, including extreme anger, heightened fears, and/or feelings of guilt and shame because of the actions they took or failed to take during their deployment (see Moore & Penk, 2011). What this means is that military personnel may censor what occurred in the war zone and what their own actions were to avoid social censure or other serious consequences. This can prevent them from receiving effective treatment and support.

## PROTECTIVE FACTORS

There are protective factors that can help to shield families with returning members who have been traumatized. Professionals can assist families by helping them to identify these factors and capitalize on them. This includes helping the family to reconnect with extended family and friends who are able to provide social support, helping couples to learn the ways that they can be supportive to each other while ensuring that their own needs for autonomy and support are also met, helping children to engage with friends and learn pro-social coping strategies, discussing ways to promote role flexibility within the family, aiding the family and the returning individual to see the value of their military service to the country and the value of being in the military generally, and outlining the many strengths in the family and in each family member and how these can be used to help the family through this period (Van Hook, 2014).

## TREATMENT AND SUPPORT OPTIONS

It is important for professionals working with returning military personnel to know the range of treatment and support options available to them and their families, provided that they are able to overcome natural reluctance, stigma, and fears of repercussions in order to take advantage of them. Some of these include prolonged exposure therapy, cognitive processing therapy, eye movement desensitization, psychodynamic psychotherapy, and conjoint psychopharmacology where required. In many cases, couple and family therapy will be helpful.

## PROLONGED EXPOSURE THERAPY

Prolonged exposure therapy targets the negative thinking that causes generalized fear responses to environmental triggers (for example, loud noises such as a truck backfiring may trigger the experience of being under fire and cause someone to run for cover). Peterson, Foa, and Riggs (2011, p. 43) suggest that there are two types of negative thinking that "underlie the excessive fear and other negative emotions associated with the trauma memory in patients suffering from PTSD." These have to do with seeing the world as extremely dangerous, and questioning their own competence and ability to remain in the military. In prolonged exposure therapy, which can take up to 15 sessions or more, individuals examine the memories of their trauma and begin to reduce any unrealistic fears they may have. Specifics involved include retelling the story of the trauma until it loses its intensity. The individual thereby regains a more integrated and realistic perspective, and realizes that recounting the trauma is not the same as re-experiencing it. Some individuals fear that they will "go crazy" if they retell the story, and this type of therapy helps them to see that they will not. By re-encountering triggers, they see that these are in and of themselves not dangerous.

## PSYCHOEDUCATION

Psychoeducation is a significant part of this type of therapy, and it can be helpful for families as well as traumatized individuals. All can learn that the person's symptoms are normal under the circumstances, but that they have been overgeneralized to include many other situations and events not related to the actual trauma. The symptoms themselves are PTSD-related and they will improve with help. Helping the person to slow and relax their breathing, perhaps with the assistance of their partner or other family member, can help to alleviate anxiety (Peterson et al., 2011).

## COGNITIVE PROCESSING THERAPY

According to Williams, Galovski, Kattar, and Resick (2011, p. 62), cognitive processing therapy involves three phases. In the first, individuals begin to make sense of the traumatic event and find meaning in it. Discussion occurs regarding how the trauma has affected their beliefs about "safety, trust, power/control, esteem, and intimacy." This is the phase that examines thoughts and feelings and how realistic these are. In the second phase, individuals are encouraged to challenge their own belief systems and feelings about the trauma in an attempt to balance the way they see what happened as well as their world view in general. In phase three, individuals focus primarily on "stuck points" in each of the areas identified above, focusing on alternative ways of thinking about them that are intended to become "current beliefs."

Because military culture itself promotes avoidance of emotions related to the trauma of combat, it can be a challenge to use this approach with military personnel. However, if individuals are able to recover their feelings and thoughts about the event and reorient them to a more balanced way of thinking, they are likely to see significant improvement in trauma-related symptoms.

## EYE MOVEMENT DESENSITIZATION AND REPROCESSING

In describing why eye movement desensitization and reprocessing (EMDR) is helpful, Russell, Lipke, and Figley (2011, p. 75) state that "dysfunctional stored information in memory (neural) networks often 'derived from earlier life experiences that set in motion a continued pattern of affect, behavior, cognitions, and consequent identity structures' that both influences and is triggered by present experience" is what is at the heart of symptom development in PTSD. This is the brain's attempt to heal, but in a maladaptive way. Information is stuck and sometimes mixed up with earlier information in a way that causes emotions, behaviour, and thinking to become disrupted or distorted.

Russell et al. (2011, p. 75) describe EMDR as "an integrative psychotherapy that focuses on all aspects of the traumatic memory, including visual imagery, cognition, emotion, and sensation, as well as preferred modes of functioning, to provide the desensitization and reprocessing that provides relief of traumatic stress symptoms." Essentially, EMDR attempts to take the sting out of these stuck memories, emotions, and thinking by reprocessing them in such a way that an individual can experience them differently. It has eight phases, beginning with a phase in which a client history is taken and rapport is built, a preparation phase in which coping skills are taught and the therapy is explained, an assessment phase in which distressing memories are targeted and rated from worst to no distress, a desensitization phase in which traumatic memories are "reprocessed," and an installation phase where preferred cognitions are paired with a therapist's hand movements until these seem well habituated. In phase six, the individual determines whether or not negative physical sensations still occur related to a traumatic memory. In phase seven, a debriefing session is held in which relaxation techniques are used to attempt to eliminate any remaining distressing feelings or images. Finally, in phase eight, that of re-evaluation, a therapist ensures that all distressing memories have been processed so that current triggers can begin to be eliminated. Arkowitz and Lilienfeld (2012) admit that there are numerous studies that demonstrate EMDR's success in symptom alleviation for people with PTSD over no treatment, and that some preliminary evidence exists pertaining to its efficacy in treating anxiety disorders. However, they point out that it does not work better than standard therapies like cognitive behavioral or imaginal exposure (where someone is gradually exposed to an image in their minds). In fact, some suggest that the reason EMDR works is because of the imaginal exposure aspect of it. So, while it is better than doing nothing or engaging in a simple supportive listening approach, it is not better than cognitive behavioral therapy, for example, in the treatment of PTSD and anxiety.

## PSYCHODYNAMIC PSYCHOTHERAPY

The Canadian Association for Psychodynamic Therapy defines this type of psychotherapy as an "exploration and discussion of the full range of ... emotions [wherein] the therapist helps the patient describe and put words to feelings, including contradictory feelings, feelings that are troubling or threatening, and feelings that the patient may not initially be able to recognize or acknowledge" (Shedler, 2010, p. 99). In contrast to cognitive behavioural therapy, it tends to focus on emotions as opposed to thoughts and beliefs. Proponents believe that focusing on deeper feelings and understanding the reasons for them is more likely to result in change than having an intellectual understanding of beliefs and thoughts. This type of treatment recognizes the impact of earlier traumas in a person's life that may be contributing to the onset of PTSD and/or making it worse. Methods such as "free association," which allows the individual to discuss freely whatever comes to mind, irrespective of its content, is intended to help the person discover the beliefs, thoughts, and feelings that contribute to the development of ideas concerning what is acceptable or not, and what psychological defences they may use to prevent thoughts or actions that may not be acceptable (Kudler, 2011). It is thought that a considerable amount of what someone experiences consciously, or is aware of, is driven by unconscious forces within them of which they are not aware.

For this reason, dreams, termed by Freud as "the royal road to the unconscious" (American Psychoanalytic Association, 2014), are considered to be helpful, and dream interpretation is likely to be a part of this therapy.

## DEFENCE MECHANISMS

Defence mechanisms are the ways in which human beings try to cope with internal conflicts caused by the sexual and sometimes aggressive impulses that cause internal tensions (Freud, 1894/2013), and are also considered an important aspect of psychodynamic theory. The focus is on understanding and overcoming them where they are impeding a person's daily functioning. Defence mechanisms are considered to play a role in "mediating between an individual's wishes, needs, and affects on the one hand, and both internalized object relations and external reality on the other" (Northoff & Boeker, 2006). What this means is that everyone has an ego, an id, and a superego. In simple terms, this means that everyone has a core personality, the ego, that is generally exhibited in their day-to-day presentation of themselves in the world. The id refers to darker impulses that sometimes cause people to behave in ways that are considered socially inappropriate. The superego is often thought to refer to a person's conscience—the part that puts the brakes on id impulses, requiring them to think twice before engaging in behaviour that is socially or morally inappropriate. Defences are thought to be part of this mediation process. They are also considered to be part of the process of helping a person to adapt to the external world, and this requires examining their feelings toward others. These feelings may be based on their earliest experience of important caregivers in their lives, and individuals need to recognize that the people they encounter in their present lives are different, even though they may remind them of those who had an early impact. When individuals relate to others as if they were those early caregivers, it is called "transference."

The most "primitive" defence mechanisms are considered to be denial (a "refusal to accept reality"), regression ("reversion to an earlier stage of development"), acting out (extreme behaviour that expresses thoughts or feelings that cannot be expressed otherwise), dissociation (losing track of time and oneself), compartmentalization (where parts of oneself are separated from awareness of other parts—this can manifest in different values being expressed at different times), projection ("the misattribution of a person's undesired thoughts, feelings or impulses onto another person" who does not have them), and reaction formation (changing thoughts considered to be unwanted or dangerous into their opposites—usually good or pleasant thoughts) (Grohol, n.d.).

Helping individuals to gain insight into themselves through the use of the above concepts and others is the goal of psychodynamic therapy. While there is little research one way or the other to support this type of therapy, some have found it very useful in coming to terms with the various conflicts they experience in their lives and the symptoms that these may generate.

## PSYCHOPHARMACOLOGY

In some cases, therapy alone does not sufficiently alleviate the symptoms of those who have suffered post-traumatic stress disorder and of their families. Where this is the case, doctors may prescribe particular medications that can be adjuncts to therapy. It is generally thought that use of medication on its own is not the best practice since it can lead to dependency, but that use of medication as part of a broader range of treatment can be helpful. Common medications used to help individuals with PTSD include medications for depression and anxiety, such as selective serotonin reuptake inhibitors (SSRIs). Older forms of tricyclic anti-depressants may also be used if SSRIs are found not to be particularly effective. Benzodiazepines are also sometimes used but usually with extreme caution because of concerns about possible abuse and creation of dependency. Prazosin and trazodone may be given to individuals experiencing nightmares and sleep disruptions (Sauve & Stahl, 2011). As with all medications, side effects can be problematic, and in some cases individuals will refuse medication because they find the side effects too distressing.

## CHAPTER SUMMARY

This chapter has covered the many challenges facing military families during the three phases of relocation, deployment, and reunification. It has touched upon the stressors faced by military personnel, including PTSD symptoms because of wartime experiences, and the after-effects of rape by other military personnel. While no one chapter can capture the totality of a family's experience during these phases, readers can now think about the many stressors that these individuals and their families face, in an effort to increase sensitivity to their plight and acquaint professionals with some of the treatments available to assist them.

## FURTHER READING

Canadian Forces Moral and Welfare Services. (2018). Profile of military families in Canada. https://www.cfmws.com/en/AboutUs/MFS/FamilyResearch/

Documents/2017%20RegF%20Demographics%20Report%20FINAL%2015%20
June%202018.pdf

Canadian Military and Veteran Families Leadership Circle & Vanier Institute for
the Family. (2019). Early learning and child care professionals and practitioners
working with military and veteran families. https://vanierinstitute.ca/new-resource-
for-early-learning-and-child-care-professionals-and-practitioners-working-with-
canadian-military-and-veteran-families/

Vanier Institute for the Family. (2019). Work-family conflict among single
parents in the Canadian Armed Forces. https://vanierinstitute.ca/
work-family-conflict-single-parents-canadian-armed-forces/

## CLASSROOM RESOURCE

*Children of soldiers.* (2010). NFB. https://www.nfb.ca/film/children_of_soldiers/

## CLASSROOM ACTIVITY

### Text Read-Aloud

Ask students to read aloud a passage from the text or additional readings that held
particular meaning for them and explain why.

## QUESTIONS FOR REFLECTION

1.  Has someone you know served in the military? What challenges might they
    have related to the phases of military life?
2.  Was any of the information in this chapter surprising to you? If so, why?
3.  Which of the types of treatment available do you feel might be most useful for
    military personnel and their families? Explain your choice.
4.  If you, or someone you love, were to be deployed overseas to a war zone, how
    do you think you might react?

## REFERENCES

American Psychoanalytic Association. (2014). Freud quotes. Baltimore, MD.

Arkowitz, H., & Lilienfeld, S. O. (2012, August 1). EMDR: Taking a closer look.
*Scientific American.* Retrieved from https://www.scientificamerican.com/article/
emdr-taking-a-closer-look/

Armstrong, K., Best, S., & Domenici, P. (2006). *Courage after fire: Coping strategies for troops returning from Iraq and Afghanistan and their families.* Berkeley, CA: Ulysses Press.

Boss, P. (2006). *Loss, trauma, and resilience.* New York, NY: Norton.

Freud, S. (2013). *A general introduction to psychoanalysis.* Thompson Dickerson Books (Original work published 1894, 1900).

Grohol, J. M. (n.d.). 15 common defense mechanisms. *Psych Central.* Retrieved from http://psychcentral.com/lib/15-common-defense-mechanisms/0001251

Kudler, H. (2011). Psychodynamic psychotherapy. In B. A. Moore & W. E. Penk (Eds.), *Treating PTSD in military personnel* (pp. 107–124). New York, NY: The Guilford Press.

Moore, B. A., & Penk, W. E. (Eds.). (2011). *Treating PTSD in military personnel.* New York, NY: The Guilford Press.

Northoff, G., & Boeker, H. (2006). Principles of neuronal integration and defense mechanisms: Neuropsychoanalytic hypothesis. Retrieved from https://www.tandfonline.com/doi/abs/10.1080/15294145.2006.10773514

Palmer, C. (2008). A theory of risk and resilience factors in military families. *Military Psychology, 20*(3), 205–217.

Peterson, A. J., Foa, E. B., & Riggs, D. S. (2011). Prolonged exposure therapy. In B. A. Moore & W. E. Penk (Eds.), *Treating PTSD in military personnel* (pp. 42–58). New York, NY: The Guilford Press.

Pryce, J., Pryce, D., & Shackelford, K. (2012). *The costs of courage: Combat stress, warriors and family survival.* Chicago, IL: Lyceum Books.

Russell, M. C., Lipke, H., & Figley, C. (2011). Eye movement desensitization and reprocessing. In B. A. Moore & W. E. Penk (Eds.), *Treating PTSD in military personnel* (pp. 74–89). New York, NY: The Guilford Press.

Sauve, W. M., & Stahl, S. M. (2011). Psychopharmacological treatment. In B. A. Moore & W. E. Penk (Eds.), *Treating PTSD in military personnel* (pp. 155–172). New York, NY: The Guilford Press.

Shedler, J. (2010). The efficacy of psychodynamic psychotherapy. *American Psychologist, 65*(2), 98–109.

Snyder, V. (2013). Caring for each other, together and apart: Military families in Canada. Vanier Institute for the Family. *Transition, 43*(1), 5–7.

University of Alberta Sexual Assault Centre. (n.d.). Rape trauma syndrome. Retrieved from https://view2.fdu.edu/metropolitan-campus/public-safety/threat-assessment-team/rape-trauma-syndrome/

Van Hook, M. P. (2014). *Social work practice with families: A resiliency-based approach.* Chicago, IL: Lyceum Books.

Williams, A. M., Galovski, T. E., Kattar, K. A., & Resick, P. A. (2011). Cognitive processing therapy. In B. A. Moore & W. E. Penk (Eds.), *Treating PTSD in military personnel* (pp. 59–73). New York, NY: The Guilford Press.

# CHAPTER 16

# Grieving Families

*I have never climbed Mt. Everest, but I sometimes think it would be easier than navigating the pathway through grief.*

—K. Shear (2012)

## CHAPTER OVERVIEW

Like individuals, families grieve for many different reasons. They grieve for a lost family member or friend. Parents who have a child with a disability or a mental health issue, or one who ends up in conflict with the law may grieve for the child they thought they were going to have or for the person someone was before they became ill. In some families having a child who is gay or lesbian is cause for grief. Families sometimes experience intense grief when a pet dies or is lost. Military families may experience grief and ambivalence when a family member is missing in action. How, or even whether, a family grieves is as individual as the family members themselves, and often depends on existing family dynamics, as well as their belief system and culture. There is no right or wrong way to grieve.

Grief can be intense or gentle. It can bring family members closer together or cause extreme conflict, especially when a parent dies. It can remain painful for short periods of time, or it can last for months, years, and sometimes decades. What is certain is that grief changes families and everyone in the family in a variety of ways, and it is highly personal.

Where a spouse or child dies, the loss may change the identity of the survivors. Someone may now be a widow or widower rather than a husband or wife. They may no longer be a parent. Loss of a breadwinner may greatly change a family's economic circumstances. If someone was a caregiver for a family member with a terminal illness, their loss will completely change the caregiver's life. "Accepting the unacceptable" is what grief is all about (Family Caregiver Alliance, 2014).

Grief occurs in stages. Kubler-Ross (1969) identified these stages in her landmark book *On Death and Dying* as denial and isolation (as a defence against overwhelming loss); anger (this can be at others, the person who is gone, or even inanimate objects); bargaining (when feeling helpless, this can be an attempt to regain some control by trying to make a deal with God); depression (worry, sadness, and sometimes regret); and acceptance (a stage of calm that not everyone reaches). These stages do not usually happen sequentially, but individuals and families can expect to experience some aspects of each stage as the grieving process evolves.

There are also often symptoms associated with grieving. These can be physical, such as lack of energy, gastrointestinal problems, headaches, and feelings of exhaustion; cognitive and emotional, such as irritability, resignation, rage, and inability to focus; or spiritual, where someone may either feel closer to God or anger at God. Some even feel cut off from God, as if God does not care for them anymore.

In some cases grief can be anticipatory, where family members grieve the person's "former self" even before they are lost, especially where there is a terminal illness. This stage may involve feelings of guilt as some may wish a long illness was finally over. It can also allow people to share intimate moments with the person and process unresolved issues before the person dies. It may also be a time to talk with them about end-of-life decisions and what arrangements they want after their passing (Family Caregiver Alliance, 2014).

Where a loss is sudden or unexpected, family members may experience shock and, in some cases, symptoms of post-traumatic stress. Their sleep may be impaired. They may have intrusive images of their loved one, and they themselves may feel unsafe, especially where a crime has been committed or someone has died in an accident or committed suicide. There can be strong feelings associated with losses of this kind that leave family members shaken and overwhelmed, perhaps feeling guilty, or lost, asking unanswerable questions.

## SUICIDE AND MURDER

When a family loses a member to suicide, the grief reactions can be traumatic, especially if a family member found the person. Survivors who are still in shock may have to deal with the police and answer heart-wrenching questions. Survivors are likely to replay over and over again the days and weeks before the family member committed suicide, attempting to determine whether or not there was something they could have said or done. They may experience shame and guilt and feel stigmatized by a family member having committed suicide and this may cut them off from others who would otherwise provide support. Keeping the suicide a secret can lead to a family feeling isolated and removed from others. Other family members may feel extremely angry at the person who committed suicide, seeing them as having assaulted the family through their actions.

Perhaps most importantly, professionals working with families that have lost a member to suicide should be particularly watchful for signs that other family members may also be contemplating it, making it clear that, whatever thoughts and feelings they may be having, it is safe to share these with the professional. Assisting family members to link to others who have also lost someone to suicide can be particularly helpful in easing feelings of social isolation (Harvard Medical School, 2009).

When someone is murdered, family members can direct their anger at the perpetrator; however, this does not ease grief. The loss of a loved one to violence is one of the most traumatic experiences a person can have. That loss is especially horrendous when a child has been murdered. When family members experience traumatic grief, it is difficult to comfort one another, and the resulting isolation can be devastating. Whether or not a perpetrator is caught, families do not experience closure. The pain and anguish will go on for years, possibly for an entire lifetime. Where someone's body is never found, that anguish can be multiplied. Not knowing where the person's remains are is particularly devastating.

Children who have lost a sibling to murder often experience intense feelings of despair and hopelessness, and professionals working with them should be on the lookout for survivor guilt. Children will often ask "why not me instead of them"? Siblings are especially vulnerable, as parents' grief is centred on the lost child (Canadian Parents of Murdered Children and Survivors of Homicide Victims, 2018).

In cases of traumatic loss to murder or suicide, there will be a temptation among family members to self-medicate away their intense pain. The professional will need to be aware of this possibility and pay special attention to the family member whose grief is so intense that they feel unable to bear it. Helping them to understand that their deep grief is equal to the love they felt for the person and the difficulty of letting them go can be useful.

Professionals also need to be on the lookout for triggers—reactions that re-occur over time, and to help family members to address these when they occur. Suicide and homicide survivors are at greater risk for post-traumatic stress, and therefore using trauma-informed practices to assist them may be the most helpful option. Mindfulness, helping the person to centre themselves in the present using grounding exercises focusing on slowing down the breath and becoming acutely aware of one's surroundings, can sometimes pre-empt panic attacks and settle flashbacks (Living Well, 2019). Spending time in nature and paying particular attention to one's surroundings can also be helpful.

For both children and adults who have experienced the traumatic stress of losing a loved one to murder or suicide, referring them to a professional ther-apist to assist them in the weeks and months after the loss will be a prudent decision. Individuals who have experienced loss this traumatic will need the assistance of others who understand and can help them to work through their distressing emotions.

## COMPLICATED GRIEF

Shear (2012) describes a condition termed "complicated grief," which she says af-fects about 7 percent of people who have suffered a loss. Shear (2012, p. 2) defines normal grief as "the psychobiological response to bereavement whose hallmark is a blend of yearning and sadness, along with thoughts, memories, and images of the deceased person." But those with a complicated grief reaction "are caught up in rumination about the circumstances of the death, worry about its consequences, or excessive avoidance of reminders of the loss. Unable to comprehend the finality and consequences of the loss, they resort to excessive avoidance of reminders of the loss as they are tossed helplessly on waves of intense emotion" (Shear, 2012, p. 1). Mourning is the usual set of processes that accompany grief, where an individual attempts to integrate their loss by coming to terms with it and by becoming more accustomed to a world where a loved one is not present.

Those considered most at risk of a complicated grief reaction are those who have lost a child or a life partner, and their grief can be intense for up to a de-cade after the loss (Lannen, Wolfe, Prigerson, Onelov, & Kreicbergs, 2008). Additionally, those who may have been absent at the time of death, or who had argued with someone prior to their death, or who disagreed with treatment, or who have doubted their own ability to help or comfort the person they have lost may excessively focus on these things, and this can lead to a complicated grief reaction (Shear, 2010).

Shear (2010, p. 4) informs us that common symptoms of a complicated grief reaction include "intense yearning or longing for the person who died, intrusive or preoccupying thoughts or images of the deceased person, a sense of loss of meaning or purpose in a life without the deceased … incessant questioning, worrying, or ruminating over some aspect of the circumstances or consequences of the loss." "If onlys" and catastrophizing occur frequently, often accompanied by excessive and incessant worry. There may also be excessive expressions of bitterness, guilt, and anger, with little to no breaks in which positive emotions occur. In fact, any positive emotion may cause guilt. Those suffering complicated grief reactions may also avoid any reminders of what they have lost or alternatively may seek closeness to anything related to the person whom they have lost. Suicidal thoughts may accompany the person's grief, and the person may be greatly impaired in their day-to-day functioning even after an extended period of time.

Shear (2010) recommends several strategies to professionals seeking to help someone experiencing a complicated grief reaction. These can include helping people to approach and move back from difficult emotions and thoughts, and, wherever possible, replacing negative emotions with more positive ones by re-framing a thought; helping individuals to plan for the future while incorporating memories of the person they have lost; and assisting people to regulate their emotions by spending time with those who offer comfort and support for healing and by observing and reflecting on their thoughts before letting them go. She recommends using a grief monitoring diary and including highest and lowest ratings of the level of grief they are experiencing. This allows them to see patterns and begin to recognize that the intensity of grief changes over time, allowing them to feel less out of control. Where counselling and support alone do not help, short-term use of antidepressants can help to alleviate symptoms.

Many issues can arise for families as someone is dying. Family members will have had different relationships with the person who is lost, and this can cause conflict with other family members. In some cases, sons and daughters may have unresolved issues with each other or with a parent, and these can play out in extremely negative ways when a parent or sibling dies. Families may argue over an end-of-life decision, such as whether or not to raise the level of pain medication in a way that could lead to an earlier death. Families' belief systems come to the fore in circumstances like this. People who believe strongly that where there is life, there is hope may fight to keep someone alive against the wishes of other family members, who see this as only prolonging a dying person's suffering. In some cases, family members who are expecting a large inheritance will want someone to die sooner, and this can place them in direct conflict with other family members who consider them to be greedy and self-serving.

Treatment decisions can also cause family fights. Depending upon family members' knowledge, trust in the medical and nursing professions, or desire to avoid them altogether, battles can ensue about whether to treat or not to treat if someone has a chronic or terminal illness.

Family member hierarchical patterns also often emerge during times of extreme stress such as the loss of a parent. One son or daughter may step forward and attempt to control decisions, thereby alienating other siblings. This can engender hostilities that may last to the end of their lives and result in hurt and pain that makes the grieving process much worse. A similar process can occur if one sibling wants to force a parent to accept placement in a long-term care facility, while another considers this to be an unconscionable treatment of a parent whom they believe should be cared for at home until the end of their days.

Other arguments can involve the funeral service itself. Family members may have very different views of the person who is gone, and may therefore want different types of services. Arguments can ensue about choice of music, what will be said, and who will say it. Old arguments about religion may surface in the choice of clergy.

The following three scenarios illustrate the kinds of arguments that can occur between family members going through the grief process.

Mary's father divorced her mother and remarried when Mary was in her twenties. She had nothing against her father's new wife or her family, and occasionally spent social time with them. Her mother, however, was extremely angry about the divorce and remarriage, and Mary's younger sibling shared this anger. This caused considerable stress in the family. During her father's illness, when Mary brought him some of his favourite food, she was criticized for it by her step family. This was likely the result of their long-standing resentment of Mary because of her continuing closeness and good relationship with her father. When her father died, Mary was also horrified at the behaviour of her "step family." As he lay dying, they sat at his bedside and discussed funeral arrangements. Before he died, they convinced him to change his power of attorney and his will, cutting both daughters from his original family out of the will. At the funeral, Mary was not even left alone to grieve at her father's casket. His wife sent a minister over to her to try to convince her to meet with her "step family." At the service, the man they described was not the man she had known all of her life. Her sister did not attend the funeral, so she was the sole representative of the "original family." Afterward, one of the step siblings kept her father's ashes. When she asked if she might have them, she was refused, but was told they could "divide" up the ashes—something she was completely unwilling to do. The extremely hurtful and insensitive way she was treated complicated and prolonged her grief. It was only after several years that she was able to separate the warm memories she had of her father from the pain she had suffered at the hands of her step family during and after his death.

Paul has two siblings—a brother and a sister. He is not close to either of them but sees them socially from time to time. When their mother passed away fairly suddenly, and no previous arrangements had been made concerning her wishes regarding treatment or her funeral, Paul, in an attempt to be fair, got his brother and sister together to be there at her passing and to share in making arrangements for her and for their widowed father. However, in the aftermath of her death, old resentments surfaced, as his sister wanted nothing to do with helping their father remain in his own home. This caused a huge argument between Paul and his sister when he could not understand why she was unwilling to help. This placed an extra burden on him to spend more time caring for his father, and he resented his sister for this. He developed stomach problems in the aftermath of his mother's death.

Catherine had a complicated relationship with her father, who was an alcoholic. When he became seriously ill, she was faced with having to execute his power of attorney—something she did not want to do but which neither of her two brothers was willing to do. Her aunt, who had an aggressive personality, had been close to Catherine's father all her life. She now stepped in, raising concerns about his treatment and Catherine's lack of caring. Catherine did not like this aunt, and tried to curtail her involvement, but the aunt fought back. In the end, she got her way by having him transferred to a hospital farther from Catherine, and Catherine felt angry and powerless about it. When her father died, the funeral was a difficult event. However, another aunt was kind to her and made the service easier. Nevertheless, Catherine continues to harbour angry feelings for her aunt. She feels her aunt has never understood her feelings about her father and believes her aunt criticized her unfairly during his illness and after his death.

## POWERS OF ATTORNEY

Some of the issues that occur around a parent's death can be forestalled by use of a power of attorney for finances, and a power of attorney for personal care. In the former, the person appoints someone to execute their wishes with regard to their property and financial affairs. This is a legal document that allows someone to access another person's financial holdings in the event that they become incapacitated or are unable to do so themselves.

A power of attorney for personal care allows someone to spell out their wishes with respect to care and treatment should they be unable to instruct health care professionals themselves. The person holding a power of attorney for personal care is obliged to carry out the wishes of the individual with regard to their care and treatment as well as end-of-life decisions, such as whether or not to use "heroic measures" to keep someone alive when there is no hope that they will recover.

Although these are by no means foolproof if a family member decides to challenge the holder of the power of attorney, they can nevertheless greatly ease things for a grieving family if family members know a person's wishes in advance. Having funeral arrangements finalized can also greatly help a grieving spouse and other family members and prevent arguments, because the dying person themselves will, in essence, have made their own funeral arrangements and paid for them.

## WHAT CAN PROFESSIONALS DO?

There are several things that professionals can do to help ease the situation for a family, and the first is to recognize that there are probably longstanding family dynamics at play during the grieving process and this is not the best time to attempt to resolve them. Offering all family members care and comfort in the way that seems most acceptable to them is helpful. Often this involves simply listening and responding empathically to them without offering advice or self-disclosure. This is a time when family members need to be heard, and they often do not want to hear about anyone else's grief or personal losses.

If possible, normalize expressions of grief by saying "It is pretty understandable that you would feel this way at this time." Professionals cannot take away someone's pain; they can, like everyone else, only commiserate. One could say "I can't imagine your pain in having lost...." If someone does not want to talk, don't force the issue. Sometimes people prefer silence and just having someone sit with them while they cry. Offer a Kleenex and perhaps a supportive touch on the arm at times like this. Even though boundaries require that professionals not engage in physical touch at most times, this may be a time when a hug or a touch on the arm or shoulder is appropriate, provided that there is no specific reason to refrain. One reason for not doing so may be if a person of the opposite sex has shown romantic interest in the professional. If that is the case, a handshake and words of condolence will suffice.

Attending to the family during the funeral as well as after everyone has gone home, and in the weeks and months after their bereavement, can help them to make sense of what has happened and begin to regain their footing. Noting the loss in a family's file and remembering to acknowledge the anniversary of the bereavement a year later, especially if the family is exhibiting distress at this time, can be helpful in bringing some of the reasons for the distress to consciousness.

## HEALING

Healing after a significant loss takes time. Intense grief can last from a few months to a year, and, in some cases, longer. Where grief is extended, individuals may feel that there is something abnormal occurring, and they may need reassurance that everyone grieves differently. How long it takes for someone to recover will depend on many factors, including their personality, their belief system, their culture, previous experiences of loss, the type of loss they suffered, and the circumstances of their loss. Everyone will need to take whatever time they require to process their grief.

Family members who feel intense guilt will need to embark on a process of self-forgiveness. Where a loved one has committed suicide and there is a sense of anger, they may also have to forgive the loved one. Forgiveness can be an important aspect of overcoming grief. The Mayo Clinic (2014) defines it as "a decision to let go of resentment and thoughts of revenge," recognizing that these negative thoughts and feelings only hurt the person experiencing them. Replacing these kinds of thoughts with compassion, "the ability to understand the emotional state of another person or oneself [and] alleviate their suffering" (Engel, 2008), can help with healing.

## CHILDREN AND GRIEF

Children find grief after the loss of a family member to be a bewildering experience. Depending upon their ages they will react differently, with young children expecting the loss to be temporary, while older children are more likely to experience stages of grief similar to adults. All children will be shaken by seeing older family members experiencing grief, but will take their cues from them. It is not unusual for children to be in denial, especially about the death of a parent; however, if the denial persists for more than a year, it can lead to a complicated grief reaction. Children will display sadness over long periods of time, and this is normal.

Questions are sometimes asked about whether or not children should attend a funeral. Some children may not want to, and should not be forced to do so; however, something should be done to memorialize the person who has been lost. It is suggested that prayer, lighting a candle, making a scrapbook of pictures of the person, telling stories, and encouraging children to express their feelings of loss are all helpful (American Academy of Child and Adolescent Psychiatry, 2018). A search for meaning and answers will often follow the loss of someone close—a reflection on one's own life, its meaning, any regrets, as well as joys and sorrows. It may become necessary to find people with whom family members can discuss larger questions concerning the purpose of life and death so that they can make sense of what seems senseless. Clergy, wise family members, friends, and sometimes books can be helpful during this period of reflection.

Helping a family to engage neighbours, friends, and other family members to make their lives easier at this time can also be helpful. Neighbours can cut the lawn, rake leaves, or shovel snow. Friends can bring food or contribute to a cause the person believed in, or look after pets or small children to give a bereaved spouse a break. Sometimes helping with transportation to and from the funeral home is a help. Essentially, the professional's role at this time is to try to make a family's life easier. Showing gentleness and compassion will always help the situation; this, and refraining from judgments.

## CHAPTER SUMMARY

This chapter has outlined the various stages of grief and the types of grief reactions common to families. Also discussed are the ways professionals can be of assistance to families in dealing with grief and help them to find meaning in their loss.

## FURTHER READING

Australian Child & Adolescent Trauma, Loss and Grief Network. (n.d.). Children, adolescents, and families: Grief and loss in disaster. http://earlytraumagrief.anu.edu.au/files/Disasters%20grief%20children%20and%20families_0.pdf

Schuler, T., Zaider, T., & Kissane, D. (2012, September). Family grief therapy. https://aifs.gov.au/publications/family-matters/issue-90/family-grief-therapy

## CLASSROOM RESOURCE

*Grief in the family*. (2013). Concord Media. https://www.youtube.com/watch?v=nI-rjKl9r3E

## CLASSROOM ACTIVITY

Ask students to journal their own experiences with loss, then come to class prepared to discuss what they learned from their journalling experience.

## QUESTIONS FOR REFLECTION

1.  Have you ever lost someone close to you? If so, what type of grief reaction did you have?
2.  Have you been a support to a friend or family member who has lost someone? If so, how did you support them?
3.  Given what you have read in this chapter, are there ways that you might behave differently now to help someone cope with a loss?

## REFERENCES

American Academy of Child and Adolescent Psychiatry. (2018, June). Grief and children. Retrieved from https://www.aacap.org/AACAP/Families_and_Youth/Facts_for_Families/FFF-Guide/Children-And-Grief-008.aspx

Canadian Parents of Murdered Children and Survivors of Homicide Victims. (2018, June 24). Health and social issues following the murder of a loved one. Retrieved from http://canadianpomc.ca/resources/the-impact-of-murder-on-the-family-unit/health-and-social-issues-following-the-murder-of-a-loved-one/

Engel, B. (2008). What is compassion and how can it improve my life? *Psychology Today*. Retrieved from www.psychologytoday.com/blog/the-compassion-chronicles/200804/what-is-compassion-and-how-can-it-improve-my-life

Family Caregiver Alliance. (2014). Grief and loss. Retrieved from www.caregiver.org/ caregiver/jsp/content_node.jsp?nodeid=404

Harvard Medical School. (2009, July). Left behind after suicide. Retrieved from https:// www.health.harvard.edu/newsletter_article/Left-behind-after-suicide

Kersting, A., Brahler, E., Glaesmer, H., & Wagner, B. (2011). Prevalence of complicated grief in a representative population-based sample. *Journal of Affective Disorders, 131,* 339–343.

Kubler-Ross, E. (1969). *On death and dying.* New York, NY: MacMillan.

Lannen, P. K., Wolfe, J., Prigerson, H. G., Onelov, E., & Kreicbergs, U. C. (2008). Unresolved grief in a national sample of bereaved parents: Impaired mental and physical health 4 to 9 years later. *Journal of Clinical Oncology, 26,* 5870–5876.

Living Well. (2019). Grounding exercises. Retrieved from https://www.livingwell.org .au/well-being/mental-health/grounding-exercises/

Mayo Clinic. (2014). Forgiveness: Letting go of grudges and bitterness. Retrieved from www.mayoclinic.org/forgiveness/art-20047692

Shear, K. (2010). Complicated grief treatment: The theory, practice and outcomes. *Bereavement Care, 29*(3), 10–14.

Shear, K. (2012, June 14). Grief and mourning gone awry: Pathway and course of complicated grief. *Dialogues in Clinical Neuroscience, 14*(2), 119–129. Retrieved from www.ncbi.nlm.nih.gov/pmc/articles/PMC3384440/

## CHAPTER 17

# Common Pitfalls in Working with Families

*The greatest good you can do for another is not just to share your riches but to reveal to him his own.*

—Benjamin Disraeli

## CHAPTER OVERVIEW

Working with families can present numerous challenges. Among them is the temptation to side with one family member, or one half of a couple where a divorce is underway and there is a custody dispute. Maintaining confidentiality when family members are confiding in a professional, sometimes about each other, can also be challenging. So, too, is obtaining informed consent, especially in situations where family members may be attempting to coerce someone to accept intervention.

A particular difficulty occurs when a family has been referred by the courts or a child protection agency and is resisting professional involvement. All of these issues and more will be outlined in this chapter, which describes ethical and practice dilemmas that may confront professionals working with families.

## ALIGNMENT WITH FAMILY MEMBERS

Margolin (1982) has pointed out that the way that a professional works with one family member may not be beneficial to other family members. This can be avoided to some extent by professionals not becoming too heavily aligned with one member of a family and, instead, seeking to engage all family members. Alignment with one particular family member can occur if that person's beliefs and values more closely align with the professional's, or in the case of a romantic attraction, which would require that the professional immediately seek supervision and be honest about their feelings. Romantic thoughts about anyone with whom a professional is working is a danger signal that needs to be immediately addressed by involving a supervisor who can assist, especially if a professional's clinical judgment is impaired in this or any other way.

For this reason professionals need also always be aware of how their own attitudes, beliefs, and behaviour toward family members can affect family dynamics and how the family responds to them. This can become especially challenging when child-rearing practices and couple interactions confront a professional's own belief systems. By using an empowerment approach that stresses family members' autonomy when making decisions, and working with them in a neutral way, professionals can avoid forcing their own values and beliefs on the family. However, where it is clear that a child or children may be in danger because of abusive or neglectful child-rearing practices, professionals must make a report to child protection authorities. Where family violence is occurring, the same may be true if children are at risk, which they generally are in these situations.

## CONFIDENTIALITY

Confidentiality is a particular challenge when working with families. Professionals, especially those bound by the requirements of their professional colleges, must be careful to maintain confidentiality according to their codes of ethics (American Association for Marriage and Family Therapy, 2012). Professionals are advised to inform families about their rights to confidentiality; specifically, that the professional cannot share with one family member what another has said in private, but also the limits to that right in the case of perceived child abuse and family violence. Professionals will need to use their judgment as to whether or not they are prepared to meet with family members privately as well as in a group.

## INFORMED CONSENT

Where a professional is asked by a family member for help in working with the entire family, it becomes especially important to ensure that other family members consent to be involved of their own free will, understanding the risks and benefits of doing so, as well as what other options may exist for them. It is not until a professional is certain that all family members who are participating understand these risks and benefits, as well as the other options that are available to them, that it can be said that they have given informed consent (Shaw, 2011). Shaw suggests that failing to ensure the rights of all family members to equitable treatment in this regard can result in the professional being seen as an accomplice of one family member in the intervention process. This can be especially true if one family member always becomes the point of contact between the family and the professional.

## TRANSFERENCE AND COUNTERTRANSFERENCE

A particularly thorny issue arises in working with families when transference and countertransference occur. This can also occur ethnoculturally. Transference refers to "the redirection of feelings and desires and especially those unconsciously obtained from childhood to a new object" (Howes, 2012). Your professor reminds you of your mother with whom you did not have a good relationship, and so you don't like her. Your doctor reminds you of your father with whom you *did* have a good relationship, so you respect him and take his advice. So how can a professional deal with transference when it arises in their work with family members? Howes (2012) suggests it be discussed openly and "normalized": "I seem to remind you a bit of your own mother, but I'm sure there are differences between us. What do you see as some of those differences?" Since transference is so common, it is fine to acknowledge it with a family member, but it is also important to explore what unresolved issues might be behind the transference reaction. One might ask, "How are you feeling about your mom these days?" or, if noticing a particular interaction when meeting with the whole family, one might say, "I noticed you making an attempt to get closer to your mom there. How did you feel about her response?"

When the repressed feelings of the professional are aroused by work with a particular client, it is called countertransference. A child in a family reminds the professional of their own child. A parent reminds the professional of themselves. It is tempting to project particular characteristics onto the other person because of a countertransference reaction. A professional might say, "Oh, I know just how you feel" to the person who reminds them of themselves, or perhaps feel that a child in the family is likely to act out because they are reminded of their own son or daughter, or brother or sister. A professional may be intimidated by a family member who reminds them of an authoritative figure from their own childhood. These kinds of reactions can be dangerous because, if denied, professionals can model denial for the family members with whom they are working and also fail to deal with the uncomfortable feelings that have been evoked (Murphy, 2013). According to Rasic (2010, p. 252), feelings generated in professionals by countertransference reactions include feeling "overwhelmed/disorganized, helpless/inadequate, positive, special/overinvolved, sexualized, disengaged, parental/protective, criticized/mistreated." Seeking the input of colleagues or supervisors is important when experiencing these kinds of reactions.

## ETHNICITY AND CULTURE

Comas-Diaz and Jacobsen (1991, p. 401) state that "ethnicity and culture can touch deep unconscious feelings in most individuals and may become targets for projection." What this means is that the way an ethnocultural group is portrayed in the media and elsewhere may cause professionals to inadvertently project stereotypic beliefs onto a family. Ethnocultural identification may result in both the professional and the family projecting certain qualities and characteristics onto the other. Is a professional more concerned that children from one racial and/or ethnic group are likely to get in trouble with the law? Is there a feeling that because a professional comes from the same culture that they know exactly how a family is likely to process information or handle things, and therefore proceed based on those assumptions? Is a family more likely to trust someone from their own culture and therefore project onto them particular understandings that they may or may not have? All of these questions are valuable in helping professionals to maintain perspective and check their assumptions before reaching conclusions.

## WORK WITH HIGHLY RESISTANT FAMILIES

In some cases professionals are attempting to work with highly resistant families who may have been forced to accept professional help. The North East of Scotland Child Protection Committee (NESCPC) (2008) outlines some characteristics of such families. These include ambivalence or avoidance (missing or being late for appointments, refusal to talk about any topic that is uncomfortable); confrontation (not answering or slamming doors in professionals' faces, arguing); or outright violence.

In these instances, it is important for professionals to look at the whole picture. Are there cultural differences that are creating discomfort in the family? Does the family understand what to expect from professional involvement? Is the professional misinterpreting their behaviour for cultural or other reasons? Has the family had bad experiences with previous professionals? Is the family attempting to hide a family secret about which they feel ashamed? Do they fully understand the impact on children of the way the family functions? Some of these can be addressed by the professional clearly explaining their role and the reason for their involvement, by expressing concern for the family and a sincere desire to help them, and finally, openly discussing the family's behaviour and seeking clarification from them about why this is occurring (NESCPC, 2008).

## WORK WITH HOSTILE FAMILIES

A major issue in working with families is that professionals can become intimidated. The NESCPC (2008) says that "despite sensitive approaches by professionals, some families may respond with hostility and sometimes this can lead to threats of violence and actual violence. It is, therefore, important to try to understand the reasons for the hostility and the actual level of risk involved."

Recognizing what constitutes threatening behaviour is important for professionals who are working with families where violence is possible. The NESCPC (2008) suggests that the following may be warning signs and should not be ignored: an overabundance of emails and phone calls, including written and verbal threats, "deliberate use of silence," "intimidating or derogatory language, discriminatory attitudes and remarks, domineering body language," dogs or other animals used as a "veiled threat," and "swearing, shouting, throwing things or actual violence." Some threats may be implied, such as threats directed toward others.

Where families argue loudly or are abusive or neglectful, or where family members are aggressive, professionals can feel intimidated and fail to address issues of vital importance in an effort to avoid conflict (Herefordshire Safeguarding Children Board, 2011). The authors of the Herefordshire Safeguarding Children Board report suggest examining both the family's previous experience and the professional's own way of working with them to determine what is at the root of this aggressiveness. Is the worker angry with the family? Is the family frustrated with the worker for some reason? What is causing anger in a particular family member? Is the family intending to be abusive or threatening, and aware of the impact it is having? Is the aggressive behaviour habitual? (Herefordshire Safeguarding Children Board, 2011).

Professionals need to examine their own reactions as well. Is their reaction disproportionate to what the family is doing? Is the professional taking things personally when they may not be intended that way? Providing a family with feedback about their impact in a calm and constructive way can sometimes be helpful: "Wow, you're very powerful when you get angry. Are you aware that you may scare people when you shout like that?"

Since professionals are generally working with families that are under extreme stress, aggressiveness may be a symptom of this. Naming it as a function of stress and working with the family to reduce their stress levels offers the professional and family an opportunity to work together to confront the problem of stress-related aggression in the family.

If professionals do not feel safe working with a particular family, it may be necessary to work in tandem with another professional or agency, or to institute special safeguards, or to meet particular families in the office rather than in their homes. Managers should be informed if a professional feels threatened and, at times, police attendance may be warranted. It is important that professionals understand the limits of their own skills and tolerance regarding threats and hostility, and set personal limits in a tactful way.

Working with very difficult families can take a personal toll on professionals:

> Working with potentially hostile and threatening families can place professionals under a great deal of stress and can have physical, emotional and psychological consequences. It can also limit what the professional can allow themselves to believe, make them feel responsible for allowing the violence to take place, lead to adaptive behavior and also result in a range of distressing physical, emotional and psychological symptoms. Professionals experiencing depressive or post-traumatic stress related symptoms such as hypervigilance, numbness, rumination (repetitive thoughts), sleep disruption, intrusive images, or feelings that nothing they do has any impact need to seek supervision and seek help in addressing these symptoms. Compassion fatigue is rife in the human services and it is important not to ignore symptoms. Similarly mental health issues can ensue for professionals who ignore the impact of prolonged stress. (NESCPC, 2008)

## PROFESSIONAL SELF-CARE

Today's professionals work with families who are often in tragic circumstances: the military family that has lost someone; the newcomer family that is splintered, poor, and faces discrimination; the Indigenous family experiencing substance abuse, discrimination, and violence; the family with a child with a severe disability, who cannot get help and are on the brink of collapse. In all of these instances, professionals are directly affected by the pain and distress of the people with whom they work. Some things may resonate for them, such as the eldest sibling struggling to keep younger siblings on track, or the single mom fighting depression and isolation, or the father who believes tight control is the answer to keeping his family together, or the family who decides to place Grandma in a nursing home. Any and all of these issues can resonate for a professional and bring painful feelings to the surface. Continued exposure to others' pain can also place professionals at risk of developing stress-related symptoms or more serious mental health challenges of their own. No one is immune to others' pain.

Neglecting self-care can become dangerous under these circumstances. Volk, Guarino, Grandin, and Clervil (2008) state that "we may not need hats, pads, or protective eyewear—but if we want to continue to be safe and effective in our work, we do need to have self-care tools that we use every day." They point out some of the warning signs that a professional is becoming overstressed, such as feeling indispensable and being unable to take time off without feeling guilty, negative thinking, overreacting to relatively minor things, not taking vacations, dreading going to work, feeling overwhelmed and making mistakes, not sleeping enough, irritability and argumentativeness, and a poor social life.

Many of these may be the result of what is known as compassion fatigue, vicarious traumatization, or secondary traumatic stress (Babbel, 2012). According to Babbel (2012), "The helpers' symptoms, frequently unnoticed, may range from psychological issues such as dissociation, anger, anxiety, sleep disturbances, nightmares, to feeling powerless. However, professionals may also experience physical symptoms such as nausea, headaches, general constriction, bodily temperature changes, dizziness, fainting spells, and impaired hearing. All are important warning signals for the caregiver that need to be addressed or otherwise might lead to health issues or burnout." Hearing horrible stories of abuse and violence and being with others who are experiencing extreme psychic pain are very stressful for professionals, but they may remain unaware of just how much stress they are experiencing.

> [Self-care is necessary to help] reduce susceptibility to the internalization of traumatic stress and compassion fatigue.... Paying attention to and being aware of physiological signals and somatic countertransference such as "dizziness, emptiness, hunger, fullness, claustrophobia, sleepiness, pain,

restlessness, sexual arousal, and so forth" can be an important method of preventing and managing compassion fatigue. Somatic countertransference entails the psychotherapist's reaction to a client with bodily responses such as sensations, emotions, and images that can only be noticed through body awareness. Since somatic countertransference is often neglected in both the literature and in the caregiver's training, many are not aware of the somatic countertransference elicited in the helper-patient relationship. (Babbel, 2012)

Volk et al. (2008) offer some approaches that can be helpful to professionals working with families in crisis. They point out that we model self-care for others. Too often "helpers" tend to neglect their own needs and constantly respond to the needs of others both on and off the job. This can deplete them. Workplaces need to recognize the needs of those working with individuals whose lives are painful and chaotic.

Self-care crosses several domains: physical (getting enough sleep; eating regularly and healthily; exercising, especially with activities that bring us pleasure; obtaining regular medical care and taking time off when sick; engaging in healthy sexuality; taking vacations and getaways; turning off phones); psychological (taking time for self-reflection; journalling to record your thoughts, dreams, and experiences; reading for leisure; learning a new creative skill; attending artistic, musical, or other cultural events; seeing a counsellor if necessary; being able to set limits and say no); and emotional (spending time with positive people; remaining in contact with those you respect; changing inner talk from negative to positive; engaging in comforting practices; crying and grieving when needed; going to a comedy show; expressing angry feelings in as constructive a way as possible; getting a pet).

Babbel (2012) adds, "Studies have also shown that a positive attitude toward life such as a sense of humour, self-confidence, being curious, focusing on the positive, and feeling gratitude ranked high in being helpful in treating traumatized people. Additionally, support, supervision, balancing work and private life, relaxation techniques, and vacation time have been useful." All of these are ways to get life back on track and maintain perspective, and they are especially important for anyone working in the human services.

There is growing recognition in some health and human services organizations of the need to ensure that front-line professionals are properly supported in their roles and that steps need to be taken to prevent compassion fatigue. Walker, Morin, and Labrie (2012), in preparing a manual for the Region of Peel, found that maintaining professional boundaries and being able to obtain support from team members was very helpful to professionals working with children at risk of poor developmental outcomes. Having strong professional experience, recognizing milestones in their work, and developing new coping strategies that fostered resilience helped them to overcome some of the more negative aspects of their work.

Agencies can also do a number of things to assist professional staff, including providing specialized training related to their work, introducing reflective practice and collaborative case review during team meetings geared toward helping staff to find meaning in their work, establishing specialized consultations with others to provide direct support to staff, creating policies supportive of service delivery, maintaining reasonable caseloads, and including self-care activities in staff meetings. All are of some help. However, prolonged exposure to stressful situations without a break is likely to be the biggest threat to a professional's mental health.

Taking regular breaks, maintaining a personal life outside work, and having a social support network not related to work may be among the best defences against compassion fatigue. When individuals who help others for a living also overburden their personal lives by taking on the problems of others in their families and friendship circles, they place themselves at significant risk for compassion fatigue. Learning to set limits and to know when not to help are important steps professionals can take to protect themselves.

## CHAPTER SUMMARY

This chapter has examined some of the pitfalls professionals encounter when working with families, including the danger of enmeshment or alignment with one family member, difficulties maintaining confidentiality and obtaining informed consent, the need for self-awareness, understanding one's impact on a family and their impact on the professional, working with resistant and sometimes violent families, transference and countertransference (including cultural transference), and finally, the urgent need for professionals to engage in self-care. All of these issues confront professionals every day in their work with families, and wise professionals develop skills in each of these areas to assist them in their work.

## FURTHER READING

Debicki, A. (2009). Wraparound in Canada. http://www.wrapcanada.org/html/pdf/
    CanadaWrapOverviewMarch12,2009.pdf

Jackson, K. (2014, May/June). Social worker self-care: The overlooked core competency.
    *Social Work Today, 14*(3), 14. https://www.socialworktoday.com/archive/051214p14
    .shtml

Social Policy Evaluation and Research Unit. (2015, November). Families with complex needs: International approaches. https://www.superu.govt.nz/sites/default/files/Families%20with%20complex%20needs.pdf

Stanley, N., & Humphreys, C. (2017). Identifying the key components of a "whole family" intervention for families experiencing domestic violence and abuse. University of Central Lancashire. https://pdfs.semanticscholar.org/15e3/7d893afc9b532f6be3e86a4c49af14c536dc.pdf

## CLASSROOM RESOURCES

*Drowning in empathy: The cost of vicarious trauma.* (2016, April 15). TED Talk. https://www.youtube.com/watch?v=ZsaorjIo1Yc

*Portraits of professional caregivers: Their passion, their pain.* (2015). National Academy of Television Arts and Sciences. https://caregiversfilm.com/

## CLASSROOM ACTIVITY

Break the class into two groups. One group is required to research the wrap-around approach and present it in class, and the other is required to research the whole-family approach and present it in class. A debate can follow concerning which approach is likely to work best with families that have complex needs.

## QUESTIONS FOR REFLECTION

1. Have you ever felt tempted to align yourself with one family member? If so, why?
2. Have you ever found yourself becoming angry or resentful of a particular family or family members? Why did this occur? What values of yours may have been challenged?
3. How do you feel that your own ethnicity or cultural background affects your work with families?
4. Have you ever become intimidated when working with a family? If so, how did you handle it?
5. Do you have any symptoms of compassion fatigue, depression, or traumatic stress? If so, through what self-care activities do you plan to address these?

# REFERENCES

American Association for Marriage and Family Therapy. (2012, July 1). Code of ethics. Retrieved from www.aamft.org/imis15/Content/Legal_Ethics/Code_of_Ethics .aspx

Babbel, S. (2012). Compassion fatigue: Bodily symptoms of empathy. *Psychology Today*. Retrieved from www.psychologytoday.com/blog/somatic-psychology/201207/ compassion-fatigue

Comas-Diaz, L., & Jacobsen, F. M. (1991, July). Ethnocultural transference and countertransference in the therapeutic dyad. *American Journal of Orthopsychiatry*, *61*(3), 392–402.

Herefordshire Safeguarding Children Board. (2011, August). Practice guidance: Working with resistant, violent and aggressive families.

Howes, R. (2012). A client's guide to transference. Retrieved from www .psychologytoday.com/blog/in-therapy/201206/clients-guide-transference

Margolin, G. (1982, July). Ethical and legal considerations in marital and family therapy. *American Psychologist*, *37*(7), 788–801.

Murphy, S. N. (2013). Attending to countertransference. Retrieved from http:// ct.counseling.org/2013/09/attending-to-countertransference/

North East of Scotland Child Protection Committee. (2008). Guidance for working with uncooperative families. Retrieved from www.childprotectionpartnership.org. uk/nmsruntime/saveasdialog.aspx?lID=153

Rasic, D. (2010, November). Countertransference in child and adolescent psychiatry: A forgotten concept? *Journal of the Canadian Academy of Child and Adolescent Psychiatry*, *19*(4), 249–254. Retrieved from www.ncbi.nlm.nih.gov/pmc/articles/PMC2962536/

Shaw, E. (2011). Australian Psychological Society Ethics and the practice of couple and family therapy. Retrieved from www.psychology.org.au/publications/inpsych/2011/ feb/shaw/

Volk, K. T., Guarino, K., Grandin, M. E., & Clervil, R. (2008). *What about you? A workbook for those who work with others*. The National Center on Family Homelessness. Retrieved from https://www.homelesshub.ca/resource/ what-about-you-workbook-those-who-work-others

Walker, E., Morin, C., & Labrie, N. (2012). Supporting staff at risk for compassion fatigue. Region of Peel Public Health. Retrieved from www.peelregion.ca/health/ library/pdf/cf-rapid-review.pdf

# Index